W9-AVZ-495

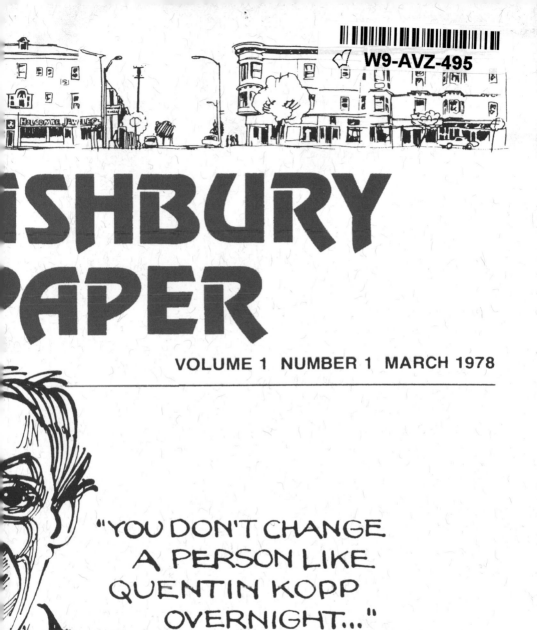

SHBURY PAPER

VOLUME 1 NUMBER 1 MARCH 1978

"YOU DON'T CHANGE A PERSON LIKE QUENTIN KOPP OVERNIGHT..."

HARVEY MILK

—INTERVIEW

THE HARVEY MILK INTERVIEWS™

In his own words

Harvey Milk was named "one of the 100 most important people of the twentieth century" by *Time Magazine*. His life and work have inspired millions of people around the world. *The Harvey Milk Interviews: In His Own Words* is the first book in which Milk explains his life, struggles, and dreams in his own words.

The Harvey Milk Interviews provides the texts of 39 interviews Milk made for newspapers, radio, and television. It includes transcripts from three famous debates in which Milk and John Briggs brawl over the notorious Proposition 6 Briggs Initiative. None of the contents of *The Harvey Milk Interviews* have ever been published in a book before. Much has never been published in any form.

Harvey Milk's unrehearsed, unguarded conversations give readers a first-hand connection with his sense of humor, sense of outrage, and love of dramatic confrontation. *The Harvey Milk Interviews* is a groundbreaking treasure trove for anyone wanting a deeper understanding of who Harvey Milk was as a person and how he inspired the world.

About Harvey Milk

When Harvey Milk (1930-1978) was elected a supervisor of the City and County of San Francisco, he became the first openly gay person elected to office in California. In spite of death threats, he supported a wide range of human rights, environmental, labor, and free speech issues across North America. Milk and San Francisco Mayor George Moscone were assassinated in 1978.

Since then, Milk's life and work have inspired millions of people around the world. Milk was portrayed by Sean Penn in the Academy

Award-winning film *Milk*, and by Peter Coyote in *Execution of Justice*. Milk's life has also been the subject of books, plays, a grand opera, and the Academy Award-winning documentary *The Times of Harvey Milk*. In 2009, President Barack Obama posthumously awarded Milk the Presidential Medal of Freedom, America's highest civilian honor. A plaque before Milk's San Francisco residence states: "His life is an inspiration to all people committed to equal opportunity and an end to bigotry."

A. O. Scott, *New York Times:* "Milk, among the first openly gay elected officials in the country, had a profound impact on national politics, and his rich afterlife in American culture has affirmed his status as pioneer and martyr."

President Barack Obama: "His voice stirred the aspirations of millions of people . . . and his message of hope—hope unashamed, hope unafraid—could never be silenced."

Sean Penn: "This great, great, beautiful, brave man . . . Harvey Milk was such a powerful personality and person, and left behind such a legacy."

Senator Dianne Feinstein: "The fact of his homosexuality gave him an insight into the scars which all oppressed peoples wear; it was undoubtedly the genesis of his admirable commitment to the cause of individual rights. He believed in what he was doing. He believed that no sacrifice was too great a price to pay for the cause of human rights."

Jack Davis, *The Sentinel:* "Harvey died doing what he did best: serving his constituents, looking for answers to the tough questions, fighting bigotry, and working to create a better world. His total devotion and commitment to the cause of dignity and personal freedom is a tribute to his humanity and an example for us all."

San Diego City Councilmember Todd Gloria: "Harvey Milk was more than a politician. He was a visionary who saw a future in which all races, genders, classes, and sexual orientations stood together to support justice and equality."

About Vince Emery

The editor of *The Harvey Milk Interviews*, Vince Emery also wrote the best-seller *How to Grow Your Business on the Internet* and edited *Lost Stories* by Dashiell Hammett. He has contributed research and articles to several books about San Francisco history and authors.

JUN 1 2 2012

979.461 MILK
Milk, Harvey.
Harvey Milk interviews

"I stand for the equal rights of all people."

THE
HARVEY
MILK
INTERVIEWS™

In his own words

By Harvey Milk
Edited by Vince Emery

Vince Emery
PRODUCTIONS
SAN FRANCISCO

The Harvey Milk Interviews: In His Own Words by Harvey Milk
Edited by Vince Emery

Published by Vince Emery Productions
P.O. Box 460279
San Francisco, California 94146 USA
www.emerybooks.com

Vince Emery Productions produces books and videos to give readers
a deeper, closer connection with their favorite authors.

FIRST EDITION, first printing. Printed in USA.
Publication date May 1, 2012. © 2012 Vince Emery Productions.

The "Acknowledgements" section is an extension of this copyright page.

ISBN 978–0–972589888

[4]

Also of interest
*Double Play: The Hidden Passions Behind the Double Assassination
of George Moscone and Harvey Milk* by Mike Weiss

Weiss provides much information available nowhere else. He gives the first
mention anywhere of Harvey Milk's earliest time in San Francisco in the 1950s,
the most detailed account of Milk and Scott Smith's first year in San Francisco,
the most complete coverage of Milk's activities as a supervisor, the best explana-
tion of the complex, shifting relationship between Milk and Dan White, and
the only detailed account of White's trial, life after prison, and suicide.

Includes 90 photos and illustrations, and a 2-hour DVD with video inter-
views of White and George Moscone, recorded phone calls from City Hall
immediately after the assassinations, police dispatch recordings of the police
responding to the murders and hunting for the killer, Dianne Feinstein on dis-
covering Milk's body, and White's confession to shooting Moscone and Milk.

Hardcover + DVD
Double Play ISBN 978-0-9825650-5-6
$39.95 U.S./$43.95 Canada

LC: 4/17 TC. 6 (2/20)

Dedicated to

Tom Ammiano	Greg Gordon	Sean Penn
Toni Atkins	Tory Hartmann	John Perez
Allan Baird	Tom Hayden	Doug Perry
Herbert Baker	Lorri Jean	Nicole Murray Ramirez
Dustin Lance Black	Cleve Jones	Stephen Rivoli
Jason Edward Black	Natalie Jones	Frank M. Robinson
Kate Brandt	Christine Kehoe	Juana Samayoa
Harry Britt	David Kilmnick	Mark Segal
Rea Carey	Anne Kronenberg	Carol Ruth Silver
Jose Cisneros	John Laird	Alan Smith
Bruce Cohen	Krystian Legierski	Denton Smith
Mike Colby	Mark Leno	Mary Stanfield
Danny Dromm	Tim Lewis	Robert V. Taylor
Bevan Dufty	Patricia Loughrey	Tania Unzueta
Manohar Elavarthi	Nathan Manske	Gus Van Sant
Rob Epstein	Armistead Maupin	Jack Veasey
Wayne Friday	Stuart Milk	Jessica Wakeman
Janet Fries	Ed Miskevich	David Weissman
Karl Frisch	David Mixner	Calvin Welch
Sally Miller Gearhart	Charles E. Morris	Chuck Wolfe
Todd Gloria	Dan Nicoletta	Michael Wong

[5]

and the millions of other people
who have been inspired to take action and improve their world
by knowing Harvey Milk or his story

E N T S

[7]

Harvey Milk Chronology

Please note that Milk's activities as a member of the San Francisco Board of Supervisors are not provided in this chronology. For those activities, please see "Milk's Supervisorial Activities" on pages 317-339.

1930

May 22. Harvey Bernard Milk is born in Woodmere on Long Island, New York, to William "Bill" Milk and Minerva "Minnie" Karns Milk.

1945

After May 8, VE-Day. The Milk family moves to Bay Shore, New York.

1947

June 23. Milk graduates from Bay Shore High School. His high school nickname is "Glimpy," after the character played in sixteen Bowery Boys movies by Huntz Hall, whom his schoolmates thought Milk resembled.

August. In New York City, police arrest 17-year-old Milk in a gay cruising area of Central Park for having his shirt off, then release him without booking him.

September. Milk enters State Teachers College in Albany, New York.

1951

June 17. Milk graduates with a Bachelor of Arts degree in teaching, with a major in history and a minor in mathematics.

June or July. Milk enlists in the United States Navy.

July 16. In the Navy, Milk is arrested for unknown charges.

September. Milk enters U.S. Navy Officer Candidate School in Newport, Rhode Island.

1952

Milk graduates from U.S. Navy Officer Candidate School.

1952–1955

Milk serves as a deep-sea diver and later as a deep-sea diving instructor in the U.S. Navy. He is stationed for six months in San Francisco and falls in love with the city. Milk later claims to have received a dishonorable discharge in 1953, but letters survive from Milk

in the Navy in 1954. In 1955 Milk receives an honorable discharge. Afterwards he lives near San Diego, where he falls in love with John Harvey.

1956

Spring. Milk and John Harvey move to Miami, where they break up.

April 21. The Miami police arrest Milk for "Inv Vag-Pervert," or "Invert Vagrant-Pervert."

May. Milk moves back to his parents' house in Long Island.

July. Milk meets Joe Campbell. They move into a place of their own.

Fall. Milk teaches high school math at George W. Hewlett High School in Hewlett, New York.

1957

June. Milk tells Campbell that they will move to Dallas. They move, but Milk has trouble holding a job. He works as an assistant credit manager in a department store, then sells sewing machines.

1958

February. Milk and Campbell move back to New York. Milk gets a job in New York as a statistician with the Great American Group of Insurance Companies.

1961

July. Campbell breaks up with Milk.

1962

November 27. Milk's mother Minnie dies of a heart attack after carrying a 24-pound turkey to a settlement house.

[10]

1963

January or February. Milk quits his job with the Great American Group and meets Craig Rodwell.

1963

March 6-8. Milk moves to San Juan, Puerto Rico and looks for work. He finds none. Feeling rejected by Campbell, he sinks into a deep depression.

March 9. Still depressed, Milk moves to Miami Beach and looks for work.

April. Milk has a personal epiphany from which he feels the beauty of living and determines to spend his life helping others.

May. Milk returns to New York. He seeks work, resumes seeing Rodwell.

By August. Milk gets job as a securities research analyst with Bache & Co. in New York.

1964

After Labor Day. Craig Rodwell is arrested and jailed for indecent exposure. Milk stops seeing him, and volunteers to work on Republican Barry Goldwater's presidential campaign.

Late that year. Milk and John "Jack" Galen McKinley move in together.

1965

May 26–30. Milk and McKinley act in the play *Saint Siegfried, or How to Make a Hero* at Café La Mama, written and directed by Tom O'Horgan.

July 14–18. Using the stage name "Basil Farckwart," Milk acts in the play . . . *And Now the Weather* by Paul Rawlings at Cafe La Mama, directed by Tom O'Horgan.

1967

January 4. Robert Downey, Sr.'s movie *Chafed Elbows* opens, with Milk acting the small part of Reggie the prisoner.

January. Milk transfers to Bache & Co. in Dallas, where he moves with McKinley, and their dog Trick.

February or March. McKinley hates Dallas. He moves back to New York with Trick. Milk stays in Dallas.

1968

January. O'Horgan takes over as director of a faltering off-Broadway musical, *Hair*, and makes many revisions to move it to Broadway.

April 29. O'Horgan's version of *Hair* opens on Broadway and becomes the most successful musical of the year.

[11]

1969

Milk asks for a transfer from Dallas and returns to work at Bache & Co in New York. Eventually he quits Bache to work with O'Horgan.

Milk catches hepatitis and stops drinking alcohol for the rest of his life except for a rare glass of beer or wine with dinner.

June 28-July 1. After police raid the Stonewall Bar on Christopher Street in New York, bar patrons riot for four nights. Craig Rodwell prints and distributes flyers calling for gay liberation.

August 29. The San Francisco production of *Hair* opens, directed by O'Horgan. McKinley has moved west to take a job as "Special Assistant to Tom O'Horgan" in San Francisco.

September. To join McKinley, Milk moves to San Francisco where he is hired as by investment firm J. Barth Co. as director of retail research (in other words, as a securities research analyst).

1970

April 29. U.S. announces the invasion of Cambodia. In a lunch hour protest at the Pacific Stock Exchange, Milk burns his BankAmericard.

Milk quits, is fired, or is laid off from his J. Barth Co. job.

December. Milk and McKinley move to Los Angeles to work as assistants to O'Horgan, who is writing music for the movie *Alex in Wonderland* and trying to persuade a movie studio to film Julian Barry's screenplay *Lenny*, about comedian Lenny Bruce.

1971

February. Milk and O'Horgan give up on the movie *Lenny*. Milk leaves Los Angeles and drives Route 66 back to New York.

March. Milk arrives back in New York City and goes to work as "Assistant to Mr. O'Horgan" on a stage play version of *Lenny* that O'Horgan is directing.

May 22. On his forty-first birthday, Milk meets Joseph Scott Smith, a former accountant now acting and working in theaters, at the Christopher Street subway stop. They begin a passionate romance.

May 26. The stage play version of *Lenny* opens on Broadway, a big hit.

Early August. O'Horgan begins direction of *Jesus Christ Superstar*.

Autumn. Milk gets Smith hired to be assistant stage manager for *Lenny* and to act in three small roles.

October 12. *Jesus Christ Superstar* opens on Broadway and is a huge success. Milk is credited as "Assistant to the Director."

December 19. *Inner City: A Street Cantata*, a musical directed by O'Horgan, opens on Broadway. Milk is "Assistant to Mr. O'Horgan," then promoted to "Associate Producer" when he persuades wealthy heirs to invest in the show. As "Joe Scott," Scott Smith is assistant stage manager. Milk also invests $2,500 in the production for one-half percent of the net profits, if any. Cheered by audiences but savaged by critics, *Inner City* struggles financially.

1972

January. Milk moves to San Francisco, sharing an apartment with friends at 1757 Grant Avenue in the North Beach neighborhood.

March 11. *Inner City* closes its Broadway run, a failure. Milk loses his entire investment. Scott Smith follows Milk to San Francisco. They live mostly on $91 per week unemployment they each receive from their theater jobs.

October. To be close to the Midnight Sun bar on Castro Street and the Bud's Ice Cream store on 24th Street, Milk and Smith move to 577 Castro Street, apartment 304.

1973

February or March. Milk travels to Los Angeles to play the part of a chef in Tom O'Horgan's film of Eugene Ionesco's play *Rhinoceros*.

March 3. Milk and Smith open Castro Camera at 575 Castro Street, financed by their savings and a loan from O'Horgan.

July 10–12. Former U.S. Attorney General John Mitchell prevaricates during three days of televised Senate Watergate hearings, angering Milk and inspiring him to enter politics.

July 26. Milk announces that he will run for the San Francisco Board of Supervisors.

August 23. On the first day that candidates can file to run for office, Milk files his candidacy.

November 6, Election Day. Milk loses his first campaign.

November. After the election, Milk and Smith take a 3-day vacation together in Monterey. It will be their only vacation together during the six hectic years Castro Camera is open.

1974

January 21. The movie *Rhinoceros* opens and Milk's part has been cut.

Summer. Milk's local merchants' association refuses membership to Castro Camera because its owners are homosexuals. Milk becomes the founding president of the Castro Village Association, a competing neighborhood association that admits both gay and straight merchants.

Coors refuses to hire union drivers for its delivery trucks in San Francisco. Local Teamsters official Allan Baird starts a boycott of Coors beer and asks Milk to get gay support. Milk says if the Teamsters hires gay drivers, then he will support the boycott. The Teamsters hire gay drivers within a week, so Milk spreads the Coors boycott to gay establishments across the entire state. The boycott costs Coors millions of dollars and lasts four years.

August 18. Milk and Smith produce the first Castro Street Fair mostly to register voters. 5,000 people attend, a huge success.

[13]

September. Milk becomes a member of the Board of Trustees of the Friends of San Francisco Deputies and Inmates.

October 15. Milk attends Tunbridge in San Francisco, an evening workshop planning adult education courses.

November 9. Milk campaigns to become elected as a delegate from the Sixth Congressional District to the National Conference on Democratic Party Organization and Policy in Kansas City. He fails to become elected.

November 10. The movie *Lenny*, which Milk had unsuccessfully pitched in Hollywood three years ago, opens. It stars Dustin Hoffman, is directed by Bob Fosse, and is nominated for six Academy Awards, including Best Picture.

1975

April. Milk and Smith move to 573 Castro Street, an apartment above Castro Camera.

August 10. Milk and Smith produce the second Castro Street Fair and 25,000 people attend.

August 18. Two-thirds of San Francisco policemen go on strike.

August 20. Milk and others file a lawsuit against Mayor Joseph Alioto and Chief of Police Donald Scott for endangering San Franciscans by their handling of the police strike.

August 21. The first day candidates can file to run for office in the 1975 election, Milk files to run for supervisor again. He cuts his hair, stops smoking marijuana, and stops going to gay bathhouses.

August-November. In addition to running his own campaign for supervisor, Milk supports George Moscone for mayor.

November 4, Election Day. Milk loses and makes a concession speech at The Island restaurant. Moscone drops by unannounced and promises Milk that if Moscone wins the runoff election for mayor, he will appoint Milk commissioner of a city board.

November 5. Milk makes Castro Camera the neighborhood headquarters for the Moscone campaign.

December 11. Moscone wins the runoff election for mayor and in his acceptance speech publicly thanks Milk for his support.

December 25. Milk's father Bill dies without knowing his son is gay.

1976

January 8. At noon, Milk attends Moscone's swearing-in ceremony as San Francisco's 37th mayor in the City Hall rotunda. That night he attends Moscone's inaugural party in the civic auditorium.

January 30. Milk is sworn in as one of Moscone's appointees to the Board of Permit Appeals, making Milk the first openly gay person appointed to a city government position by Moscone, and the first openly gay city commissioner in the nation.

February 2. Milk attends his first weekly meeting as a commissioner of the Board of Permit Appeals.

March 4. Milk and two others sue California Secretary of State March Fong Eu for invasion of privacy due to the Sexual Initiatives Statute, which they interpret as making unmarried sexual activities a crime.

March 9. In a speech at the San Francisco Press Club, Milk announces he will run against Moscone's political ally Art Agnos as a candidate for state assemblyman. Within four hours, Moscone fires Milk from the Board of Permit Appeals.

June 8, Election Day. Milk loses the election for state assemblyman.

July or August. Milk and Scott Smith break up as lovers but remain business partners. Smith moves out of their apartment.

August 15. Milk and Smith produce the third Castro Street Fair.

December 31. At a New Year's Eve party in the Castro, Milk meets John "Jack" Lira, Jr., and the two begin an intense affair.

1977

June 7, Orange Tuesday. After singer and star of Florida orange juice commercials Anita Bryant leads a campaign against an ordinance prohibiting discrimination based on sexual orientation, voters in Dade County, Florida repeal the ordinance. Thousands of angry gays mob Castro Street. Police fear a riot and ask Milk to calm the mob. With Cleve Jones, Milk averts violence using a "March 'em 'til they drop" strategy, keeping the crowd moving for three hours over a five-mile course up and down San Francisco hills, ending at midnight at Union Square, where he gives a speech. The crowd marches back to Castro, where 1,000 protesters stage a spontaneous sit-down protest, blocking the three-way intersection of Castro Street, Market Street, and 17th Street. Milk persuades the protesters to clear the intersection.

June 14. Exactly one week later, State Senator John Briggs stands before San Francisco City Hall and announces his campaign for a law removing all gay teachers from California schools.

June 24. Milk announces his fourth candidacy, this time for District 5 supervisor.

[15]

June 26. 200,000 people (San Francisco police estimate) to 375,000 people (*Los Angeles Times* estimate) march in or watch the San Francisco Gay Freedom Parade.

June 29. The windows of Castro Camera and four other Castro Street businesses are blown up with M-80 firecrackers.

August 14. Milk and Smith produce the fourth Castro Street Fair.

November 8, Election Day. On his fourth try for office, Milk finally wins and is elected supervisor for District 5.

November 18. After closing the Castro Camera store for the night, Milk records cassette tapes labeled "In case . . .". Milk has received hundreds of death threats, and he intended for the tapes to be played only in the event of his assassination as his political will. (See *The Mayor of Castro Street*, pages 372–375.)

December 9. Supervisor-Elect Milk is the keynote speaker kicking off a three-day meeting in Los Angeles to organize people across the state to defeat the Briggs Initiative.

1978

Monday January 9. At 10:00 a.m., Milk gathers at Market and Castro Street with supporters, his lover Jack Lira, and a class of sixth-graders studying government. They parade thirteen blocks down Market Street to City Hall.

At 11:00 a.m., because the supervisors' formal swearing-in ceremony will not be open to the public, Milk and fellow supervisors-elect Gordon Lau, Carol Ruth Silver, and Ella Hill Hutch hold an informal swearing-in ceremony outdoors on the steps of City Hall open to everyone.

At noon in the supervisors' grand chambers in City Hall, all supervisors are formally sworn into office.

At 2:00 p.m., the year's first regular session of the Board of Supervisors begins. (**For Milk's activities as a supervisor, see "Milk's Supervisorial Activities" on pages 317-339.**)

That evening, Milk appears at Bear Hollow restaurant and bar on Castro Street, where David Goodstein, publisher of the national gay magazine *The Advocate*, throws an invitation-only hors d'oeuvres-and-drinks party honoring Milk as a step toward ending years of conflict between the two men.

Tuesday January 10. Milk's supporters hold a $50-per plate-dinner at the Galleria, to help retire $8,000 of Milk's campaign debts. The event is emceed by Democratic Party activist Tory Hartmann. Speakers include Republican Lt. Governor Mervyn Dymally

and Milk, who gives his first major speech as supervisor (printed as "A City of Neighborhoods" in *The Mayor of Castro Street*, pages 353–358). Guests include Mayor George Moscone, Chief Administrative Officer Roger Boas, Fire Chief Andy Casper, District Attorney Joe Frietas, City Attorney George Agnost, San Francisco Giants baseball team owner Bob Lurie, Pier 39 owner Warren Simmons, Bank of America executives, labor leaders, and Supervisors Dianne Feinstein, Ella Hill Hutch, Gordon Lau, Carol Ruth Silver, and Dan White.

After his Galleria dinner, Milk appears at three discos (Alfie's, Bones, and the I-Beam) from 10:00 p.m. to 1:00 a.m., where David Goodstein throws three simultaneous parties honoring Milk and open to the public. Anonymously produced flyers denounce their rapprochement.

Wednesday January 11. Milk testifies in Sacramento, the California state capital, before the State Assembly's Ways and Means Committee on behalf of A.B. 1302, which would have prohibited employment discrimination based on sexual orientation. The bill never makes it out of committee.

Saturday February 19. Milk is interviewed in his office at Castro Camera by Greg Gordon for KPFK radio and the IMRU Gay Radio Collective.

Saturday-Sunday March 4-5. Milk flies to Chicago to campaign for a gay political candidate running for the Illinois House of Representatives.

Tuesday-Thursday March 7-9. While Moscone is in Europe, Milk serves as acting mayor of San Francisco, making him the first openly gay mayor of an American city.

[17]

Friday March 10. Milk flies to San Diego where he gives his "Hope Speech" to the gay caucus of the California Democratic Council. (Printed in *The Mayor of Castro Street*, pages 359–363.)

Wednesday March 22. Tom Hayden interviews Milk in his Castro Camera store.

Friday March 31. The Castro Camera landlord raises the rent from $350 to $1,200 per month. Milk and Scott move their store to 2362 Market St. Milk and Jack Lira move to a flat at 18 Henry Street.

Tuesday April 11. At a ceremony in the mayor's office, Mayor George Moscone signs Milk's anti-discrimination Human Rights Ordinance into law.

Tuesday April 25. Voters in St. Paul, Minnesota repeal a three-year-old law prohibiting discrimination based on sexual orientation. In reaction, angry demonstrators gather at San Francisco City Hall, where Milk addresses them.

Sunday April 30. The first Haight Ashbury Community Street Fair is held, which Milk helps produce.

Monday May 1. State Senator John Briggs turns in signed petitions to the California secretary of state so his initiative, formally named the School Employees Homosexual Initiative, will qualify to be placed on the ballot for the November election.

Tuesday May 2. Milk goes to Sacramento to speak before the Senate Industrial Relations Committee, which then votes 4-0 to endorse legislation sponsored by Republican State Senator Milton Marks to prohibit job discrimination based on sexual orientation.

Friday May 5. Milk speaks at a Harvey Milk Tribute dinner at the Bonaventure Hotel in Los Angeles, hosted by Don Amador (Los Angeles Mayor Tom Bradley's liaison to the gay community) and Tony Karnes (California Gay Caucus coordinator).

Saturday May 6. Milk speaks at the California Gay Caucus in the Bonaventure Hotel in Los Angeles.

Tuesday May 9. Anita Bryant leads an effort in Wichita, Kansas, which defeats a proposed anti-discrimination law.

Monday May 22. Milk's 48th birthday is Youth in Government Day, so Carol Ann Ravano of Presentation High is Milk's student counterpart for the day.

Tuesday May 23. Voters in Eugene, Oregon repeal an anti-discrimination law. In San Francisco, an angry crowd gathers at 18th Street and Castro. Milk speaks, then leads the crowd on a march.

Wednesday May 24. Milk speaks at a birthday party held for him at the Gay Community Center.

June. Milk and San Francisco State University professor Sally Miller Gearhart form United Fund to Defeat the Briggs Initiative with offices at 1 United Nations Plaza in San Francisco. They select Cleve Jones to head the organization.

Saturday June 10. Milk speaks at the Texas Gay Conference in Dallas.

Saturday June 24. Milk is the keynote speaker at the Third Annual Gay Freedom Day Rally in St. James Park, San Jose, California.

Sunday June 25. At Gay Freedom Day in San Francisco, the rainbow flag designed at Milk's request by Gilbert Baker is displayed for

the first time. In spite of a death threat, Milk speaks to a crowd of more than 100,000 in front of City Hall. (For more information, see *The Mayor of Castro Street*, pages 223–226. For the text of Milk's speech, see *The Mayor of Castro Street*, pages 364–371.)

Sunday July 2. As part of Gay Pride Day in Los Angeles, Milk speaks to a rally in DeLongpre Park.

Thursday July 20. Milk attends Dan White's fund-raising party on the sailing ship *Balcutha*. (See *Double Play*, pages 176–181.)

Sunday August 20. The fifth annual Castro Street Fair features 200 booths from vendors and attracts 20,000 to 30,000 attendees.

Monday August 28. After the Board of Supervisors meeting adjourns at 6:55 p.m., Milk attends an evening committee meeting. About 9 p.m. Milk arrives home at 18 Henry Street, the apartment he shares with Jack Lira, to find his lover hanging from a ceiling beam on a rope, a suicide.

September. Milk moves to a flat at 28 Henry Street.

Wednesday September 6. Milk debates John Briggs about Proposition 6 at the New San Remo Restaurant in San Francisco..

Friday September 15. Milk debates John Briggs at the Northgate High School auditorium in Walnut Creek.

Sunday September 24. Milk speaks as part of the Gay Rights under the Law Symposium hosted by the University of California Hastings College of the Law in San Francisco.

Tuesday September 26. Milk is interviewed by Juana Samayoa live on KBHK TV's program *News Talk*.

October. Milk gives up his car, a leased 3-year-old Volvo, because he can no longer afford it.

Tuesday and Wednesday October 10 and 11. For the first time in many years, Milk attends Yom Kippur services. He tells the gay Congregation Sha'ar Zahav's rabbi Allen Bennett that he feels good to "be home."

Wednesday October 11. A debate on Proposition 6 is held at Mission High School in San Francisco. KQED TV reporter Belva Davis moderates. John Briggs and Rev. Raymond Batema speak in favor of Proposition 6, and Milk and San Francisco State University professor Sally Miller Gearhart speak against it, with questions from KQED reporters Randy Shilts and Rollin Post. Milk and Gearhart also speak at a rally afterwards.

Later that night, Milk celebrates his friend Cleve Jones' 24th birthday at the Elephant Walk bar on Castro Street.

Wednesday November 1. Milk and Briggs debate at Pacifica High School in Garden Grove, a town in Briggs' district.

Thursday November 2. Milk and Briggs debate in Los Angeles live on KABC TV and/or KABC radio.

Friday November 3. Milk and Briggs debate at Temple Sinai in Oakland.

Sunday November 5. Milk and Briggs debate on KJAZ radio in San Francisco.

Tuesday November 7, Election Day. Voters defeat Proposition 6.

Friday November 10. Dan White resigns from the Board of Supervisors.

Monday November 13. The Board accepts White's resignation.

Tuesday November 14. White changes his mind and asks to have his resignation withdrawn. Because the Board has already accepted White's resignation, it cannot be withdrawn.

Wednesday November 15. Mayor Moscone promises White that if Moscone has the power to do so, he will reappoint White to his supervisor's seat. White overhears a phone call between Milk and the city attorney's office which he construes as Milk trying to block his reappointment.

Milk sponsors a meeting in the San Francisco Public Library to form a gay library and archival collection. His concerns will lead to the formation of the GLBT Historical Society and the James C. Hormel Gay & Lesbian Center.

Sunday November 26. White is aware that Moscone changed his mind and will appoint someone else to White's former seat, and that Milk is working against his reappointment. He feels that Moscone and Milk are humiliating him.

[20]

Monday November 27. Shortly before 11:00 a.m., White shoots and kills Moscone in the mayor's private sitting room in City Hall. White runs a full city block to the other side of City Hall, where he shoots Milk five times, killing him.

After the coroner autopsies Milk's body, his eyes and heart are donated to organ transplant recipients.

That night, in a spontaneous demonstration of grief, 25,000 silent mourners carry candles along the route that Milk had led marchers to City Hall for a candelit memorial. Among the speakers is Harry Britt, who says, "Harvey was a prophet. Like Dr. [Martin Luther] King, he lived by a vision. As I look out over this crowd, I think this city has bought this vision. Something very special is going to happen in this city, and it will have Harvey's name on it."

PART ONE

1930 – 1973,
The First
Eight Lives of
Harvey Milk

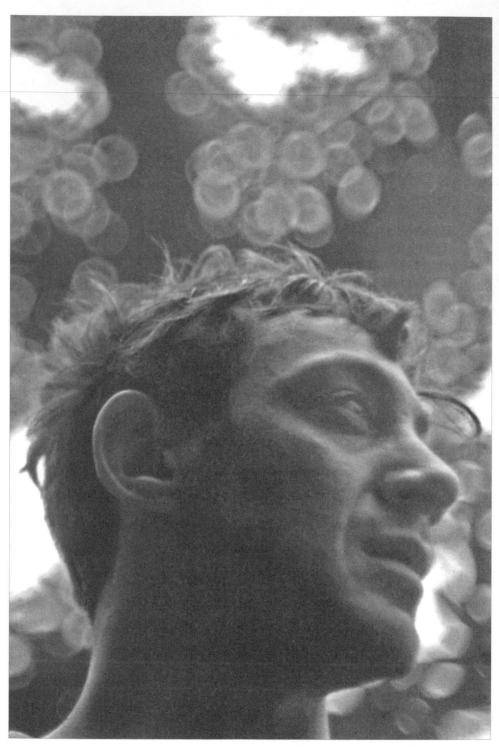

Milk in his twenties or early thirties

W HY a book of interviews?
Because in these interviews Harvey Milk reveals himself.

The interviews here span Milk's political career from his first days as a candidate in 1973 to shortly before his assassination in 1978. They are arranged chronologically, so we see his thoughts changing over time, both his political ideas and his concept of himself.

He presents himself formally in some interviews, casually in others, but always remains aware he is the center of attention (which he loved), a performer communicating to his audience. Milk's best interviews also expose some of his personal qualities. Within these interviews, none of which have ever been published in a book before, we find much of significance which is preserved nowhere else. All in his own words.

If you are just beginning to learn about Milk, this may not be the best book for you. But if you want to go deeper, to find out more about what Milk believed, how he felt, how he expressed himself, welcome. This book is for us.

The first eight lives of Harvey Milk

If asked "What was Harvey Milk's occupation?" most people would say he was a politician. They would be only partly right. Milk's political life made him inspirational and famous, but he was a political candidate just during the last five-and-a-half years of his 48-year life, and a political officeholder (for two offices, one appointed and one elected) for one year total.

Like a cat with nine lives, Harvey Milk had nine occupations. His political life was his last incarnation. He spent most of his 48 years in other fields: retail clerk, deep-sea diver, teacher, insurance statistician, securities research analyst, theaterman, camera store proprietor, writer. Each shaped his personality and his life and contributed to his slowly emerging sense of himself as a leader.

Retail clerk

Harvey Milk started life in a store. When he was born in Woodmere, New York, on May 22, 1930, his grandfather Morris owned Milk's Dry Goods. Morris built it into the largest department store on Long Island and later sold it to Macy's. Harvey played in his grandfather's store as a child and may have worked there. When he was fifteen, his family moved east on Long Island to the town of Bay Shore, where his father Bill opened his own shop: Bay Shore Furriers. Harvey later said he worked for years in his father's shop. He also worked at a local grocery store, packing groceries and carrying them to customers' cars. When he was thirty, he worked nights and Saturdays in a men's clothing store his father opened in Manhattan. From Harvey's experience in retail, he learned to influence customers, a type of persuasion based on making many quick person-to-person emotional ties, very different from the step-by-step calculation practiced by attorneys who enter politics. Customer persuasion is based on charm.

Deep-sea diver

Milk wanted to become a teacher. But after he earned his B.A. in teaching from the State University of New York College for Teachers at Albany in 1951 with a major in history and a minor in mathematics, he felt so strongly about the need to defeat Communists in Korea that he enlisted in the United States Navy. In 1952 he graduated from U.S. Navy Officers Training School in Newport, Rhode Island. For three years, during the end of the Korean War and afterwards, Lieutenant (junior grade) Milk served in the Navy first as a deep-sea diving officer and later as a deep-sea diving instructor. This was not scuba diving, but dropping underwater to far more dangerous depths to perform

[24]

Milk's Master Diver belt buckle shows a Mark V diving helmet, a trident, and two classical-style dolphins. Oddly, Milk was a Master Diver in the Navy, but his buckle shows the Master Diver insignia for the Army.

submarine rescues, encumbered by a helmet, a thick suit, and high-pressure air hoses. As an instructor, he needed to communicate clearly and vividly; in a diving crisis, a mistake could kill his students. He was stationed in San Francisco for six months. He fell in love with the city, and was always proud of his Navy service. Years later, when Milk was elected a supervisor of the City and County of San Francisco, he wore a Master Diver belt buckle to work every day, even the day he died.

Teacher

After the Navy, Milk returned to Long Island. He taught math to tenth and eleventh graders at George W. Hewlett High School, but he lived in fear. He was a gay teacher living with another man, Joe Campbell, so the slightest sourceless whisper could kill his teaching career. Even though Milk enjoyed being the center of attention in front of a class (and would later make at least two attempts to return to teaching), he decided to change occupations.

Actuarial statistician

After a brief, unproductive move to Dallas in 1957, Milk and his lover Campbell relocated to Manhattan, where he embarked on a new career. In February 1958 he leveraged his mathematics education to get hired by Great American Insurance Company as an actuarial statistician. Milk's income enabled them to live the good life in New York City until late 1962, when Campbell broke up with him. He soon found another lover, Craig Rodwell. Milk hated his insurance job, so in early 1963 he quit Great American.

[25]

Securities research analyst

Depressed over the end of his relationship with Campbell, Milk moved to Puerto Rico. He could not find work there. Then he tried Miami. Same problem. By May 1963 he was back in New York City looking for work. Once more he used his math education to change occupations. By August he was hired to work as a securities research analyst at 51 Wall Street with Bache & Co., one of the largest brokerage and investment banking firms.

He was seeing Craig Rodwell again, but in 1964, when Rodwell was arrested for indecent exposure and jailed for three days, Milk broke up with him. He did not want anything to disturb his conservative life—so conservative that he volunteered for Barry Goldwater's presidential campaign.

Late in 1964, a new lover moved into Milk's apartment: John "Jack" Galen McKinley. He took Milk into a completely new world. McKinley worked for his friend Tom O'Horgan, one of the top directors of off-Broadway plays. The gravitational field of the theater had attracted Milk since he was a boy, and now pulled him into O'Horgan's orbit. Weekdays Milk worked on Wall Street, but nights and weekends he threw himself into O'Horgan's plays, loaning money to the director, working backstage, sometimes even acting.

In January 1967, Milk transferred to Bache & Co. in Dallas and moved with McKinley and their dog Trick. McKinley hated Dallas and soon fled with Trick back to New York City. Milk stayed in Dallas until early 1969, when he returned to Wall Street for Bache again.

Theaterman

While Milk had lived in Dallas, O'Horgan had taken over an off-Broadway musical named *Hair*, revising it extensively and moving it to Broadway, where *Hair* became a smash hit. Milk eventually quit his job with Bache and went to work with O'Horgan. He let his hair grow long.

O'Horgan launched productions of *Hair* in Los Angeles, London, and then San Francisco. McKinley moved west to become the "Special Assistant to Mr. O'Horgan" for *Hair* in San Francisco. In September 1969, Milk followed McKinley to San Francisco, getting a job as director of retail research (in other words, as a securities research analyst) with J. Barth Co., an investment company on Montgomery Street, the so-called "Wall Street of the west."

The next year, 1970, J. Barth Co. told Milk to cut his long hair. He quit or was fired. That ended Milk's career in the financial industry.

By December 1970, Milk was working for O'Horgan again. He and McKinley moved from San Francisco to Los Angeles to act as assisstants to O'Horgan, who was composing and conducting the music for the movie *Alex in Wonderland* and trying to convince a film

Milk worked on several plays off Broadway and these four Broadway shows.

[27]

studio to make *Lenny,* a movie about comedian Lenny Bruce. Milk pitched the movie unsuccessfully until late February, then gave up and drove Route 66 back to New York. He worked as "Assistant to Mr. O'Horgan" on a stage play version of *Lenny* that O'Horgan was directing. On May 22, 1971, Milk's forty-first birthday, at the Christopher Street subway stop he met Joe Scott Smith, a former accountant now acting and working in theaters. They began a passionate romance. *Lenny* opened on Broadway on May 26 and was a great success. Milk was now a hotshot in the glamorous world of show business. He got Smith hired to work on *Lenny* as an actor in three small parts and backstage as assistant stage manager.

O'Horgan and Milk also worked on a third show, *Jesus Christ Superstar.* It opened on October 12 with the largest advance ticket sales in Broadway history, a spectacular success. Milk was credited as "Assistant to the Director." O'Horgan now had three hits—*Hair, Lenny, Jesus Christ Superstar*—playing on Broadway at the same time. He and Milk started on a fourth Broadway show, a musical called *Inner City.* Milk began work on it as "Assistant to Mr. O'Horgan," then was promoted to "Associate Producer" when he persuaded the heirs to a tea fortune to invest in the musical. Milk also invested $2,500 in the production for one-half percent of the net profits—if any. He brought his lover Scott Smith aboard as assistant stage manager. *Inner City* opened on December 19. It drew cheering standing ovations from audiences, but because it was savaged by critics it had trouble selling tickets.

One month later, in January 1972, Milk turned his back on Broadway and returned to San Francisco, moving in with friends in the North Beach neighborhood. *Inner City* limped along without him until it closed on March 11, a financial flop. Milk lost his entire investment. Smith followed Milk to San Francisco, where they mostly lived on unemployment checks from their jobs in the theater.

Camera store proprietor

In October 1972, to be close to the Midnight Sun bar and the Bud's Ice Cream store, Milk and Smith moved to an apartment at 577 Castro Street. In a few months their unemployment payments ran out, and they needed a way to make money. When a local store mis-developed photos by Milk and ruined them, he got an

idea. He could use his retail experience, his enjoyment of photography, and their dwindling savings to open the only camera store in the Castro neighborhood. He tapped his friend O'Horgan for a loan. Milk and Smith opened Castro Camera on March 3, 1973 at 575 Castro. Their shop would never be a gold mine, but would generate enough income to pay most of Milk and Smith's living expenses for the next five years.

A different dividend was generated as Milk and Smith became involved in their Eureka Valley-Castro Street neighborhood. Milk became a problem-solver for his customers—not just their photography problems, but difficulties with their families, their loves, their careers. With a dumpy old couch and a barber's chair he turned Castro Camera into a neighborhood social center.

Writer

Throughout Milk's adult life he considered himself a writer. He wrote about sports in his college newspaper. He wrote humorous articles for a gay liberation newsletter that Craig Rodwell published. He wrote a weekly newsletter for his Bache & Co. office about business trends. Milk's managers were so impressed with his newsletter that they sent it to Bache offices nationwide. He worked on publicity for plays in New York. He wrote for gay publications in San Francisco. He even applied for a job as a columnist with the *San Francisco Chronicle*.

An unlikely contender

Unlike many American political candidates, Harvey Milk was never a lawyer. But his grab-bag of occupations taught him skills and fattened his resume in ways that made his unlikely candidacy stronger:

- From working as a retail clerk, he learned how to persuade people with charm.
- Working as a deep-sea diving officer taught him how to lead and inspire his troops, and later, as a deep-sea diving instructor, his students.
- As a math teacher, he honed his ability to instruct (which is a form of persuasion) and practiced how to keep an audience's attention in front of a room of teenagers. He loved being in front of an audience.

- Four years as an actuarial statistician polished his ability to estimate probabilities and costs.
- He spent six years in the securities industry discovering trends and investigating cashflows to find hidden flags that signaled problems.
- Show business gave Milk familiarity with how drama attracts and holds an audience, and how to work with publicists and media.
- At Castro Camera, he became a visible figure on his street, a leader in his neighborhood.
- From his writing he was able to write speeches and communicate in print.

Connecting. Persuading. Leading the troops.

These were Milk's strengths. All were spawned from his irrepressible urge to communicate, a passion fundamental to his nature. Combined with his energy, his self-deprecating sense of humor, and his anger at unfairness—especially against the little guy—they helped him become, against all odds, a viable political candidate.

Harvey Milk jumped into politics one summer day in July 1973, wearing casual clothes, a moustache, and shoulder-length hair. In an era when people spat on gays, he was an openly queer hippie of no consequence, the co-owner of a tiny business, an outsider with no legal background and no financial resources. What happened when such an unlikely person ran for office?

We'll let Milk tell us in his own words.

PART TWO

1973 – 1975,
Two-Time Loser

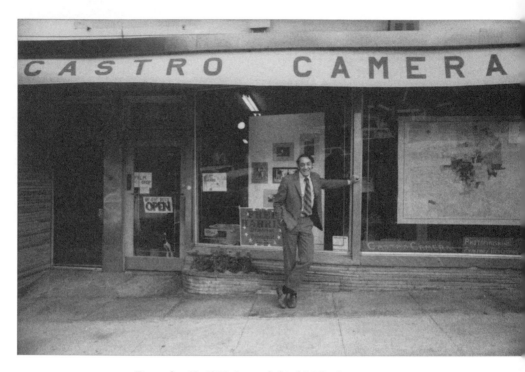

December 19, 1975: A map behind Milk shows precincts
he lost and won in the 1975 election.
Milk and Smith's dog The Kid stands behind the door.

I.

Shopowner runs for supervisor

We have President Richard Nixon and his former Attorney General John Mitchell to thank for Harvey Milk's leap into politics. During the summer of 1973, weekday business in Castro Camera was slow, so Milk and Scott Smith watched the Senate Watergate hearings on television. Mitchell testified for three days in July, obviously not telling the truth. Milk swore loudly at Mitchell's lies and grew so angry that he decided to change the political system by taking part in it. Exactly two weeks after Mitchell's last day of testimony, Milk announced he would run for office as a candidate for a seat on the Board of Supervisors of the City and County of San Francisco. This article in the July 27, 1973 *San Francisco Examiner* quotes the unlikely candidate.

H ARVEY MILK, 43-year-old Castro Street camera shop owner, has announced his candidacy for San Francisco supervisor.

"Having a small business and being one of thousands of people whom no one in government will listen to, I have decided to run for supervisor as a person," he said yesterday.

He said he was "fed up" with taxes, moralization by self-serving politicians and lack of respect by "our so-called leaders" because he represents no large voting block or monied group.

Individual Rights

"I stand for all those who feel that the government no longer understands the individual and no longer respects individual rights.

"I will vote to stop the endless, useless and senseless spending of our government . . . the waste of money spent trying to enforce victimless crime laws while our schools need improvement and while there is still a need for decent housing.

Shopowner Harvey Milk

Former Analyst

"I will strive to bring the government to the people, be they intellectuals or fellow homosexuals, be they blacks or fellow Jews, be they the tax-starved elderly or fellow small shop owners, be they taxi drivers or newspaper reporters," he said.

Milk is a graduate of the Albany State College for Teachers in New York, [and] spent eight years as a research analyst for stock brokers in New York City, San Francisco, and Dallas.

He helped produce several plays and musicals on Broadway and first moved to the City in 1969.

He is co-owner of Castro Camera at 575 Castro St.

2.

"What is obscene, except people who think that they can tell others how to live?"

An organization preparing a pamphlet about candidates sent Milk an interview questionnaire. On August 7, 1973, Milk filled it out. His answers here give a more revealing, detailed look than any other source at his lack of resources and experience as a candidate. In transcribing Milk's hand-written answers, I have retained as closely as possible his eccentric capitalization and punctuation. My editorial corrections are indicated by [square brackets].

(Personal Background)

Please attach a biography. If not included, please answer the following:

1. *What public elective offices have you previously held? Please give dates.*
 Milk: NONE

2. *What other public offices have you run for? Please give dates.*
 Milk: NONE

3. *What public appointive offices have you held? Please give dates.*
 Milk: NONE

4. *What is your current employment?*
 Milk: CO-OWNER of CASTRO CAMERA 575 CASTRO ST.

5. *When and where were you born?*
 Milk: WOODMERE / NEW YORK / MAY 22, 1930

6. *Where did you grow up?*
 Milk: WOODMERE & BAY SHORE NEW YORK

7. *When did you first reside in San Francisco?*
 Milk: SEPT–1969

8. *Have you lived here continuously since then? If not, where else have you lived since then? (Please give dates.)*
 Milk: N.Y.–MARCH 1971–JaN 1972
 L.A.–DEC 1970–FEB 1971

9. *To what clubs and organizations do you belong?*
 Milk: NONE

10. *What community projects have you worked on?*
 Milk: NONE

11. *What is your net worth? If married, what is your spouse's net worth?*
 Milk: $2,000 IN DEBT
 CAR WORth $1,000
 FURNITURe $5,000 $4,000 at most

12. *What was your gross income in each of the past three years?*
 Milk: 1972–apx $1,000
 1971–apx 10,000
 1970–apx 10,000

13. *What is your party affiliation?*
 Milk: DEMOCRAtic

(General)

1. *Why are you running for the Board?*
 Milk: Waste of tax payers money by government
 Misdirection/misuse of tax payers money on priority of spending
 Victimless crime laws must be removed
 election of supervisors by district

2. *How much do you estimate it will cost you to run your campaign?*
 Milk: 5–10 thousand

3. *What do you estimate the various costs of your campaign for the Board will be? (Please also attach a campaign budget if you have one.)*

a) Campaign staff	**Milk:**	$None
b) Office rent	**Milk:**	$None
c) Printing of posters, etc.	**Milk:**	$5,000
d) Mailings	**Milk:**	$1,000
e) Newspaper advertising	**Milk:**	$3,000
f) Radio & TV spots	**Milk:**	$None
g) Office supplies	**Milk:**	$500.00
h) Opinion surveys	**Milk:**	$None
i) Other (please specify)	**Milk:**	$None

4. *Are you at a disadvantage as a non-incumbent in raising campaign funds? Explain.*
 Milk: Yes–no one will give unless they know you — & you can't be known unless you advertise & the Chronicle & Progress refuses to print my announcement

5. *What other problems have you had or do you anticipate as a non-incumbent?*
 Milk: Press–lack of reportage

[37]

6. *What will be your sources of campaign finance?*
 Milk: passing the hat for dollars & coins

7. *What individuals or groups have endorsed your candidacy?*
 Milk: None

8. *In your appeals for voter support, how do you plan to take account of:*

 a) *Differences in voters' ages?*
 Milk: None

b) *Differences in voters' religion?*
Milk: None

c) *Differences in voters' occupations?*
Milk: None

d) *Differences in voters' ethnic background or race?*
Milk: None

e) *Differences in voters' geographic location in San Francisco?*
Milk: None
1 campaign for all – No division to appeal to groups by eating blint[ze]s & pizza

(Policy)

1. *What is the most important recommendation you would make for Board action in each of the following areas as they concern San Francisco[?]*

Civil Service (municipal)
Milk: [blank]

[38]

Health Care
Milk: Expand – esp for elderly – i.e. dental care

Employment
Milk: encourage spending money on operation bootstrap for black, Spanish, welfare, young[.] In short <u>all</u> people as they can go into business for themselves.

Consumer Protection
Milk: Set up a commission with power to investigate complain[t]s & take action to correct wrong & publish findings

Cable Television
Milk: [blank]

Economic Development
Milk: Instead of going [with] more tourist & conventions I would go into self employment & an operation bootstrap, so we would not need to rely on tourists & conventions.

Public Utilities
Milk: Should be owned by city—would save money i.e.—advertising & salaries right away[.] Should be able to lower rates.

Culture and the Arts
Milk: encourage local centers—that is the best way to develop new talent

Housing
Milk: Massive drive to renovate run down areas through principle of self help

Transportation
Milk: do away with "schedules" & any charge—put cost of running under tax budget & then encourage people to use this "free" system

Older Persons' Problems
Milk: this is a crisis—from health, food & shelter & is being ignored at present

[39]

Environmental Quality
Milk: a much more stringent control on autos, factories, etc & restrictions on Building heights

Street Crime
Milk: Put ALL vice squad & police iNto uniforms & on the beat & cut all efforts now spent on victimless crimes

Civil Rights
Milk: For all, - esp. gay
esp. black
esp. Mexican
esp. Oriental

For a city made up of minorities there is no "equal"

Local Taxes
Milk: Must be lowered thru better use of funds & CONTROLL of TAX revenues

Zoning
Milk: [blank]

Open Space and Recreation
Milk: Much more is needed[.] Could institute a citywide, street by street voll[e]yball league for [illegible] together

Other (specify)
Milk: [blank]

Which five of your recommendations do you consider the most important?

Milk: END WASTE of TAXpayers money – misdirection & misuse of government spending
election of supervisors by district
end all victimless Crime Laws
put all police into uniform & on the beat
SET an example to State & Federal gov't on how to LOWER taxes & better use the money for NEEDED priorities

 7. What should the Board do about the following:

 a. Regulation of building height and bulk.
 Milk: Yes – strict code to break up congestion downtown & encourage new buildings in undeveloped areas

 b. Yerba Buena [convention center].
 Milk: less emphasis on tourists & conventions – more emphasis on "operation bootstrap" programs

 c. Hunters Point Naval Shipyard
 Milk: turn its facilities into finding ways to build new low cost houses

d. *Childcare centers*
Milk: [blank]

e. *San Francisco airport expansion*
Milk: Nothing—expansion for expansion sake is wrong—

f. *Downtown traffic*
Milk: ban autos in the core area
free bus rides
restrict parking greatly

g. *Development of the northern waterfront.*
Milk: better use as a place to develop shipping, [illegible]
tourist ships

h. *Halfway houses and board and care homes in residential areas.*
Milk: if people who call themselves "Christians" are Christians then the only answer is "of course"

i. *Street artists.*
Milk: More, more, more, more—

j. *Rent control.*
Milk: No

k. *Pornography and obscenity.*
Milk: what is obscene except people who think that they can tell others how to live

[41]

l. *Organized crime*
Milk: end police efforts against pornography & other victimless crimes & into uniform & on streets—divert effort now after prostitutes toward crime

m. *Drug abuse.*
Milk: legalize marijuana. help hard drug addicts

(The Board)

1. *What powers should the Board have that it does not now have?*
Milk: —

2. *What responsibilities should the Board not have that it now has?*
Milk: to the "people"

3. *In what ways, if any, should the Board's organization or proce-dures be changed?*
Milk: —

4. *Do you believe citizen participation in activities of the Board should be expanded? How?*
Milk: through election by district & district offices

(Electoral Process)

1. *What changes in the laws affecting campaign finance would you recommend?*
Milk: No contribution in any way over $100.00 – all money goes into city board of control who have record of all income & outgoing funds for all candidates

2. *What changes in the number and length of terms of Board mem-bers would you recommend?*
Milk: None

[42]

3. *Do you favor district elections of supervisors? Please explain your answer.*
Milk: yes—it will bring the supervisors back to the people & find out about the problems of the city

4. *Should candidates for the Board run on party tickets? Why?*
Milk: No[.] Parties mean nothing: i.e., Wallace & McGovern are both Democrats!!

5. *Do you favor the disclosure of contributors' names and amounts donated to supervisorial campaigns, regardless of amount and whether made through a committee or not?*
Milk: Yes!! —

(*Law Enforcement*)

1. *Do you favor deemphasizing current enforcement of laws against so-called "nonvictim" crime (such as prostitution, certain sexual conduct, marijuana use)? Please explain.*
 Milk: Yes—either you are God or you don't try to be go & tell people how to run their lives because of your own problems—

(*Political Forces*)

1. *Who do you think runs City Hall? (The Board? The Mayor? The Bureaucracy? Labor? Business? No one?)*
 Milk: a combination of Bureaucracy the Mayor & Business

2. *Are there political factions or machines in San Francisco? If so, describe them. Where do you fit in?*
 Milk: don't know
 don't fit in

3. *If you are elected, how could citizens most effectively influence your views as a Board member?*
 Milk: write to me
 talk to me

(*Finance and Budget*)

1. *How should San Francisco meet its revenue needs?*
 Milk: through better use of the tax revenue it now has

2. *What changes, if any, do you favor in the budget process?*
 Milk: Open disclosure of all spending esp the police budget

Additional comments on other matters:
 Milk: [blank]

Thank you.
Date:
 Milk: 8/7

3.

"Taxes and priorities change from year to year, but freedom does not."

In the 1970s, the most respected national gay news publication and the one with the widest circulation was *The Advocate*. An openly gay candidate running for office was a rare and groundbreaking occurrence in 1973, and therefore worthy of attention for *The Advocate*'s national audience. In its October 10, 1973 issue, in an article entitled "S.F. gay campaigning for the straight vote, too," an unknown author interviewed Milk about his run for office.

H IS NAME is unlikely and his current enterprise is unlikelier yet—or seems to be.

Harvey Milk is gay, and he's running for a seat on the Board of Supervisors, the governing body of the City and County of San Francisco.

Gay candidates come and—so far—mostly go. If Milk succeeds in his ambition, he will have scored an historic first. But someday, a gay candidate will be elected at the municipal level or higher, and Milk obviously figures it might as well be him.

He denied he is a token candidate.

"I am not running just for the gay vote to show our strength. I am out on the buses every morning. I am in the shopping centers or the financial district every day. I want the straight vote, and I'm going after that vote," is the way he puts it.

Unlike some of the other gay candidates who continue to pop up here and there, Harvey Milk is not exactly a glamour boy. Born in 1930, he looks a bit like a slightly overage hippie, with longish hair and mustache, and a bit like a neighborhood shopkeeper—which he is.

Behind the image is eight years of experience as a research analyst for several member firms of the New York Stock Exchange

here, in New York, and in Dallas. He also spent a year working on Broadway, helping to produce such shows as *Lenny, Jesus Christ Superstar,* and *Inner City.*

There are many reasons why he is running for supervisor, he says, "from the waste of city tax money to the crazy sense of priorities that the city supervisors now have. However, there is one reason that probably does stand out as without question the most important. For taxes and priorities change from year to year, but freedom does not."

Milk wants to make supervisors elected by district, to make them more responsible to the voters. He wants taxes cut, because he says tax money is being wasted. And not least, of course, he wants an end to victimless crime laws.

This last relates directly to the reasons why he thinks a gay person should be elected.

Forcing the Issue
"It will force the issue. How will it look if the people who are making the laws have amongst them a fellow legislator who is a criminal under the law? Something will have to be done. Freedom is the only answer. This is needed in order to stop the burning down of our churches, in order to stop the beating up of Gays on the streets . . . As long as we are legislated into second-class citizenship and are criminals under law, it gives a left-hand[ed] sanction to the burnings and beatings."

And if that's not enough of an argument, Milk offers this one: "To see and hear a gay legislator argue for people and individual rights changes the image overnight and brings respect to all Gays."

He describes himself as an exponent of "Jeffersonian democracy as stated by Lincoln: Of the people, by the people, and for the people, and not a Nixonian philosophy that stands for a government of the few, by the few, and for the few. We have enough Nixons, Reagans, and Aliotos."

On Campaign Promises
He has a lot to say about the record of the city's supervisors on government "of, by, and for the people," too. The supervisors are good

[45]

at promising things when they're up for election, he notes, but "what happens after Election Day is another matter.

"For example, last November the people of this city voted against the death sentence, and then the supervisors passed a resolution in favor of the death penalty. Is that what one can call representing the people? This same board also recently voted ten to one in favor of closing down the nude shows in the city . . ."

In the same way, "a few crumbs" get thrown to Gays during an election year. "They want us; they want our votes. But it's just lip service so long as we remain criminals and nothing is done to change it.

"They say they can't do anything because it's a state law, but they can cut the balls off the police department by cutting the budget. But they pass the police budget like Washington passes the Pentagon's: without questioning it."

Milk has a simple answer for *San Francisco Chronicle* humorist Herb Caen, who awarded "single entendre of the week honors" to the candidate in a recent column for saying he was running "because I'm tired of the election year lip service given to the gay community by our officials." "What do these people WANT?" Caen inquired archly.

"I want freedom for gay people," says Milk. "I reach out to my gay brothers and sisters. I reach out so we can grab each other's hand and fight for what God and the Constitution has given us and man has taken away from us."

4.

A gay candidate with something for all

For a first-time political candidate, one of the most difficult and most essential tasks is to build credibility by earning endorsements from prominent people, organizations, and the press. This interview by John Bryan appeared in a November 1973 issue of the alternative newspaper *The Phoenix*. Headlined "A gay candidate with something for all," it represented a triumph for Milk: one of his very first press endorsements.

A 43-YEAR-OLD Castro Street camera store owner named Harvey Milk is making the first serious attempt in San Francisco history to get a homosexual on the Board of Supervisors.

As this year's supervisorial campaign neared its end just before *Phoenix* press time, Milk (who has "Something for Everybody") was out at dawn at bus stops handing out buttons and pamphlets. He was speaking before every gathering that would hear him—including one sponsored by conservative University of San Francisco students and another held by pensioners living in condemned downtown hotels.

Although the native New Yorker who came here in 1969 is perfectly open about the fact that he's gay, Milk is not putting any unusual emphasis on it. Instead, he's talking about a wide variety of issues which affect everyone. (Interestingly enough, the most politically powerful gay organizations which might support him have turned their backs on Harvey Milk. He does not expect to get more than 20,000 gay votes . . . although he estimates there are at least 90,000 gays in the city and about 40,000 of them are registered voters.)

Instead, Milk is doing a lot of talking about such primary issues as better Muni service, making all city employees (INCLUDING cops) live in the City and putting an end to enforcement of the victimless crime laws.

Some recent Milk quotes on these matters:

"Before each election, the supervisors throw a crumb or two to minority groups like homosexuals . . . after the election they promptly forget it. Dianne Feinstein said before the election two years ago that reform of the vice laws against gays was 'long overdue.' It's two years later, she's done nothing, but she's still saying the same thing. What we need are elections every six months to make the politicians responsible . . .

"I'm for total repeal of all the victimless crime laws. You can't legislate morality . . . If certain cops want to be ministers, fine. Let them join the clergy. But they have no right to enforce nineteenth-century Christian morality while wearing policemen's uniforms . . .

"Let's tell the Police Department to close down its vice squad or promise them that we'll cut off the fifty percent of the police budget that now goes to enforce victimless crime laws . . . Let's instruct the city attorney to bring suit against the state demanding the repeal of victimless crime laws. The publicity that would result from this would be worth it alone. It would make the voters all over the state face the issue . . .

"Let's stop entrapping prostitutes in downtown hotels. Put those same men on traffic detail enforcing a 25 mile-per-hour limit on Doyle Drive. Get the police out of the Hilton Hotel [where they try to catch prostitutes] and into the streets!

"The entire Yerba Buena convention center project is a stinking albatross which will hand around the necks of the taxpayers for generations. The politicians are afraid to allow the public to vote for Yerba Buena bonds—general obligation bonds which have the lowest interest rate. So they are financing through lease revenue bonds which are twice as expensive. This kind of deception makes Candlestick Park and BART look like small potatoes . . ."

Milk also has strong criticism for the entire concept of making San Francisco a "high income" city dependent entirely upon big business and tourism to keep its residents alive. He'd like to see money spent on making this a city all kinds of low income people can afford to live in and to hell with big business.

This is Milk's first campaign for public office. He's aware that he has little chance to win this time but plans to run again two years from now. He thinks the issues he is now bringing up so dramatically will become even more important by then and that people will remember his pioneering stands.

For whatever it's worth, the *Phoenix* likes Milk. We like his program and his candor. We'd recommend you vote for him.

In spite of his endorsement by *The Phoenix,* Milk lost his campaign for a seat on the Board of Supervisors. However, for a candidate with little money and no recognition, he did much better than most people expected.

5.

"Shop owner / social organizer / politician"

Once bitten by the political bug, Milk was determined to run for office again. During 1974 he laid the groundwork for a future candidacy by joining local organizations and working to register voters. He tried to join his local merchants' association, but was refused membership because Castro Camera's owners were gay. In response, Milk became the president of the Castro Village Association, a competing but dormant neighborhood group that admitted both gay and straight merchants. He became active in other local groups as well. As a voter registration event, he and Scott Smith produced the first Castro Street Fair, which everyone considered a big success because it attracted 5,000 people.

On October 21, 1974, an organization called Tunbridge in Boston held a meeting in San Francisco to begin a Tunbridge in San Francisco branch, bringing together people who are not professional teachers but are interested in teaching adult education courses. Milk's brief answers to the Tunbridge in San Francisco membership questionnaire reveal a changed view of himself compared to the questionnaire a year before when he answered "To what clubs and organizations do you belong?" with "NONE."

[. . .]

10. *Your vocational field*

Milk: Shop owner / social organizer / politician

11. *Your job title and a brief description of what this job entails*

 Milk: To bring gov't to the people by organizing the people

12. *Avocational interests in which you have considerable skill and experience*

 Milk: Theater producer
 Stock market analyst
 Newspaper writter [sic]

13. *Areas of involvement and access*

 Milk: Active in Gay Civil Rights
 Trustee Friends of S.F. Deputies & Inmates
 Write for several papers
 Head of Voter Registration Drive
 Pres. Castro Village Assoc.

6.

The second time around for Milk

In the next year, 1975, Milk and Smith produced the second Castro Street Fair, and 25,000 people attended. To increase his credibility as a candidate, Milk cut his shoulder-length hair, stopped smoking marijuana, and stopped going to gay bathhouses. He worked with labor unions and advocacy groups on their issues in hopes of receiving their endorsements. In August, he filed to run for the Board of Supervisors a second time.

At the same time that Milk ran his own supervisorial race, he made Castro Camera the neighborhood headquarters for another campaign, that of George Moscone, the president of the California State Senate, who was running to be mayor of San Francisco. Milk supported Moscone, and Moscone supported Milk.

Milk's pre-campaign efforts paid off, giving him more endorsements and higher visibility than in his previous campaign. The *San Francisco Chronicle* covered his candidacy in this October 23 article by reporter Julie Smith, who later became famous as an Edgar Award-wining mystery novelist. Smith toured with Milk through different neighborhoods for a day, giving us a portrait of Milk as he campaigned.

I N 1973, the first time Harvey Milk ran for supervisor, he told people he was a Democrat, a Jew, and a gay white male, just so there'd be no mistake.

At that time, "people couldn't get past the word 'gay'." Milk got fewer than 17,000 votes.

Now he's running again and he feels things are going much better: "People know the city's hard up and they don't care if I'm green with two heads."

The last time he ran, Milk remembers, "People who weren't out of their closets wouldn't put my signs in their windows.

"Now that my creditability is established, being gay is not an issue. When you've been endorsed by the groups I have, it's ALL straight."

His list of endorsements includes groups as diverse as San Francisco Tomorrow, the National Women's Political Caucus, the Union Labor party, the San Francisco Building and Construction Trade Council, and the San Francisco Black Political Caucus.

Milk, who came to San Francisco from New York in 1969, is a former Montgomery Street financial analyst [with J. Barth Co.]. He gave up that job on the day Nixon invaded Cambodia: "I made a protest speech on the steps of the Pacific Coast Stock Exchange and my speech beat me back to the office."

He is 45, talks non-stop, enjoys a good argument and can't resist clowning now and then. Sometimes, in profile and at just the right angle, he resembles Dustin Hoffman.

He lives what he describes as a "very quiet" life in a two-bedroom flat over the camera store he operates with a business partner. And his lifestyle is so modest he has only three suits to campaign in, one of which is so old it had to go to the tailor's last week for emergency repair.

Because he cannot afford a high-powered media blitz, he campaigns on the streets, in Golden Gate Park, and at bars, coffee shops, street fairs, movies, church bingo games and Sunday services and conventional political events.

As he walked down Castro Street the other day, slender young men wearing Levi jackets and one earring each waved and called him by name, but the person who greeted him most warmly was a heavyset man with some of his teeth missing. Milk says the man is a hardhat who lives in the neighborhood.

Later, at the opening of a mayoral candidate's headquarters in the Mission District, Milk was approached by a young man with a heavy Spanish accent.

The young man introduced himself and promised to work for Milk in Visitacion Valley. This happens even though, according to Milk, prejudice against gays is heaviest in the Spanish-speaking community.

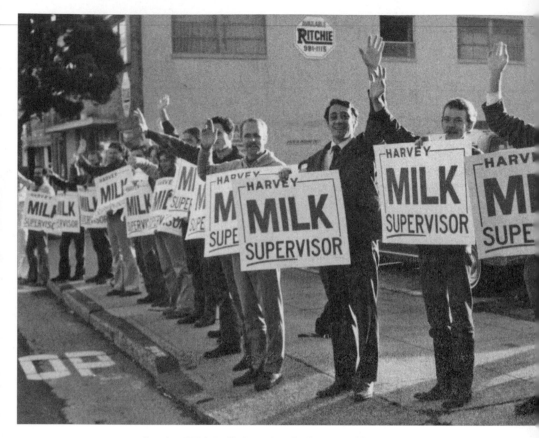

[54]

October 1975: Milk, Scott Smith (their raised hands overlap),
and friends form a human billboard on Market Street.

At a Howard Street tavern, Milk hands a leaflet to a red-nosed
man who asks what Milk intends to do about taxes. The man says he
is a retired post office worker.

"I'm so mad," he says, "I'd join any group to fight those people
(the incumbents). I'd even join a revolutionary group."

Milk says later that people don't want to talk about gay issues:
"They're concerned about their day-to-day life, their jobs, taxes . . ."

In a Clement Street coffee shop, a middle class man and woman
recognize Milk. "What are you doing here?" the woman asks. "Why
aren't you over in . . ." She seems embarrassed to mention Milk's

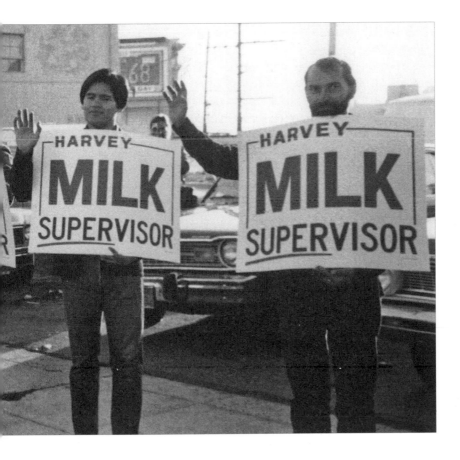

neighborhood. But she says, "I hope you make it." Her companion shakes Milk's hand and observes that "we need to see some new faces at City Hall."

In Golden Gate Park, a young man sees Milk's name on his campaign button and gets off a quick pun. "What are you running for?" he asks. "Dairy queen?"

Afterward, he says he did not know Milk is gay. But the unintentional double meaning is not lost on the candidate, who laughs it off.

"I sort of enjoyed it," he says. "I don't get defensive about things like that. If I turned around every time someone called

me a faggot, I'd be walking backwards and I don't want to walk backwards."

Another man, an older one, refuses Milk's leaflet. "I'm against gay people," he announces. Milk asks why.

"Because they go around molesting people."

Milk counters by quoting statistics that indicate the great majority of child molesters are heterosexuals.

The anti-gay is one of only three Milk says he has clashed with during the entire campaign. "When I run into that," he says, "I have to take off my candidate's hat and try to find out where their prejudices are and do a little educating process.

"As a pure candidate, I shouldn't waste my time—I'm not going to get their votes—but that's the other part of my life. I'm a gay person."

In the gay community, though, this does not entitle him to wholesale support. According to gay spokesmen, there is some opposition there, especially from women who believe Milk is poor on feminist issues.

Partly because of this opposition, Milk did not get the endorsement of the Alice B. Toklas Democratic Club. Despite that, Jim Foster, its former president, estimated Milk has "most" of the gay votes.

That, of course, is to be expected. But Milk's enormous support from labor is something else again.

It grew out of Milk's alliances with labor on several issues—most notably his backing of a recent Teamsters' boycott of Coors beer and his opposition to labor-opposed Proposition B, which would eliminate the crafts pay formula from the city charter if approved by voters.

The fact that he is gay "comes along with the usual jokes," said Stan Smith of the Building and Construction Trades Council. "But nobody's standoffish with Harvey."

"I've seen many a Harvey Milk button on construction workers I thought would be slightly opposed to a gay candidate."

Milk acknowledges that his gladhanding relationships with the hardhats "just destroys every stereotype." But he claims not to be surprised by it.

"I had a very good argument," he says. "I pointed out that labor can't trust the incumbents."

Another union leader, J. B. Martin of Automotive Machinists Local 1305 thinks "the working people of San Francisco have come to realize that, listen, the gay community is here to stay. It's not looked on like it was in the past—like some kind of disease that has to be pushed away."

Milk believes that "once the first gay is elected to the Board, it'll never be an issue again." He gives himself an "outside chance" to set the precedent.

Milk says he is running for supervisor because he is "mad"—about inequitable taxes, strikes and poor city services. His campaign is based largely on a "throw-the-bums-out" philosophy.

"I point to the incumbents and say 'If you like what you're getting, vote for them" he says repeatedly.

7.

"*I'm not a gay candidate, but a candidate who happens to be gay.*"

The day after the *Chronicle* story appeared, this article by David Johnston appeared in the weekly counterculture newspaper, the *Berkeley Barb*. It was titled "Harvey Milk: One gay candidate runs to win." My editorial insertions appear in [square brackets].

W HEN HARVEY MILK ran for San Francisco supervisor two years ago he wore a mustache and a pony tail in a quick campaign that was as hard on shoeleather as it was low on cash. Pulling 17,000 votes, he wound up 19th in a 32-person heat.

This year Harvey Milk has a haircut. He's wearing a coat, a tie and according to the "secret polls" he has a better-than-even chance at unhorsing one of the six incumbents on the Board. If Milk wins, he will be the first gay member of the city's Board of Supervisors.

"I changed my image," he said this week, "but I haven't changed one word of what I've always said. People must understand, it doesn't matter what you look like."

To win, Milk, like the five other challengers in the race, has to beat at least one of the six members of the Board up for re-election. Four of the six are considered all but locked in; two, depending on whose poll you believe, are shaky. Milk thinks that Supervisors [Robert] Gonzales and [Terry] Francois—the only Latin and black seatholders—are weak and could be taken by either himself or the other highly-ranked contender, Joyce Ream.

So far the race hasn't generated much smoke. With the [Patricia] Hearst case [she was arrested in San Francisco on September 18], the Sally Moore affair [housewife Sara Jane "Sally" Moore fired a shot a President Gerald Ford and missed him by six inches in San Francisco on September 22], the lost UFO people [on September

14 in Waldport, Oregon, twenty people disappeared who claimed they were going to be taken by a UFO] and the mayoralty race, the election of supervisors hasn't had much play. And frankly, while the election may be critical, the race is almost always ho-hum anyway.

The reason it's boring is built in. The rules make any juicy hair-pulling between two candidates all but impossible. It is a race where everybody runs and the highest vote-pullers win. This year the first six will get seated, the rest will simply mutter and fade away.

Such rule-induced boredom makes running for supervisor a question of getting visibility over the rest of the field, and here the incumbents—who already have name recognition and money to buy more—hold a heavy natural advantage.

Challengers like Milk, even though his $6,000 budget is double what he had in 1973, have little choice but to flail away at the big issues while scuffling in the streets for votes. For two years Milk has hit the bars, worked the parks and the community organizations, and has picked up support from a surprising array of groups.

With his salvoes against downtown corporate interests and backing for neighborhoods, social services, and unions, Harvey has been endorsed by the National Women's Political Caucus, San Francisco Tomorrow, and none other than the powerful Building and Construction Trades Council, who feel the current Board is out to skin them alive in its attempts to pare crafts pay salaries of city workers.

Stanley Smith of the Council said flatly, "We aren't supporting any of the current members. We're agreeable with Harvey on most issues." And apparently such big labor, pro-Manhattanization support has not hurt Milk, not even among the anti-building environmental groups like San Francisco Tomorrow. "We know where he stands," said Sue Bierman, a director of the organization.

"I'm not opposed to all building," explains Harvey, "just some kinds of it."

Milk's knack for picking up support from such disparate forces as the traditionally hostile unions and environmentalists explains his rise as a major contender, but the "new" Harvey may have lost some of his support from his gay community base in the process. There he has been criticized for downplaying gay issues to curry favor with the straight, but politically potent, organizations.

"A number of gays worked very hard for Harvey," says gay attorney B. J. Beckwith, "but he hasn't even seen fit to list them on his campaign literature as endorsers. I'm very disappointed."

Milk counters these complaints by pointing to his support from organizations like the Gay Voters League. "I would have put them on my masthead, but I heard that they weren't going to endorse me," says Milk, who dismisses criticism as part of a power struggle within gay community groups. "Some people don't like me because I showed that anyone in the community could run," he says.

But Harvey admits to taking sex out of the campaign. "I'm not a gay candidate, but a candidate who happens to be gay. I'm trying to break down stereotypes and if I win it will be victory for everybody, including the gay community."

Six supervisors' seats were open in the 1975 election, and Milk came in seventh, by far the strongest showing of any candidate who was not an incumbent. On election night, Milk made a concession speech thanking his supporters. George Moscone, who was leading the race for mayor but would still need to win a runoff election, came by unannounced and promised that if he (Moscone) won, he would appoint Milk the commissioner of a city board.

A little over a month later, Moscone won, and in his acceptance speech publicly thanked Milk for his support. The next year, 1976, would be the bicentennial celebration of the Declaration of Independence, and Milk looked forward to harvesting the results of his own political efforts. For a two-time loser, his future looked bright.

1976,
Harvey Milk
vs. The Machine

Harvey Milk

On THE ISSUES

These are some of the major issues affecting our lives. There are others. Too many seem to arise from an insensitivity or unwillingness of our legislators to involve themselves with the real issues. The fact that so many of the controversial issues come before the public only through the petition process points to the fact that our legislators don't want to risk taking stands on the issues that concern people the most.

Legislators try to buy favors by doling out stop-gap programs here and there in the community. Most programs come too late, are wasteful and don't work. We need to *prevent* future problems by attacking their causes, instead of just covering over their symptoms with bureaucratic red tape. This takes sensitivity, foresight and aggressive leadership.

Jobs

Light industry must be brought back into the city. Our elected officials watched silently as major industries in San Francisco packed up and left—taking thousands of jobs with them: Hunter's Point Shipyard closed, the Port moved to Oakland, and Third Street, China Basin, India Basin and Yerba Buena have become deserted wastelands.

Without these jobs the people in the district have no money to spend. The Result: White Front closed, Sears in the Mission closed—and still more jobs were lost.

Instead of fighting to keep these jobs in

Leaflet promoting Milk's 1976 candidacy for California state assemblyman representing the Sixteenth Assembly District.

8.

"If we are to live in harmony, we have to build bridges from community to community."

San Francisco Mayor George Moscone kept his promise to Harvey Milk. On January 30, 1976, he appointed Milk a member of the powerful Board of Permit Appeals. This made Milk the first openly gay person appointed to any city government position by Moscone, and the first openly gay city commissioner in the nation.

In early February, the following interview entitled "Harvey Milk" was done for *San Francisco Interview,* volume 1, number 2. Milk was interviewed in the Delancey Street restaurant, operated by a non-profit group that rehabilitates drug users and convicted criminals. In the boldface paragraph below, the people mentioned include Milk's friend Dennis Peron, who owned the Island restaurant and the Big Top marijuana dispensary and was an activist for the decriminalization of medical marijuana; Rick "Slick" Thomas, a producer of entertainment events who worked with Milk and Scott Smith to produce the Castro Street Fairs; attorney Carol Ruth Silver, who the next year would run for a seat on the Board of Supervisors; Tom Hayden, who was running in the Democratic primary for the U.S. Senate; and his wife, the movie star Jane Fonda.

Eureka Valley, gay Mecca of the world's gay magnet, has been placed firmly on the political map of this city by the fearless, dauntless, persistent efforts of its most public character, the owner of a small camera shop on Castro Street. (He says he's a

film seller.) It is not enough to say that Harvey is blessed with good looks, a tremendous smile, hearty handshake if it's needed, and the first outspokenly gay city commissioner in S.F., the U.S., maybe the WORLD. It is not enough to say that he has influenced city government over the years, fighting people's causes for gays, blacks, Chicanos, and Chinese, all minorities. The underprivileged, the oppressed, and the worker. It is not enough to say that at this point in his life he is seriously challenging to overturn a ten-year political plan by the state power machine.

Harvey Milk is much more. He is responsible for the gay vote in San Francisco. He is the symbol of gay pride. He is the creator of the city's most spectacular street fair.

Here are his own words on the subject.

Harvey sits with Dennis Peron and Slick at Delancey Street, while photographer Alan Kucheck snaps, on the occasion of a fundraiser hosted by Carol Ruth Silver and the Golden Gate Demo[cratic] Club, with special guests, Tom Hayden and Jane Fonda.

Rick Slick: *You can come over and sit and chat occasionally if you want to, Harvey.*

Milk: We could do it right this minute.

Slick: *You want to make it current?*

Milk: No, it'll be dated. What am I? What's Harvey Milk all about? (laughs) We don't really know.

Slick: *Yeah, that's what I want.*

Milk: It's a whole new thing. Let me give you an up-front example.

There's a fairly wealthy gentleman in this city who has contributed to many political campaigns in the past. Everybody's. His voting record and my voting record on issues would be identical. He's a liberal. He stands for everything I stand for. He won't give me a penny because he chokes on the word "gay." He admits it. He says he's got a hangup, and, in essence, he'd vote for [Alabama Governor George] Wallace before he'd vote for me, even though Wallace stands for everything he's against. Because of that one thing.

There's an awful lot of that in this city. You don't hear about it, but it's there. It exists. It's deep. So there's two ways. One, you can take a twenty-year, thirty-year approach and educate people. Slowly educate, and hope to change people's views. That will be done, but what about people that exist today? What you have to do is confront them.

What Harvey Milk is all about, I guess, is confronting them. The government is screwed up. They give us little crumbs, and we go back happy. In the meantime, they rip off millions and millions for themselves. Then they pull their hypocrisies and their prejudices. Somebody's got to call it.

Right now, most of the political people are in this crazy game. The Lockheeds, the Northrops. Congress knows about this. Nobody ever seems to want to challenge this and say, "What's democracy about?" and "What's government about?" So you have that on one side, and coming from a gay person, it kind of throws them in a tailspin. First of all, to be challenged, to start with, and second, to be challenged by someone whose lifestyle they disapprove of because of their prejudices. So you're hitting on two fronts.

But sooner or later, though they might not admit it, they're going to say, "Hey, this guy is really fighting for what I stand for." When he realizes that I'm on his side on the issues, the Nixons are on the other side, then he'll accept me as an individual because we're fighting the common enemy. Once he accepts me as an individual and joins me in the battle, then he will overcome some of his prejudices and some of his hangups.

I think a clear-cut example of that is in the last supervisorial race, where the hardhats, the Archie Bunkers, the San Francisco construction and building trades not only endorsed me, but worked for me, campaigned for me, wore buttons, handed out literature. These are the people that are stereotyped as anti-gay. I was fighting for them. I was fighting their battle, because I believed in it. Once they understood that, the fact that I was gay had little significance. I'm fighting not only for gays, but for blacks, and all minorities, and people in the street.

The politicians and some of the "leaders" have to understand that when we have common battles, we have to fight together. I think that's what Harvey Milk stands for, in essence. The fact that

someone's willing to get up there and fight those battles because he believes in them, because he's dedicated to them.

At the same time, I'm trying to build bridges between the different communities. Sometimes the bridges are shaky, but they're bridges that didn't exist before. I think it's vital that the larger the population grows, the more we'll have to live in harmony, or it'll be an awful place to live. If we *are* to live in harmony, we have to build bridges from community to community. That doesn't mean that we have to accept their lifestyle or they have to accept our lifestyle. But there has to be tremendous respect. They have to realize that we have a common goal, and that is to live and to enjoy life.

You can't sit down and discuss intelligently and logically with political leaders, because they're not into that. You can't throw stones and bricks, because that won't achieve anything. So you have to work through the system. Work hard at it. Learn it. When they realize that you're working in the system, they help build their bridge, and we finally achieve what we all want to achieve—through the system.

I guess that's what I'm all about.

9.

"I will fight for freedom of speech and for democracy."

Milk quickly made splashes in George Moscone's pond. Milk thought he would have a good chance of election as the representative to the California State Assembly for the Sixteenth Asembly District. He found that Moscone and Leo McCarthy, the powerful speaker of the California Senate, had agreed to back McCarthy's aide Art Agnos to run for that assembly seat.

Before Milk made his final decision to run, he spoke with George Mendenhall of the *Bay Area Reporter*. The resulting article, "Finding the Answers: Harvey Milk vs. The Machine" appeared in the February 19, 1976 issue of the *Reporter* and sums up Milk's situation. (Ellipses in the text are not my deletions, but are part of Mendenhall's writing style.)

"HARVEY MILK and every citizen has a right to present his credentials to the voters. I have an absolute duty to appoint commissioners who would use their time to serve the city . . . If he runs, he will set the record for the shortest commissioner in history. And I am not talking about his size . . . A guy cannot serve the public and campaign at the same time."

Mayor George Moscone surprised friend and foe with the above statement early this month. Milk is the Castro Street merchant who was recently appointed by the mayor to the city Board of Permit Appeals . . . the first upfront gay to be appointed by any mayor to a major city commission. In office only 30 days, Milk indicated that he might be running for a vacant seat in the 16th Assembly District. The Moscone response placed Milk in an "underdog fighting the big politicians" role . . . a role that he obviously enjoys.

The mayor's supporters state that all commissioners agreed to serve four years [as their] term. They add that the mayor had told his commissioners that he expected them to serve the city and not to use their positions as stepping stones to higher office. It was felt by many that Milk would serve effectively on the Board for a reasonable period of time and then move on to higher office, probably to the Board of Supervisors. Milk's intent to run for the Assembly was as surprising as Moscone's blunt reaction.

Moscone states that it is Milk's "absolute right" to run, a point emphasized by Quentin Kopp, president of the city's Board of Supervisors. Kopp, who had supported John Barbagelata in the recent mayor's race, seized the opportunity of the Milk-Moscone confrontation to state that an "unholy alliance" exists between Assembly Speaker Leo McCarthy, Congressman Phil Burton, and Moscone. This "alliance," he contended, was pushing a "machine-picked" candidate, Art Agnos, and attempting to squeeze Milk out of the race. Although undocumented, it made good press copy.

Milk was greatly encouraged by the Kopp attack and now talks about the "machine that dictates who your representatives are," Milk told this reporter. "There is lots of wheeling and dealing and political payoffs. That is what is wrong with politics. It doesn't have to be like that. There are some politicians that are not like that." He obviously includes himself in the latter category and adds, "It is not whether they have been good to the gay community or to people. It is, are they faithful to democracy? Are they better than this system? I don't think anybody—even Harvey Milk—is better than this system. I will fight for freedom of speech and for democracy."

How democracy works was illustrated by a telephone call that led [to] his intent to run. Milk says that McCarthy is part of the "machine" of Bay Area legislators and he made [a] "courtesy call" to McCarthy, whom he had met once before. He said he had asked for the support of several legislators and [departing assemblyman John] Foran in the future (1977) supervisorial race. He said that if he got that kind of support he "wouldn't have to think about anything else." The implication was clear—that if the "machine" supported him at a later date, he would be able to see his way to not

run for the Assembly seat. Milk says he got no assurance from any of them that they would support him in the future.

Milk says he told McCarthy on the telephone that "the big road to my being a supervisor was being blocked and that if there was a crowded field (in the Assembly race) that I would have a better chance of winning there. I [called] him to let him know. It was a courtesy call. Leo and I have gotten along well in the past . . . Those that I called may have felt that if I got enough support in the supervisorial race that I might not have to run for the Assembly. They can think what they want to think."

Speaker McCarthy told this reporter that Milk had called him with "probing comments" but that "I am not going to draw inference from it. You can draw your own." He said that Milk explained that "he was taking out papers for the 16th Assembly District—but that his real preference was to be on the Board of Supervisors. He did not specifically ask me to do anything . . . I did not react because I personally sensed what the conversation was about. I try to be fair as I can with people . . . he went on and then I told him that I didn't know what to say. I told him, 'You have a right to run for the Assembly if you want to.' Of course, he knew of Art's relationship with me. I told him that I didn't know what I could do as far as the Board of Supervisors was concerned. He did not ask me to support him if he ran for Supervisor, nor did he ask me to try to get the mayor to appoint him to the Board—and I didn't offer anything."

McCarthy added that his aide Agnos, was "unfortunately being put down in all of this crossfire with Quentin Kopp. Art has an excellent record and I hope people are not being prejudiced by all of this. Kopp supported Barbagelata and he saw this opportunity to put Moscone down. Kopp doesn't like me or Burton and he sees this as a prize occasion to make himself a hero through using Harvey Milk . . . It is ironic that I should be aligned with Phil Burton because we have been mortal enemies on at least a dozen occasions over the years, and George [Moscone] and I ran against each other ten years ago. To describe us as a kind of 'political machine' is humorous."

There is the possibility that the entire Milk vs. Agnos race could have been avoided if the "ins" had consulted with Harvey Milk in advance. Milk says, "You would think that they would have

[69]

said, 'You know, Harvey represents a certain segment. We ought to talk with him and see where his head is.'" Instead, Milk concludes, "They thought that Foster (Jim Foster, gay politico) and Goodstein (David Goodstein, *Advocate* publisher) were more important . . . They didn't inform me what they were doing. That is their problem. I had been asked to be kept informed, to prevent something like this from happening. They never told me . . . All they had to do was pick up the phone and explain the situation to me. Instead, they did it behind my back."

Milk has written to Moscone, requesting a meeting to discuss the issue. The mayor has recognized that he received the letter but has not responded. Milk says, "I would like to sit down with him and say, 'George, what did you say to the press?' Maybe he was misquoted. Maybe it was taken out of context. I want to ask him what he meant. Moscone has since repeated that Milk's position on the Board of Permit Appeals is in question but that he will wait to see if Milk files on March 12.

Milk is clearly the most well-known candidate in the race for Assembly. His image is also impressive—conservative small businessman, gay activist—with the implied implication that he is for all minority rights, and now an "underdog fighting the big political machine." He has run twice for the Board of Supervisors and made impressive showings with a minimum expense. Milk is aggressive, articulate, and highly independent. He is quick to point to the 16th Assembly District chart in his business and explain at length how well he did there in the last election. Money could be raised for a campaign, he believes, and he is already accepting checks for that purpose. He believes that he can "do it" on $15,000 but is aware that Agnos, with broad political support, could raise considerably more.

The 16th Assembly District is possibly the most interesting area in the state. It is an unusual combination of Blacks, Gays, Latinos, Italians, Chinese—you name it—plus a conservative element. The area includes South of Market, Hunters Point-Bayview, North Beach, Tenderloin, Castro, Noe Valley, Potrero Hill, Twin Peaks, and the Mission. In each of these areas there has been a continuing conflict between conservative and liberal factions.

[70]

Who is Art Agnos? He is virtually an unknown person to the general public—few know his face or his name. What he will have going for him is considerable support from neighborhood activists and leaders—including some gay community leadership . . . In his seven years in Sacramento as an aide to Leo McCarthy, he has been "the man" to contact for legislative changes and financial grants to community projects. He knows all Assembly members on a first-name basis and is an expert on state and federal funding. Many people are indebted to Agnos, who has helped the poor and disenfranchised for several years.

Milk is aware of the Agnos strength and responds that "They buy the minority communities to get their support. That is what politics has been and it is the tragedy of politics." Milk may be right but many gay activists who have walked the halls in Sacramento know how Agnos has helped with legislation. Others point to Agnos' assistance on getting gay employment counseling and gay alcoholic aid through the Whitman-Radclyffe Foundation.

Agnos is confident. He says that Milk is a novice who gets excited because his name is now in the newspapers. He says, "Quentin Kopp has seduced him for his own political needs. Kopp is using Milk in a patronizing way—as a political link to the gay community." He says that there is no "machine," but "I know the people. Isn't it great that I will be able to walk into the mayor's office or our congressman's office or the assembly speaker's office and get things done for you, like I have for the past seven years? Or do you want someone who doesn't know these people, is feuding with these people, who can't work with them?"

"This whole thing, Agnos claims, "has been blown up because Harvey wants it blown up. He is a nice guy but he is now coming on like a conniving politician. He should have to put in some time as a public servant on the Board of Permit Appeals. Instead, he announced that he is seeking higher office. He appears now to be a political opportunist." Agnos' anger and concern is justified because it will take more effort and money to defeat Harvey Milk than it will the third announced candidate, former football star Bob St. Clair.

Within the gay community, Milk is hopeful that there will be a spirit of "electing one of our own"—no matter what the "leadership" wants. There is some feeling that Milk can "do it" because he is an

amazing 18-hour-a-day campaigner, seven days a week. Whether he is or is not favored by Bay Area legislators, some gay people would like to see an elected gay person in Sacramento. How strong this feeling is cannot be determined. Milk's earlier campaigns did not rally hundreds of workers from the gay community behind him.

Has Milk enjoyed politics and has it helped him financially or otherwise? In an interview in his Castro shop, he said, "No. But it is needed. It does not have to be Harvey Milk. I kind of fill a vacuum. I saw the need and heard a good reaction. I keep battling . . . Do I enjoy it? No. It has destroyed my personal life—from sex to entertainment. It has been a tremendous financial handicap to my business. (He took $2,500 from his business to help finance his last campaign.) . . . I am the kind of guy who likes to go to movies, theatres, dinners—all of that. If I go out to relax in a bar, people stop me to talk about thus-or-that . . . I do not enjoy it [at] all, but it is desperately needed. It has to be done—so I will do it, with every ounce of energy that I have. There are some politicians who enjoy it . . . I wish others would pick up the ball but they are not.

"My business suffers because I should be spending time promoting it and working for it more. I take money from the store to help with my campaigns and that hurts the business . . . I only get $15 a week for being on the Board of Permit Appeals, which amounts to about $3 an hour. I do not ask for expenses because I want to be clean—super clean. It would disturb me to learn that the first upfront Gay, like let's say a judge or something, was on the take. We have to be like Jackie Robinson when he was the first black in baseball. I wouldn't even take the offer of a free massage although I recently spoke up for the rights of a massage parlor owner."

When he was asked, "Well, hasn't the so-called 'political machine' worked well lately for gay people?" Milk said that it was the "machine" politicians who "set up Agnos to run. They primed him, picked him for it. They locked it all up ahead for him. That is what they are trying to do . . . No, the machine hasn't worked well for us. The Willie Brown bill was not sufficient; it was a step. Foran's bill on employment rights could have passed. Do you mean to tell me that the speaker of the Assembly and the chairman of the Ways and Means Committee cannot get anything they want passed through the Assembly? They can—but they have to pay the

price for it. They do not want to pay that price for gay rights—to end discrimination of gay persons. They are not willing to pull all of the strings. They aren't willing to go all the way."

Several well-known gay activists have privately said that they will be supporting Art Agnos, because of his efforts in Sacramento. How does Milk react to this? . . . "Gay people have gotten favors from the machine because they have gotten payoffs in one form or another—aid, funds, whatever. While I certainly appreciate whatever help the gay community gets, I think that loyalty has to be based on democracy and not political payoffs. If they want to go with the man who can buy them—then fine. Prostitution exists and will continue to exist . . . Maybe they are buying off leaders in all the communities so that when the time comes to announce, there will be all those debts. Everyone is then supporting him, not knowing that he was bought with public money . . . Do we have to kiss their hem? They are just getting a tiny bit of what they owe us.

"You don't dictate to us by going to four or five so-called 'gay leaders' and making a deal. These 'leaders' can't deliver. They are not going to deliver the votes of the people in the streets. The people have minds of their own . . . They want to use the names of these 'gay leaders' in their literature. You would think that if they were going to do that, they would have come and talked with me—a long time ago."

[73]

10.

"*I try to set examples by deeds rather than simply by words.*"

In a March 9 speech at the San Francisco Press Club, Milk announced his decision: he would run against Art Agnos as a candidate for state assemblyman. Within four hours, Moscone fired Milk from the Board of Permit Appeals.

In the April 1, 1976 *Bay Area Reporter,* columnist Wayne Friday (who Dan Nicoletta says was Milk's best friend) interviewed Milk to find why he decided to campaign to represent the Sixteenth Assembly District. His interview was titled "World of Wayne: What Makes Harvey Run . . ."

A FTER LISTENING TO, *and reading about, weeks of charges, counter-charges, accusations, denials, etc., regarding the decision of Harvey Milk to challenge Art Agnos in the 16th Assembly District Primary, and being fully aware that Harvey Milk had just completed an exhausting, yet unsuccessful race for the Board of Supervisors, I had to wonder why in hell the guy would want to take on another political battle—since another writer recently stated the case for the Mayor and Art Agnos—I arrived at Milk's Castro Street Camera Shop with pen, pad, and tape recorder—the back of his shop had been turned into a very busy campaign headquarters—two phones were ringing at the same time, and five young men and a young woman were busily stuffing envelopes, etc. Harvey was happy to answer some of my questions, and here is his side of the story—this is how it went:*

Friday: *What made you decide to enter this race, Harvey? What is your reason for running, anyway?*

Milk: There is a solid two-fold reason why I am in this race; neither is *the* main reason; both are to me, vital. First, I feel that our

government on many levels has taken a turn, and a sharp turn at that, away from responding to the needs of the people—that its sense of priorities is becoming more and more misdirected. I hope to bring that sense of priorities back to the basic needs of people. All too often, we misuse what resources we have; the end result is that the general public gets very little. I'm against the large bureaucracy that has frustrated too many people.

The second reason is that I feel the gay community, the last minority that has not achieved its full civil rights, must have a voice on the floor of an important legislative body, especially in view of the recent Supreme Court ruling. It is needed not only for our own protection, but to set an example to the young gays that says the system does work. I won't go into details on this point because I think that most of us understand the importance of electing gay people to office. Every minority has learned the importance of electing their own.

Friday: *Then why not wait and run again for supervisor? You did very well last year, even though you obviously had limited funds.*

Milk: Having finished just out of the money in the last year's race on, as you so well put it, limited funds, I was seriously considering building for another try at supervisor in two years; however, several facts that were not known to the public, but only to me, made me reconsider another try for supervisor. First, there is the cost of such a race. No one who has not actually run for supervisor knows what it is really all about . . . it's about money. In order to win in San Francisco, you have to either have a great deal of money or a name that is a strong household word. The incumbents with the position of the office, the name recognition, and the ability to make news, also have the funds. And with the changing of the laws, there will be no limit on what they can spend next time. Thus, anyone who wants to challenge the incumbents must have very substantial backing. And frankly, I don't have that kind of money. Second, even if there were to be one or two openings on the present Board, for whatever reasons, the mayor himself told me that I would not be getting either the first or second vacancy that might occur on the Board of Supervisors. Thus, being appointed by the mayor was at

[75]

best a very outside chance. There would have to be some three or four supervisors leaving the Board before I would be given a shot at it. That possibility is remote. I personally don't foresee any of the present supervisors stepping down in mid-term. Besides, the mayor only appointed me to a one-year term on the Board of Permit Appeals. So there wasn't even the guarantee that I would be able to run for supervisor from a commissioner's spot. In fact, if he did not reappoint me, it may even have looked worse to some people, and that in turn could be an additional handicap to anyone, especially a gay person.

All these factors compounded the decision of attempting to run again for supervisor next year. So when the opportunity to run for the Assembly presented itself by John Foran vacating his seat to run for the Senate, I listened very carefully to those who urged me to make this race.

Friday: *In what way do you think your election could help the gay movement?*

Milk: Wayne, in all of my involvements, I always think of the effect it has on the gay movement. I have always tried to do two basic things. One, build bridges with the non-gay community. Two, not use the positions solely as platforms to make a pitch for the movement. I try to use those positions to set examples, which in the long run, I think I make for a strong voice for the movement. In short, what I could say in words from those positions is not as important as what I actually do in those positions. I try to set examples by deeds rather than simply by words.

[76]

My election and my work on the floor of the Assembly on day-to-day problems would be one of the greatest things I could do for the movement. To work with others in the Assembly on the economic and social problems would be a vital step in the right direction, and from the confidence I would be able to gain, I would then be able to fight for the necessary legislation that is so long overdue for all gay people. It will be a most solid and effective method.

Friday: *Just what are your honest chances, Harvey? I heard one politician say that if the election were held tomorrow, you would easily win.*

Milk: I promised all who urged me into this race and all who have come with us since that I would not run if I thought I would be a Don Quixote. The broad base that we had in the race for supervisor has already broadened and the race has really just gotten under way. If the present rate of help continues, then I think we have a much better chance for success this time than we had in our race for supervisor. We surprised a lot of people in that race with the finish we made on the limited funds that we had. In short, Wayne, too much is at stake here to waste it on a race without a good chance. We have that chance here.

Friday: *What is your biggest obstacle now?*

Milk: Money. As simple as that. While we do not need as much for this race as you need for a race for supervisor, since only one-third of the city is covered in the 16th Assembly District, we still badly need funds. Dollar bills and, if possible, checks for large amounts. If everyone who voted for us in the last race for supervisor sent in just one dollar, we would have enough funds to mount a very successful race.

Friday: *Two of the better-known names who have endorsed you are Carol Ruth Silver and Quentin Kopp. What part are they playing in this campaign?*

Milk: Carol is part of the Steering Committee of Advisors and one of the co-chairpeople on the campaign. She has also been my attorney. On top of that, Carol has given us a warmth and spirit that titles cannot cover. Quentin has done two things: urged me to run in the first place, then warmly endorsed me. He has been so deeply involved in the current city strike situation that he and I have not yet sat down to talk. We have greeted each other in passing and that's about it. When the strike is over, we will no doubt be getting together to see just what role he is willing to play in the campaign. Quentin's support and that of Carol is very much appreciated. Kopp was the highest vote-getter in this assembly district last November.

[77]

Friday: *Other than the endorsement of Kopp and Carol Silver, how does your support in this race compare with that in your last race for supervisor?*

Milk: Well, as I said, Quentin and Carol's endorsement[s] have already made a difference. Add to theirs, increasing support coming in from the ethnic groups which was not strong the last time; then there are those who found out what we were all about too late or after the fact the last time, who are already helping, and we see a much broader base than we ever had before. It is a wonderful thing to see the total picture of such different communities forming together in this race. We have reached way beyond our community and found tremendous help. Help from others who believe in what we are saying about the priorities of government. It's exciting!

Friday: *How has the gay community in general reacted to your candidacy?*

Milk: Almost the same as last year's race. Those who understand the importance of a gay person being elected are there. Those who understand the need of breaking down myths, stereotypes, and so forth, are there. Those who understand the social and economic issues beyond the movement are there. Those who do not agree with me politically and do not care about the movement are not there.

The importance of sending gays to the Democratic Convention are expressed by some. They ask for support because they are gay. Yet those same people support my opponent, who is not gay. They express the importance of electing upfront gays to the National Convention, and yet they in turn don't see the need to elect upfront gays to public office. I question that type of self-serving wisdom.

[78]

But in large, last year I did not receive support of many of the gay leaders and spokespersons. My strength in the gay community comes from the people in the gay community, not necessarily the leaders, although I welcome and hope for their support. It was primarily the people, not the leaders, in the gay community who helped us in the last campaign and who are there working with us now. Without their support, I would not be able to do what I am attempting to do. It honestly renews my faith in people, Wayne. And that is a good feeling.

Friday: *Harvey, what do you feel that you, as an assemblyman who just happens to be an upfront gay, can accomplish in the legislature?*

Milk: Well, the first is to present the case for the much-needed gay legislation from a gay person's point of view, rather than second-handed, without the [lack of] personal involvement that a non-gay legislator has. I think that I can present the case with more sincerity, and of course, conviction, for I would be presenting not only the case for gay people, but for myself as a gay, as well.

Second, as I have said before, working with the legislators on the many issues before the Assembly, I would be setting an example and winning friends and allies on these other issues. I would be building important bridges, and one day, they will have to say, as we all know is said about so many of us, so many times: "Hey, he's not so bad after all. What were we so afraid, uptight, etc., about in the first place?" This is an accomplishment that only a gay person, working as an equal on the floor of the Assembly, can accomplish. There is simply no substitute for the real thing.

Friday: *Your opponent once told me he felt he could be more effective, because he said he knows personally all of the members of the Assembly. What is your reaction to this?*

Milk: Well, Wayne, if effectiveness if based on popularity and familiarity, then we should never change one single legislator anywhere, and we will always elect the Nixons and the Reagans, because they knew everyone so well, for so long. But if the current lack of gay legislation, and current economic and social conditions, red tape, and lousy tax laws are a result of familiarity, then maybe we should elect a complete group of strangers; they could not do much worse. That statement on my opponent's part almost sounds like a desire to return to the womb. Just because you know a legislator by name, who might be ineffective, by the way, is no reason to be elected. This is not a popularity contest. This is a legislative body that spends our money and regulates our lives. I'm amazed at the lack of depth in that kind of thinking.

[79]

Friday: *Where can you be reached? Or what can those people who haven't already been approached do, who might want to get involved in your campaign?*

Milk: Well, we do need volunteer workers on all levels, and as I said before, we desperately need funds. Like I said, even those one dollar

bills help a great deal. The headquarters is here at my camera shop: 575 Castro Street, and the phone number is 864–1390. We would appreciate it if you would even just drop by to pick up a window sign to put in your house or store window. We try to work hard, but we also look for that laugh and warmth that happens when strangers meet to work for a common goal and that magic takes over.

11.

"If they give you a crumb, they can take that crumb away. But if they give you freedom, it's pretty hard to take that away."

After Milk's first coverage in *The Advocate* in 1974, the publication was sold to David Goodstein. He allied with politically active gays who viewed Milk as their rival. The April 7, 1976 issue of *The Advocate* contained the article below, "In San Francisco: Milk gets canned but keeps on running" by Sasha Gregory-Lewis. Milk was not happy about this article because he thought it implies that instead of the leading gay publication endorsing Milk, the only gay candidate, *The Advocate* was leaning towards endorsing his opponent Art Agnos. Milk was right; closer to Election Day, that's exactly what *The Advocate* did.

SAN FRANCISCO'S gay power exercise in mainstream reformist politics is showing unprecedented results this year: Three openly gay people have been appointed to important city commissions; the sheriff has hired an openly gay deputy; the city finally enforced its gay rights ordinance against the local arm of Ma Bell. Even the police chief supports gay rights, as are most of the city's elected officials.

This gay power exercise has taken too long, some people feel. Its results, they charge, are unsatisfactory, its politics tainted.

One of the people who isn't happy with this political exercise is Harvey Milk, a gay camera store owner who, casting himself in the role of the little guy fighting the big political machine, is making his third bid for elective office in as many years.

This time, after two unsuccessful bids for the city's Board of Supervisors, Milk is challenging Arthur Agnos, experienced politico and long-time aide to Assembly Speaker Leo T. McCarthy, in the Democratic primary race for the state assembly.

Milk's experience in government is recent and brief. He served about two months on the city's Permit Appeals Board as the first gay person appointed to a city government slot by recently-elected Mayor George Moscone. The appeals board job was viewed as a grooming position by many city politicos, including, reportedly, Mayor Moscone himself. Milk was to show his stuff and get his name in the public view, so the story goes, in preparation for a shoo-in victory in the 1977 supervisorial race.

Milk, however, didn't see the slot as a grooming job. Says Milk, "If anything, it was really to get me out of the way while they groomed someone else." Milk notes, however, that the appeals board is important to the gay community because it is a court of last resort for businesses and others who must apply for permits to sometimes insensitive city departments. The board's decisions may only be overridden by the Board of Supervisors.

When Milk announce that he was thinking of running for the assembly seat (on the same day that Agnos formally announced his candidacy), Mayor Moscone, in a statement which caused a flurry of controversy in the local media, said that he would kick Milk off of the board because he didn't think Milk could do a good job on the board and run for office at the same time.

Milk responded that elected officials don't resign from their positions when campaigning and that he saw no reason why he couldn't run for the assembly and keep his board position.

When Milk filed for the race March 12, Moscone removed him from the board, replacing him with Rick Stokes, a gay attorney with no immediate political ambitions. Milk then demanded that Agnos resign from his appointive position on the city's Commission on the Aging and from his position as McCarthy's aide. Agnos then revealed that he had tendered his resignation from the commission before announcing his candidacy. Agnos also said he was resigning from his post in McCarthy's office.

Milk also demanded that Agnos pay back the salary he had earned as McCarthy's aide since announcing his intention to run

for the assembly seat. Agnos replied that he had no intention of turning back any of his salary because "I haven't campaigned on state hours."

Although Milk is short on experience in public office, he is a tireless campaigner, having rounded up some 53,000 votes in the 1975 supervisorial race, bringing him into the position of first runner-up to the reelected incumbents.

Milk, praising himself on his campaign, says that he was able to bring out his 53,000 votes with the infinitesimally small campaign war chest of $10,090, $2,500 of which came from his own pocket. He says he can win the much more costly assembly race on a mere $30,000.

Despite the fact that Milk has been able to get impressive numbers of votes from the community at large, he has never been a favorite in the organized gay community: "I didn't have much support from any organized [gay] media or any organized political force, gay or straight.

"I am not a stereotype politico," Milk explains. "I think from the streets . . . therefore I don't play the political game and therefore I'm an outsider as far as the politicians go.

"I'm not controllable. I wouldn't be anybody's puppet," Milk says, explaining comments that mainstream gay political activists don't trust him.

Milk admits that he doesn't play by the "rules," which he contends don't work fast enough. "I demand my slice of the pie now." Milk views the city's gay rights ordinance [passed in 1972 under Dianne Feinstein's sponsorship], the state's consenting sex bill, and other signs of gay rights progress as "Crumbs. I don't care if crumbs are better than we've had before. Bull. If they give you a crumb, they can take that crumb away. But if they give you freedom, it's pretty hard to take that away," says Milk, who defines freedom as the absolute end of discrimination.

Milk charges that the reason a state gay rights law did not pass in the 1975 California legislature was that Speaker McCarthy and Ways and Means Chair John Foran (whose seat Milk and Agnos are contesting while Foran makes a bid for the state senate) didn't work hard enough to get it through: "Do you mean that the two most powerful people in the statehouse cannot get anything they want

passed through the assembly? They can, but they have to pay the price for it," Milk claims. They do not want to pay that price for gay rights. They are not willing to pull all the strings; they aren't willing to go all the way."

While Milk blames the assembly leaders for not making enough deals, exerting enough pressure, and calling in enough due bills, he claims that were he in office, he wouldn't make political deals. "I wouldn't sway my vote for somebody else's vote for something I didn't believe in.

"I may not get anything passed that way," Milk admits, "but maybe I could set an example . . . Maybe I could make them all just a shade more honest."

Milk, noting the contradiction between his demands for other legislators to use their deal-making power, and his refusal to make deals, says that he would use media pressure to help get his legislation through.

Milk also has another basic difference with the gay reformist political model. Gay San Franciscans have spent years developing a "gay vote," taking and receiving credit for using the gay vote to bring pro-gay people into top city offices.

Milk doesn't believe a gay vote exists.

"There's a myth in San Francisco about the gay vote," Milk explains, "a myth about the number of gays in San Francisco, a myth in San Francisco about the gay precinct. I live in a 'gay precinct,' and if twenty percent of the voters are gay here, then that's high," he claims.

Ironically, Les Morgan, political pollster and analyst most responsible for documenting the gay vote, recently predicted that an openly gay person will be able to win elective office in the city in the near future.

Milk did not run a gay campaign in the last supervisorial race. He didn't hide his affectional preference, but he didn't publish it in his literature, either. He was able to get endorsements and support from a variety of non-gay groups, including the construction workers' union, a Chinese publication, and several neighborhood groups. (Most of these groups haven't yet announced who they'll be backing in the assembly race.) Fourteen thousand of his 1975 votes came from the conservative Sunset district. Although the Sunset district

isn't in his assembly district (supervisorial races are at-large), Milk contends that the efforts which brought out the Sunset vote will bring out the vote in the non-gay precincts of his assembly district.

Milk counts on what he describes as the vote-getting power of his personal appearances at candidates' nights and in-person, dogged campaigning.

Milk's supporters, he says, "cut across every conceivable line. They voted for me partly to get rid of the incumbents, but more because they heard me at candidates' nights."

Milk's biggest issue in the 1975 race was "the direction the city was going. If you liked the way the city was going then you voted for the incumbents . . . If you didn't like what you were getting for your [tax] dollar, If you didn't like the Manhattanization, then you didn't vote for the incumbents."

At issue in the race, according to Milk, will be his fight against what he calls the political machine running the city.

Members of this machine, Milk charges, are Mayor Moscone, Congressman John Burton, and Speaker McCarthy, all of whom, along with other Democratic heavyweights, have endorsed Agnos.

Despite the fact that Milk doesn't campaign as a "gay candidate," he explains that he entered politics because "it's time that we had a gay person in office."

He sees his campaigns as opportunities to "build the bridges. If I can be accepted by the hard-hat construction worker, that's going to help gay people."

Milk, who is down on the organized mainstream gay movement, charging that it is part of the machine, feels the movement is dominated by "those who have the most money [who think it's enough] to show you can do it [be a successful gay person]. That's not what the gay movement is about," Milk says, explaining that he doesn't "do anything politically without three people in mind:

- One, a fifteen-year-old girl in San Francisco who told me that because she is an upfront gay she was about to be denied her high-school diploma;
- Two, Steven, seventeen, who just 'turned gay' and is terrified of what will happen if his parents find out; who called me to say he'd seen me talk, that he was watching me;

[85]

- Three, the fourteen-year-old in Des Moines, Iowa (or some other small town) who is terrified of coming out.

"That's what the gay movement is about. So that fifteen-year-old kid can walk down the street relaxed and free," says Milk.

The June 8 primary race between Milk and Agnos is developing into a bitter one, one which Milk already describes as being like "guerilla warfare."

Milk expects that, despite the antipathy of the organized gay community to him, and despite the fact that Agnos is marshalling not only support from political heavyweights but from gay heavyweights as well, he will get some gay votes in his assembly bid from those who believe, as he does, that it is time that a gay person is elected to office.

Meanwhile, the city's reform-minded gay politicos contend, as Jo Daly of the city Human Rights Commission, that Milk's opponent, Agnos, has been a longtime "supporter of gay rights and a friend of the gay community. He has been a voice for us in the capitol. I just think we should support people who have supported gay issues."

12.

"*I stand for the equal rights of all people.*"

Milk did not campaign only for gay votes in the Castro area, but to represent all neighborhoods, races, and groups across the Sixteenth Assembly District. San Francisco's large Filipino population read its own newspaper, *The Mabuhay Republic*. Its May 15, 1976 front page included this article, "Milk: 'Jobs' is key issue' by Bert Esteva.

CITING "JOBS" as the key issue in the campaign in the Sixteenth Assembly District in San Francisco, candidate Harvey Milk is walking the district for 16 hours a day to personally take his cause to the people.

"The effective unemployment in the city is twenty percent, and this has been caused by the closing of Hunter's Point [shipyards], the failure of Yerba Buena [redevelopment project], and the flight of small businesses and industry from the Army Street area and China Basin," he explained.

The powers [that] be have failed to keep the jobs in San Francisco, and without jobs people are sorely beset with the other social problems related to welfare, crime, and health, Milk emphasized.

"Our most important priority is to bring back the industries and businesses that have deserted this city, taking we them the jobs we so sorely need for the residents of this city," he stated. "Band-Aid solutions in the form of welfare programs will not solve the basic problems of unemployment—which only jobs can solve," he further noted.

A businessman—a camera store owner—living and working in the 16th Assembly District, Harvey Milk sees firsthand the concerns and aspirations of the people he wants to represent.

His candidacy has been opposed by almost every politico, except Quentin Kopp, in the city. Moscone, Burton, McCarthy, Brown, Foran—you name him, and he is against Milk for assemblyman.

This doesn't faze candidate Milk, but he instead urges the residents of the 16th Assembly District to reject the "machine politics" of his opponent, and instead join with him in returning the assembly seat to the people.

He pointed out that the so-called "machine" is not a figment of somebody's imagination, but a reality recognized by other political figures and major newspapers and magazines.

Milk has spoken and delineated his views on the issues:

Taxes

"I stand for an immediate closing of all tax loopholes and a simple graduated tax on all income for all taxpayers. I am in favor of changing the present assessment laws that favor large downtown corporations."

Human rights

"I stand for the equal rights of all people. I will fight to end discrimination in housing and jobs. I will fight to end higher tax rates for single persons. I support affirmative action in hiring for women, gays, and minority groups."

Child care

"The key to financial independence for thousands of women and low-income families is the availability of child care. I strongly support the expansion of comprehensive child care services."

Senior citizens

"Senior citizens deserve the dignity of guaranteed decent housing, food, medical care, and secure neighborhoods. Equally important, we must restore opportunities for seniors to contribute to the life of our city."

Schools

"Our schools have failed in two areas: Each year thousands of young people graduate from high school, unable to read or write.

Thousands of others who by current standards have 'done well' in school discover that their education has not prepared them for the realities of earning a living in today's job market. Not only must we revise what we teach and how we teach it, but we also must change the way we finance public education."

Criminal reform

"The root cause of crime is the lack of opportunity. As long as people are frozen out of job opportunities by the failure of our educational and economic systems, we cannot expect to lower the crime rate. An attack on poor education and unemployment is an attack on crime."

The 45-year-old candidate is the owner of Castro Camera, and has been very active in his community. He has served as a commissioner on the Board of Permit Appeals, and has been board member of the Friends of the San Francisco Public Library, Mission Mental Health, Mission Neighborhood Physical Development, and Friends of San Francisco Deputies and Inmates. He is past president of Castro Village Association.

[89]

13.

"I don't know if I'll run again."

Milk's low-budget, tiny campaign threatened Art Agnos' vastly better-funded organization backed by the full weight of the state Democratic Party, but on Election Day, Milk lost for the third time. His margin of defeat was narrow and he was bitter. Two days later, the June 10, 1976 *San Francisco Chronicle* ran this interview by Ron Moskowitz under the headline "The summing up: Harvey Milk blames 2 factors in defeat."

HARVEY MILK sidestepped the conventional political wisdom yesterday that his near victory in the 16th Assembly District Democratic primary race Tuesday would cause him to make a third try for the Board of Supervisors.

"My first priority is trying to get this camera store back into shape," he said. "I don't know if I'll run again.

"My next political effort will probably be helping Carol Silver run for city attorney."

Milk blamed "the so-called gay leadership" and Governor [Jerry] Brown, both of whom actively support his opponent, Art Agnos, for his defeat.

Milk ran as an upfront gay. Agnos, a straight, talked about gay issues more than Milk, however, especially in front of gay audiences, and has a long record of supporting gay issues.

Yesterday, Milk called the leaders of the gay establishment "a handful of self-serving people who are utilizing the movement for their own advantage and never support a gay except from their own group."

"Those people have to be weeded out for the sake of the movement," Milk said. "Every movement goes through that."

The governor, Milk said, endorsed Agnos after promising at a California Democratic Council convention he would "stay out of local politics."

Milk said he felt one of the main issues in the election was whether an upfront gay should be elected.

"With between 1.5 and two million gay people in this state, there should be a gay representative in the Legislature," he said. "Just as no white can speak out adequately for blacks, the same is true for the gay community. It is going to have to come sooner or later."

The victor, however, said he did not believe the election had anything to do with sexual orientation.

"A very rough preliminary look at the precincts shows the vote was pretty steady throughout the district," Agnos said.

"In Castro Village (a predominantly gay area), I didn't get beat that bad. And in Saint Mary's Park, which is old Irish Catholic country, Milk beat me 2–1. How do you figure that?"

Agnos, former assistant to Assembly Speaker Leo McCarthy, defeated Milk by a vote of 17,031 to 13,401.

He said the vote was close because he underestimated how much name identification would help Milk, who has run twice for the Board of Supervisors.

Milk lost, he said, because "I waited ten years to run and during those years worked with virtually every element in the district. Harvey lost because he hasn't done his homework."

The results of the race were so close they were not clear-cut enough to answer a variety of questions Milk's candidacy raised for the gay community and San Francisco as a whole.

Since virtually every major gay leader and publication supported Agnos, Milk's near win leaves open the question of whether gay leaders can deliver the gay vote.

Milk won in all 11 precincts that make up Castro Village in the 18th and Castro Streets area, but the total vote for the 11 precincts amounted to less than ten per cent of the total votes cast.

The close vote also left open the major question which has concerned the gay community—should gays vote for an upfront gay or a straight who has a proven record of helping gays?

Earl G. Rick Stokes, who replaced Milk on the Board of Permit Appeals when he announced his candidacy, was one of those supporting Agnos.

"When the two have appeared before non-gay groups, it has been Mr. Agnos who has talked about the gay issues, not Mr. Milk," said Stokes, who is also an out-front gay.

14.

"The problem with New York is it drove the middle economic class out of the city, which is what's happening here."

Sometime between June and August, Milk and Scott Smith had an angry, painful breakup as lovers, but they remained business partners. Scott moved out of their apartment above the camera store, but they still worked together in their store and on the third Castro Street Fair.

Milk had not decided whether or not he would run for office again when he was interviewed by Mark Vaz for *Zenger's*, a newspaper by and for students at San Francisco State University. The interview ran in the paper's November 3, 1976 issue, was titled "Harvey Milk: The candid political activist of San Francisco's gay community speaks," and included three photos of Milk by Henry Marx.

L OCATED ON CASTRO STREET, *in the heart of the City's gay community, is Castro Camera, a curious little camera store that could easily pass for a campaign office. During election time the window is crowded with posters and bumper stickers extolling that election's crop of progressive characters.*

Inside Castro Camera are information tables with leaflets, boxes of campaign materials piled to the ceiling, and every election sees a rigorous voter registration effort taking place from the camera store.

"We've always been more interested in the political situation than the business part," laughs co-owner Harvey Milk, who came to San Francisco from New York in 1969 and has had the store for five years.

Milk has run for political office from San Francisco three times in the short time he has been in the City, twice for board of supervisors

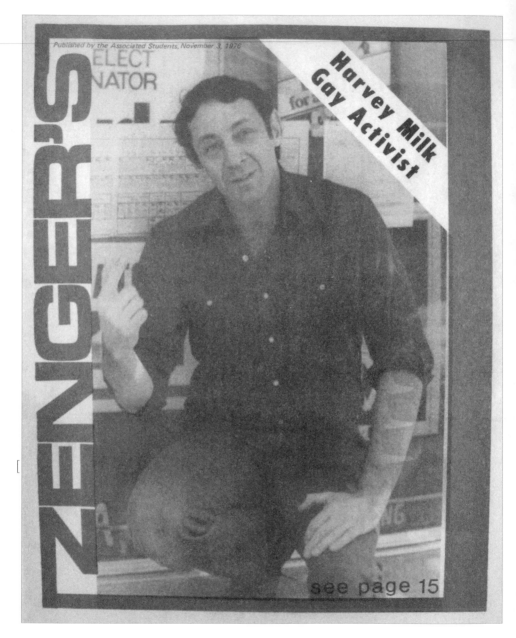

Published by the Associated Students, November 3, 1976

ZENGER'S

Harvey Milk
Gay Activist

see page 15

Milk on the cover of the November 3, 1976 issue of Zenger's.

and during the recent Democratic primary for state assembly. The 46-year-old Milk has lost all three times but he optimistically says that his share of the vote keeps getting larger each election night.

In a candid interview with Zenger's, Harvey Milk touched on what it is like to be gay and run for political office, his fears about the possibility of the Manhattanization of San Francisco, and his hopes for the City and its future.

Zenger's: *You've been involved in races for political office rather recently. What prompted your entrance into active political participation?*

Milk: I used to be a Wall Streeter and Montgomery Streeter. That ended when Nixon invaded Cambodia. I gave a speech on the steps of the Stock Exchange denouncing war profiteers. The speech beat me back to the office and I was fired [from J. Barth Co.].

My involvement in politics is very recent. All my life I would read the newspaper—and yell at it. During the Watergate hearings I started yelling at the television set.

I then realized I either had to walk away from it, or get involved. In 1973 the supervisors campaign was starting and the incumbents would come to the gay community with their attitude of "we like you." Fuck, what have they ever done? A big problem in 1973 was the police department. Many of the police were very bigoted against the gay community.

Zenger: *So you decided to run for the board of supervisors?*

[95]

Milk: It was a last-minute decision. I ran because I was mad. We had no money and I got involved late. Out of 26 candidates we came in tenth with 17,000 votes. I then had the option of saying I tried and going back to my store, or assessing that 17,000 people thought [enough] of me to give me a precious vote. I started getting involved deeper and deeper in the community on issues from prison reform to mental health.

Zenger: *Why did you leave New York, where you grew up, to come to California?*

Milk: Periodically I would get dissatisfied with New York and leave for a while and then return, but finally I realized that New York was

not going to be saved. This is a reason so many New Yorkers who come to San Francisco fight for the City—we don't want to see what happened in New York happen here.

The problem with New York is it drove the middle economic class out of the city, which is what's happening here.

In San Francisco, we're so geared to the tourists. A person from a minority community can get a job as a waiter—and that's it. No advancement. Then that person would say, "What use is an education?" Whereas, if you had some kind of light industry with the chance of advancement, there would be an incentive.

New York drove it all away, which is why it's a city of have[s] and have-nots with nothing in the middle; and the more I see it happening here, the more angry I get.

But no question that New York is the most exciting, dynamic city in the world. For instance, why does a guy drive a cab in New York? Because getting out of his cab is a delegate to the United Nations, or getting out of his cab is a pimp or dope addict, or a couple of guys who just fucked a girl in the back seat. That cab driver has to get these people to where they're going on time. That cab driver is part of it, he's making things happen!

[96]

Zenger's: *Did you have any hesitation about becoming involved as a political candidate in an era where politics and politicians are not viewed with the greatest enthusiasm by the public?*

Milk: Jefferson, Lincoln, and Truman were politicians. There's nothing wrong with being a politician. But as I got involved in politics I realized that City Hall politicians are hypocrites.

Zenger's: *How many politicians in City Hall are hypocrites?*

Milk: Every single one. I see why people get turned off.

Zenger's: *It takes a lot of money to run a campaign, especially in a large city. What is your current financial situation like after your races?*

Milk: I'm deeply in debt. My store's deeply in debt. It's a struggle to get out, not only for the money from the store but also from the energy I'm not putting in.

I just took my stand and lost, unlike other politicians who get involved just to fill their egos and their pockets. But I knew the consequences of running.

But it's vital that someone else raise the questions. Such as, "Why is there crime?" Not how to stop it by using more police. "Why is there unemployment?" and "Why has industry been driven out of town?"

Zenger's: *What forces are responsible for driving light industry out of the City?*

Milk: The current downtown Chamber of Commerce [has] driven out light industry and the middle class, and encouraged high-rise development and tourists. There are hidden expenses in building high-rise developments. It's for tourists and not for the people who live here.

Zenger's: *Is the proposed Yerba Buena project another example of manipulation by downtown interests?*

[97]

Milk: Yerba Buena is being planned for the white tourists. I'd suggest that Yerba Buena be an industrialized park where people can live and work. Secondly, I'd design it so no automobiles or trucks [would be allowed]. Traffic would not be allowed. It would be a model city. I'd have the people who developed Disneyland and Disney World, who designed a city of fun, help design a city to live and work. It would be a city within a city.

But the downtown interests don't want middle and lower income people there. They want non-union office-holders to come to it. They're so God-damn greedy for their own pocketbooks.

Zenger's: *How would you develop quality housing in San Francisco?*

Milk: I'm not so much for housing projects as rehabilitating such areas as the Western Addition, Chinatown, Hunter's Point. South of Market is so desolate it looks like a battlefield. In the South of Market area you can have playgrounds, parks, industrial areas.

If (this type of planned development) were successful, every city in the nation and the world would see that's the way to go. But not one bit of energy is going into this type of planning. All the mayor cares about is getting a convention or saving the Giants.

Zenger's: *Any other examples of the insensitivity of city government?*

Milk: Take the Muni. The supervisors encourage the public to ride the Muni and then they vote in favor of more downtown garages.

Zenger's: *Have you ever been the recipient of large campaign contributions by the downtown interests you're talking about?*

Milk: Nobody's ever given me a large amount of money. I've been influenced by issues and causes. Maybe that's why I'll never win.

Zenger's: *Do you agree with the theory that someone with progressive ideals should compromise his or her position just to get elected?*

Milk: My main goal is to raise issues. If you're elected to a position of power, you can raise the issues from a pulpit. Right now, no one presents counter-arguments. No one gives the sides of the neighborhoods.

[98] You can't compromise yourself. If you compromise one inch you might as well go all the way. I'm too old to get into that game.

Zenger's: *How have the issues in the gay community changed from the first time when you ran for supervisor? Is there still police harassment in the gay community?*

Milk: Charles Gain, the new chief of police, has changed things around. There's a big decline in police harassment. The captain of the Mission District station, which takes in Castro Street, used to preach hate. It's much better now. That's because of political power.

I have huge voter registration drives in this store—I've registered 5,000 people for this election. Registering that many street people means politicians will have to start listening.

Youth has to get the message. Politicians don't give a shit about college students. But if they [the students] ever got together it'd change the heads of a lot of politicians.

Zenger's: *Do you include the media in your list of the "downtown establishment?"*

Milk: The newspapers are tied into downtown. And take a look at the larger media situation. During the presidential debates, the press said it was dull. Oh, bullshit. The debate delineated the issues completely.

The media said that, because up until the debates, the media has told you how to vote. Up until this point, we received political coverage by a story, a column, editorial, or a thirty-second excerpt of a speech on television. Now along come the debates and you have 90 million people listening to candidates without being told who said what. I don't think the debates were like a gung fu movie, but they weren't dull.

Zenger's: *Has the local media ever misrepresented your campaign?*

Milk: I've been continuously wronged by the media. They were looking for the word "faggot." This one reporter was covering me, and she was looking for the word "faggot." We're talking multi-billion [dollar] state budgets, and all she could look for is what reaction I'd get because I'm gay.

Sensationalize is all they know. They just train for headlines.

[99]

Zenger's: *Has your being gay been a problem to some voters?*

Milk: Every now and then someone would say, "You should be hung." But I've done well in all sections of the City, from the Italians in North Beach to even voters in the Sunset, which people say is so uptight. They didn't care if I was green and had three heads, they were interested in issues.

But there are always those people who will be very prejudiced. The sick letters I've gotten—I have a collection with all kinds of gory details. People react to the fact that a gay person wants to have an effect on their lives, but that's part of the myth.

Zenger's: *You've run three times for political office and lost three times. Is there any danger that you'll be looked upon as the perennial candidate?*

Milk: Like Harold Stassen. It would be, except each time the support gets larger. A lot of people were initially uncomfortable that I was gay, but now I have appeal with the Filipino community, to upper-economic people on Telegraph Hill, to people in the Mission.

Zenger's: *Is it a myth that San Francisco is such a liberal city?*

Milk: It's a myth. San Francisco is liberal on some things and conservative on others. The City votes for McGovern and marijuana, but came close to elect-[Two lines of text are missing here from the printed newspaper.]

Zenger's: *What is your opinion of Mayor George Moscone's tenure in office?*

Milk: He was a *great* legislator, and I emphasize the word "great." But he's a lousy administrator. As mayor, you need long-range planning and the ability to handle people. As a legislator, he had a staff, he didn't have a city.

A lot of environmentalists are dissatisfied with him. A lot of people who worked for him in the past won't work for him again. As someone from one of the City's ethnic communities said, "He saved the Giants—what about us?"

Zenger's: *When you have disagreed with members of San Francisco's political establishment, have you still been able to relate to them as people?*

Milk: As long as the disagreements have been with integrity. Moscone wouldn't look me in the face for months, whereas (Congressmen) Phil and John Burton have been super warm and friendly to me. They understood our fight was one of style, and not on basic, fundamental issues.

Zenger's: *What about your political future? Do you plan to run for political office again?*

Milk: So many people say I should run for supervisor again. Customers keep coming in the store and saying, "Don't give up." The people on the street are the ones I listen to. If that support is still there, I'll do it again.

Zenger's: *From your own level of grassroots personal involvement, do you have any lasting impression of politics and politicians?*

Milk: So few of the politicians have a real sense of humor. They get so carried away with their self-importance, they forget: They represent us.

15.

"... you'll find the same people here that you'll find in the straight world. Maybe a little less inhibited, is all."

In the same issue of *Zenger's*, another writer, Jude Novi, interviewed Milk for a different article, entitled "Being gay in San Francisco."

T HE STORY has it that two little grannies were cackling to each other over their afternoon tea several years ago, discussing the fact that their Castro Street neighborhood was starting to change.

"Yes, a lot of homosexuals are beginning to move into the apartments around here," said the first. "You know, they call themselves 'gays.'"

Her friend only smiled.

"I mean, don't you disapprove of such goings on?" continued the first. "Really, Bertha, can you imagine seeing one man kiss another, right out in public?"

Bertha looked up for a moment, only to sip her tea. "Well, I think its wonderful," she said. "You watch. They'll just fix the neighborhood up so nice . . ."

Whether or not the various gay communities that have sprouted throughout San Francisco over the years have actually improved their neighborhoods is obviously a matter of personal opinion. Hosting an assortment of bars, restaurants, bookstores, and shops ("Sukker's Likkers," "Hard On Leather"), however, each neighborhood introduces its own color and clientele, unique from the others.

In the Castro Street area, for instance, many inhabitants still jokingly call their locale "the gay ghetto." The area is not necessarily rundown, but the denim, open-shirted image displayed by many males is a far cry from the sequined look of Polk Street, where you'd

be more likely to find sexy-looking transvestites and young male prostitutes, all in keeping with the latest fashions and perhaps carrying an air of snobbishness about themselves as well. The Folsom area, the city's third major gay community, represents a locale that is separate unto itself.

"Folsom is a kind of leather scene, with crewcuts and swastikas tattooed onto the earlobes—that kind of thing," noted one onlooker. "For the most part, these guys remain pretty isolated. It's like they don't need any involvement with the other communities."

A number of women's gay bars, often hosting such colorful names as La Cave (pronounced "Kahv") also dot the city.

"Actually, here in the Castro we find we have a sort of family atmosphere," said political activist Harvey Milk. "You see, a lot of gays have been condemned by their own families—'Throw the queer out of the house!'—and so the gay bar replaces that. The bar becomes the family, the church, and the social club. It's much more than just a big pick-up scene—although, of course, there's that element, too."

"Sure, basically it's a pretty mellow situation," adds Scott Goldschmidt, who works at a Castro Street pub called The Midnight Sun. "The biggest hassles come from high school kids from outside communities. They drive through and feel somehow obligated to throw a few eggs at somebody—that kind of stuff. And, well, that's the basic problem. People are too hung up on defining each other by what they do in bed—not who they are."

According to most researchers, between four and ten percent of all Americans have had at least one homosexual experience. It has not been established, however, whether tendencies toward homosexuality are due to heredity or environmental factors.

Perhaps one of the biggest myths that surrounds the gay community tells us that gays are a leering horde of perverts, and that anyone who unknowingly steps into a gay bar will be immediately pinioned to the floor and gang-raped.

"Oh, sure, there's some pretty strange things that go on under the tables and in dark corners of some of the Folsom bars," said the bartender of a Castro Street establishment. "But mostly, gay bars represent a sort of social club. There's a lot of cruising and eye

contact going on, if that's what you're looking for. But it doesn't always have to be the case."

At a bar called Nothing Special on Castro Street, for instance, the décor is very similar to anything found in straight communities. The room is graced with mirrors with ornate Victorian frames, Halloween pumpkins, and even a cardboard plaque that shows Joe Namath saying "Help us defeat leukemia." Several men mill about, sipping beers. Many of them are obviously there for no other reason than to relax, to speak to someone with whom they can relate.

"Yeah, I read the pros and cons of all those election propositions, and now I'm more confused than ever. For senator, though, I guess I'll go with Tunney."

"Wasn't his dad the heavyweight champion one time?"

"That's right, he cowtailed Jack Dempsey in the fall of 1927." A smirk, followed by a languid puff of a cigarette. "It was his one claim to fame."

At the Lion Pub, on Divisadero and Sacramento ("Where midnight thinking begins daily at 5 p.m."), the pace is slightly quicker, the music a bit louder.

"But most of these people have their heads pretty much together," said John Manley, one of the bartenders. "Sure, there's plenty of cruising going on. A lot of these people, though, have steady lovers, and the environment sort of flows with that feeling."

According to Milk, however, most gay men are not inclined towards steady relationships (although gay women are). Why is this?

[104]

"Temptation," he shrugged. "This is a very sexual city, and the availability is there. Besides, most gays realize that you want to sleep with other people, so why hide it? You see, as homosexuals, we were immediately rejected by the church. So now we say, 'To hell with the church and all its hang-ups.' For instance, how many family men do you think would just love to make it with, say, Raquel Welch? Or even that pretty little girl they see riding the bus everyday on the way to work?"

Art Bercy, a 25-year-old black man who is "just passing through the city on my way to other adventures," had his first homosexual experience when he was 21.

"It was something, because when I was a kid I'd always had these feelings for certain people. Certain guys, you know? Like it

wasn't necessarily connected with sex or anything—at least, I didn't recognize it as being that. I'd just see a person, and for some reason I'd feel very good about being near him, or talking to him, or being recognized by him—definitely in being recognized by him.

"But ever since I can remember—well, you know that whole trip you go through when you're a kid. Society and everyone else is telling you that if you don't like girls, you're a sissy; and when we see two Frenchmen kissing each other on the cheek, we're supposed to giggle. And so that's why I couldn't recognize these feelings that nature had put into me. They'd been practically smeared away and erased by society's little games."

"Sure, it's a difficult thing to make that initial plunge," said Bill Smith, who is 32. He has been openly gay for thirteen years. "And, believe me, it was a lot more difficult thirteen years ago. You're forced to overcome the hang-up that if you're homosexual, you're feminine, and you're a fag, and you're a queer, and Mommy will be oh so shocked, and the people you've grown up with will suddenly become a little bit leery when it comes time to go out drinking with you. Let's face it, your whole lifestyle takes a 180-degree turn to starboard. I think that's why so many straight guys feel they have to pound their chests and notch as many chicks on their penises as possible."

Brent Harlin, a confirmed 27-year-old bisexual, puts it this way: "Nature has got it all figured out. If everyone was bisexual, girls would still get pregnant, the species would continue, and we wouldn't be depriving ourselves of this extra pleasure our bodies are capable of giving us."

[105]

One of the more colorful aspects of the gay community is its ability to view holidays as a social occasion to the fullest extent. The Polk Street parade, which takes place every Halloween night, for instance, is a monumental event that sees literally thousands of costumed goblins, fairy princesses, and skeletons clogging and eight-block area. It is a merging of the gay and straight communities, complete with improvised sideshows, drinking in the streets, and a whooping who-gives-a-damn Mardi Gras atmosphere.

This year's parade, which took place last Sunday night, saw all varieties of characters—a 'nun' on roller skates; bearded pom-pom girls; and perhaps the most entertaining character of all—she was

the sweetest little baton twirler that anyone had ever watched dance on tiptoe. With wide, buggy eyes, she tossed her baton skyward, gulping once or twice as it flew downward, catching it, twirling it, and then tossing it up again. Her tiny skirt ruffled in the wind, and with each skipping motion she would smile and offer everyone a wave.

"Throw the baton higher!" the crowd shouted, and she obliged them. And it was only the fact that this little miss happened to host a set of bristly legs and a handlebar moustache that made her act seem, well, perhaps a little bit unusual.

"Sure the gay community has a varied atmosphere," said Milk. "On a political, social, and economic spectrum, you'll find the same people here that you'll find in the straight world. Maybe a little less inhibited, is all."

He looked up.

"I'll even say that not as many gays commit crimes. After all, most wars have been declared by straights. Right?"

1977,
Milk Fights
16 Opponents

San Francisco's First Gay Commissioner

Mayor Moscone swears in Harvey Milk (r) as a member of the Board of Permit Appeals, January 1976.

Most candidates have nothing to offer but promises.
Harvey Milk has a proven record of leadership and accomplishment.

Candidates will promise almost anything to get your vote. You can hope for the best and vote blindly on the basis of promises, or you can examine what a candidate has done in the past about the issues that concern you today. **What a candidate did yesterday tells you more than what he or she promises today.**

Harvey Milk serves on many City-wide and neighborhood boards. He's not just making promises. He's in there doing the work, taking the heat and sharing the responsibilities:

Castro Village Association: founding President
Castro Street Fair: originator and producer.
Friends of the San Francisco Libraries: Director.
Friends of the San Francisco Inmates and Deputies: Director.
Mission Neighborhood Physical Development: Director.
Gay Political Action Committee (Gay PAC): founding member
Bay Area Reporter (B.A.R.): columnist.
Society for Individual Rights: former head, Speakers Bureau
Eureka Valley Promotional Association: longtime member

Harvey Milk has been a leader in many City, neighborhood and gay rights struggles, never content to play it safe and remain silent.
You know Harvey Milk means it when he says he will:
• **Fight** to save the Gay Community Center from demolition,
• **Introduce** an anti-discrimination ordinance covering all businesses in San Francisco,

• **Work** for gay affirmative action in the police and fire departments and any other City agency that has refused as a matter of policy to hire gay people in the past,
• **Sue**, if necessary, to secure City funds for the Gay Freedom Day Parade,
• **Make sure** that the gay community gets its fair share of City services.

Harvey Milk
Supervisor/5

Endorsed by every gay political club that has endorsed in District 5:
Minuteman Democratic Club
San Francisco Gay Democratic Club
Concerned Republicans for Individual Rights
and endorsed by The Sentinel.

Friends of Harvey Milk • 575 Castro Street • San Francisco 94114 • 864-1390
William Hartmann, Treasurer • Design: Rivaldo Pabich Associates

Although Milk was a commissioner on the Board of Permit appeals for only 38 days, he touted his brief service as one example of his accomplishments.

16.

Divided they stand: The Milk-Stokes split

When Milk ran his first two campaigns to become a member of the Board of Supervisors, he lost both times. Supervisorial elections at that time were city-wide, so Milk was forced to try to win voters across all neighborhoods of the entire city, an expensive proposition.

That difficulty vanished at the end of 1976 when San Francisco switched to district election of supervisors. The city was carved up into eleven supervisorial districts. In the November 1977 election, each district would elect its own supervisor for the first time. Instead of trying to cover the entire city, candidates would need to focus only on nine percent of it, just one district.

Milk lived and worked in District 5, which included not only the Castro area, but also Haight Ashbury, Noe Valley, Diamond Heights, and other neighborhoods. When Milk ran for assemblyman he had won with margins close to 70 percent in most precincts that were included in District 5. It was an easy decision for Milk to run for his district's supervisor's seat.

Unfortunately, Milk was not the only one who decided to run in District 5. He became one of seventeen candidates, more than any other district. Other candidates had deeper pockets than Milk, plus backing from large political organizations. One of them was Rick Stokes, a gay attorney backed by well-known Democrats and the same gay political establishment that had pushed before to defeat Milk.

As before, one of the leaders of the gay political establishment was David Goodstein, publisher of *The Advocate*.

He supported Milk's opponent Stokes. But, for many reasons, most gays in San Francisco did not see Stokes as a leader. They trusted Milk.

Dramatic evidence occurred on June 7, 1977, Orange Tuesday. After Anita Bryant, a singer and star of Florida orange juice commercials, led a campaign to repeal an ordinance prohibiting discrimination based on sexual orientation in Dade County, Florida, voters overturned it. Feeling threatened, thousands of angry gays mobbed the Castro. Police feared a riot and turned to the only person they thought might be able to calm the crowd: Harvey Milk. He averted violence by leading the crowd for a three-hour march over a five-mile course up and down San Francisco hills, ending at Union Square, where he gave a speech, hoping the mob was tired and would disperse. The crowd marched back to Castro Street, where 1,000 protesters staged a spontaneous sit-down protest, blocking one of the busiest intersections in the city. Once again, the police called Milk, who persuaded the protesters to clear the intersection.

Milk was the only person trusted by both the angry gays on the street and the police. Rick Stokes was nowhere to be seen.

The Advocate covered the supervisorial campaign in this July 13, 1977 article, "Divided they stand: the Milk-Stokes split" by Bill Sievert.

THEY'RE BOTH GAY. They both have warm, friendly smiles. They're both Democrats. But that's where comparisons between the two leading gay candidates for the Fifth District seat on San Francisco's Board of Supervisors begin to pale.

Harvey Milk is flamboyant, outspoken, often wears blue jeans in his camera shop, is politically farther to the left and is a strong supporter of neighborhood politics. He says he is very distrustful of "machine" politicians.

Earl "Rick" Stokes is mild-mannered, chooses his words carefully, wears a tie to his law office, is considered more moderate and

has the backing of much of the Democratic Party organization in San Francisco. He is very distrustful of Harvey Milk.

There is a good possibility that neither Milk nor Stokes will ultimately be elected; 11 other candidates already have announced their intentions to file for the same seat, and more are expected to do so by the end-of-July filing deadline. But the two gay candidates are among the frontrunners. Both recently spoke with *The Advocate*—Milk in his cluttered Castro Street shop and Stokes in his modest law office in the shadow of city hall.

Each man believes that the first gay candidate elected will be watched carefully, not just in San Francisco but all over the country. "Whether we like it or not," Stokes says, "the gay person elected will be *the* gay supervisor. I distrust Harvey's judgment. Harvey gets too emotional, shoots from the hip, is not too cool."

"It's important," counters Milk, "that the first gay person elected is goddamn clean. I question Rick's independence from the local Democratic machine. The machine likes to divide rather than support the gay movement. Rick's a wheeler-dealer."

Stokes has been endorsed and praised by a host of big-name Democrats including Mayor George Moscone, San Francisco Assemblymember Art Agnos, and Assembly Speaker Leo McCarthy. Milk considers all three men part of an "establishment machine" that guards its power carefully and allows only "puppets" to join its ranks.

It should be noted that Milk ran against Agnos in a bid for the state assembly last year and lost. Milk blames McCarthy (for whom Agnos had once been a top aide), Moscone, and Congressmembers John and Philip Burton for splitting the gay vote in that election by their endorsements of Agnos and "big spending" on his behalf. (Agnos is and has been a supporter of gay rights. He is the sponsor of a bill pending in the California legislature to guarantee fair employment practices for gay people.)

Milk asserts that the Moscone "machine" continues to oppose him because "I won't make deals," and that the "machine" will split the gay vote again this year by backing Stokes.

"It's the red herring approach," responds Stokes. "Harvey's born to be a martyr. The truth of the matter is he's a Johnny-come-lately.

[111]

Harvey doesn't have the credentials I have." Milk accuses Stokes of the same thing.

Both candidates can rattle off long litanies of their past accomplishments. Stokes, who charges that "it helps to be an attorney if you're going to pass laws," points to a law reform package he authored (with strong gay rights provisions) that has been adopted as the policy of the state bar. Stokes has worked with the Family Services Agency, lobbied for national health care, advised Moscone in the state senate and worked with organized religion, pushing a pro-gay plank through the hierarchy of the Methodist Church. He also has been involved in many local gay organizations since 1963, when he became active in the League for Civil Education. Currently, Stokes sits on the San Francisco Board of Permit Appeals by appointment of the mayor.

Milk, a former financial analyst, had held Stoke's seat on the permit appeals board until he had to resign in order to make his run for state assembly. Claiming that "we need someone with a financial background rather than another attorney on the Board of Supervisors," Milk says it's vital that the candidate elected have experience in the "neighborhood battles."

Milk has been active in the Market Street Beautification Program, the Teamster-led Coors beer boycott, the drive for district elections, the movement to support San Francisco street artists and local child care centers. He's also been president of the Castro Street Fair, has been active in the Castro Village Association and has been a director of the Friends of the Mission neighborhood association.

In his past campaigns (two for supervisor, one for assembly), Milk has won endorsements from numerous labor unions. It's too early for most unions to have made any endorsements for the fall campaign, but Milk privately lists several major union locals that are planning to support him again. (The glaziers union already has announced its support.) Milk also boasts an endorsement from at least one major politician, popular pro-gay Republican State Senator Milton Marks.

As for endorsements from homosexual leaders, Stokes is being supported by such prominent gay locals as Jim Foster, long-time activist who recently traveled to Miami to lead the fight against

Anita Bryant; Bill Gassaway and Roberto Estevez, both past presidents of the Toklas Democratic Club; Doug de Young, another long-time activist; Darwin Jones, an early Mattachine Society leader; Roberta Babba, who has worked with the Tavern Guild; and David Goodstein, publisher of *The Advocate*. (Milk charges that Goodstein and Foster are both part of the Democratic "machine" that's out to split the gay vote.)

Milk's gay backers include Lenny Mollet and Wayne Friday, president and vice president of the Tavern Guild; Bob Ross, publisher of the *B.A.R.* (*Bay Area Reporter*); Jim Rivaldo, president of the Mint Hill neighborhood association; Hector, the current emperor of San Francisco, and former empress Flame.

Both Milk and Stokes want to see a gay person elected supervisor—though not each other. Milk criticizes those who are satisfied electing heterosexual "friends of gays," charging that "if the chips fall, it's better to have gay people in office. We need to have role models for 14-to-16-year-old kids coming out. It helps to pick up a newspaper and see that a homosexual has been elected in San Francisco."

Stokes agrees that electing a gay supervisor could create an "important role model." But, he adds, "Gays don't have to look at San Francisco politics solely as gays. I want to reflect the concerns of all the people I would represent . . . I'm always leery of one-issue politics."

Milk notes that he's never run for office as a one-issue gay candidate. "I campaign as a candidate who is gay," he says.

[113]

In an interview with *The Advocate* a year ago, Milk had said that if another gay person were to enter the race for supervisor, he would withdraw—that the important thing is to elect a gay candidate.

"I still believe in gay for gay," he says. "But it depends on who the gay candidate is. I will not support a wheeler-dealer. The gay supervisor has got to be a strong fighter."

To win, Milk and Stokes both will have to fight more than one another. A strong challenge to their campaigns is being prepared by Terence "K.O." Hallinan, a radical attorney and son of the famed leftist lawyer Vincent Hallinan. Hallinan already has made

it clear that gay rights are among his top priorities, and he's won the endorsement of the Rev. Ray Broshears.

Milk calls Hallinan's candidacy a "real threat" and charges that Moscone is backing Stokes in order to divide the gay vote and throw the election to Hallinan.

Stokes laughs off Milk's charges, but concedes that "it would be much easier without K.O. (also known as Kayo) in the race. I don't dismiss him lightly. There are people in the organized Democratic Party who will be hard put to choose between us. He's from a very wealthy family and he has some name recognition, but what has he done for the people of San Francisco?"

Name recognition, however, could be the key to election in the crowded Fifth District. Explains Stokes, "You have two kinds of voters. A few go in well-informed on the issues. I feel we won't have any problems with them. Then there are the others who vote solely on name recognition. I wish that weren't the way politics works, but it is.

"I've been working hard on name recognition the last two or three months," he says. "I'm trying to show all gay people that they can be proud to have someone like me on the Board, that they could be absolutely confident to come and talk to me."

Milk, who certainly is the better known gay candidate at the outset, claims that the reason Stokes has to work on name recognition is that he has not been involved in neighborhood or district issues. Milk is a strong proponent of district elections. He argues that they'll wrest power from the traditional "vested interests" of city hall and the downtown business establishment, giving citizens more direct participation in government. But he fears that a "low voter turnout, particularly among gays and blacks" for the coming special election could jeopardize district elections.

Stokes is less enthusiastic about district balloting, but—like Milk—is campaigning to save it. "I feel district elections are somewhere between indifferent to bad for gay people," he says. "I was slow to come to support them. The fact is that we'll probably get one supervisor who is quite supportive of the gay community instead of the four or five we have now.

"I see district elections as a vehicle for removing some people who are of questionable competence but who get elected time after

time," he says. "And there wasn't anyone representing the people who live in some areas of the city. I think district elections—in the short run—will improve the situation. They're the best way to share the pie. But in the long run, in a few years, I wouldn't be at all surprised to see a return to city-wide races."

Both Milk and Stokes say they'll continue their races even if district elections are overturned in the special August election. They'll simply have to run city-wide instead.

But Stokes says he's particularly concerned about Supervisor John Barbagelata's drive to remove the current city administration from office. "I'm very much opposed to turning over the elections now. It seems grossly unfair to those who worked hard and won. It's unfair to change the rules midway through the game."

What do the two gay candidates see as the major issues facing them and the voters in the fall campaign? Economic problems top the lists of both men.

"We're only a breath away from New York's situation," Stokes says. "There isn't anyone in the city who realizes what the economic situation is like here. In comparison to other cities, San Francisco comes out very poorly. We're the third most indebted major city per capita, and our total expenses per capita are second only to New York. To me, our economic situation is the crucial issue." Stokes says he'd particularly like to make the city's shipping port profitable again: "We had zero income from the port in 1976."

Says Milk, "Besides neighborhood issues and the matter of who's going to control the elections, the big issue is economics—particularly housing and jobs. Housing is too scarce and expensive, and there are too few jobs—particularly blue collar jobs." Milk is a strong believer in building coalitions with labor and ethnic minorities, and he would like to create incentives for blue collar industry so that it can expand the city's employment base.

Both candidates also cite street crime as a major problem for all segments of the city's population. Milk blames the high crime rate on Moscone's lack of leadership; Stokes believes the answer may lie in tougher sentencing by the courts and better media coverage of the sentences handed down to persons convicted of violent acts.

Although they disagree more often than they agree, both Rick Stokes and Harvey Milk say it's vital that more gay people get involved in the political process.

"Gay people in this city think it's so good here," Milk says. "But that's only by comparison. A lot of gays who have it made—doctors, lawyers, and the like—don't get involved. They don't realize what they have to lose. If the Anita Bryants have their way, it won't matter if you're a doctor or unemployed . . . If gays would ever realize the value of putting in an hour a week helping any candidate or giving a one-dollar bill, we'd have a gay mayor."

"We not only need to stand up," says Stokes, "we need to act responsibly." He explains that at a series of house parties he's been throwing to build support for his campaign, he repeatedly has heard "concern expressed about over-reactive behavior" along Castro Street and in the parks. "Some of us need to stop acting out our stereotypes in public," Stokes says. "There aren't so few places to get it on in San Francisco that parents should have to worry about whether their kids will walk into a restroom and stumble into a sex scene. I'm not putting anyone down, but we have to assume some new responsibilities. We're at the point of acceptance in this community where we have to clean up our act a little."

As Stokes put it at a recent political testimonial in his honor, "It would be dangerous for us to conclude that oppression is behind us. Two decades of success have bred resentment against us. Anita Bryant is not just some crazy lady. We have gone too far in this city to keep us from forging ahead in the years to come."

17.

"I don't think in terms of labels. I only think in terms of issues."

One of the neighborhoods in Milk's District 5 was Noe Valley. Its newspaper, *The Noe Valley Voice*, interviewed candidates in its September 1977 issue. Here are the paper's questions and Milk's answers.

Milk mentions that he has already debated State Senator John Briggs on television about Briggs' planned initiative to ban homosexuals from teaching in California schools. I found no record elsewhere of such a Milk-Briggs debate in 1977, which would have been the first between the two men.

B ECAUSE OF *the importance of the Nov. 8 supervisorial election to the future of San Francisco, the* Voice *asked District 5 candidates their views on both general and specific issues. Questionnaires were sent to all announced candidates as of Aug. 3. Announced candidates Marjorie Martin, Jack Schamikles, Alfred W. Williams, Natalie Bey, and Vahan Toolavian did not respond to the* Voice.

> HARVEY MILK
> CAMERA STORE OWNER
> Castro Village Ass., Eureka Valley Promotion Assn.,
> Friends of S.F Public Libraries, Mission Neighborhood
> Physical Development, Friends of S.F. Deputies and
> Inmates, Gay Political Action Caucus.

1. *Would the position of city supervisor, which pays $9,600 a year, be a full-time job for you, or would you feel the need to supplement this income with outside employment?*
 Milk: Full-time job.

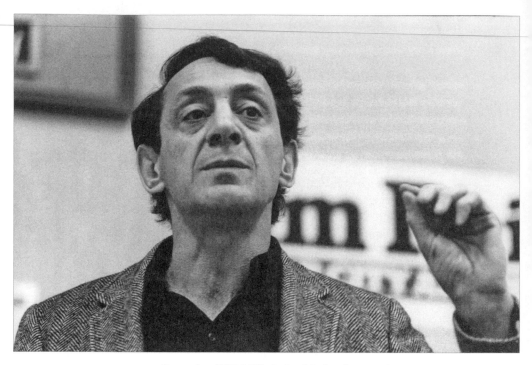

September 1977: Milk during his fourth campaign
and third attempt to become a supervisor.

2. *City residents are painfully aware of the scarcity of low and moderate cost housing and the rise in housing speculation in San Francisco. Rent control and the enactment of a graduated real estate transfer tax have been proposed as solutions to these problems. Do you favor these proposals? If not, what would you suggest as alternatives?*

Milk: Graduated real estate transfer tax—yes. Rent control— Depends on how it is written. N.Y. and Berkeley's were poor plans. The real solution won't come from these 2 plans but from a fairer tax assessment on downtown buildings, bringing industry back into the 3rd St.-China Basin area and rebuilding the port. This would put much more property on the tax rolls, and the jobs would cut into the cost of gov't services, now needed because of no jobs.

3. *After seven years of resistance, the tenants of the International Hotel were evicted from their home Aug. 4 to make way for the building's demolition and eventual development. How would you have avoided this situation?*

 Milk: The city's leaders should have raised money to buy the hotel, not talked about it. If they could raise money for football, the ballet and the Giants from the public, they should have done the same here and done a P.R. trip against the absentee landlords. At no time did they show that concept of leadership.

4. *How would you resolve the conflict presented by the City's desire for both economic growth and the preservation of existing housing and neighborhood character?*

 Milk: Start to develop the areas of 3rd St., Y.B. [Yerba Buena], China Basin as model cities with light industry—housing and services as well as parks. As long as there are indeed areas that cry for development, these areas can adequately provide for economic growth without the need to touch existing housing. I spoke out strongly at the hearing to stop 24th St. [the main street of Noe Valley] from becoming commercial on 2nd floors. As a result of my statement at least one of the planning commissioners came out and walked the area with me.

5. *Would you be satisfied to continue the City's policy of tax breaks for large downtown corporations and tax hikes on residential property?*

 Milk: No. I have been fighting that for two years. Two years ago I followed [Senator John] Tunney from meeting to meeting on this and asked in public questions others would not ask.

6. *What creative measures would you use to tackle San Francisco's unemployment rate, at a 1976 level of 12%?*

 Milk: Lobby with industry to bring new industry into the 3rd. St.-China Basin area—not just industry, but housing as well; hire by Zip codes. Am working to save Sears Mission as a gateway for Latin American tourism.

[119]

7. Is an increase in the number of police foot patrols the answer to San Francisco's rising crime rate? How would you approach this problem?

Milk: A partial answer. We know police act as a deterrent, but until we solve the unemployment problem and create a good school system, crime will exist. So jobs must be the #1 crash program.

8. How do you stand on the following issues?

a. The Bakke decision (reverse discrimination charge upheld at UC) vs. affirmative action.
Milk: Have had petitions in my store against this—signed on the top line.

b. The introduction of a bill in the State Assembly denying gays teaching jobs in the public school system.
Milk: Against this. Was on T.V. with Sen. Briggs recently arguing against him. But this is only one aspect—the opposite must take place. Gay people must be free from discrimination in all jobs. That is still not a state law.

c. A proposed fare increase in the Muni.
Milk: Should be free and totally subsidized along with higher parking rates downtown to discourage the auto. Commuters must be taxed to bring in needed revenue.

d. Possible cutbacks in city support for community-based health programs.
Milk: Against this very strongly. Our health programs must be reorganized. They are not effective at present.

e. City-funded child care.
Milk: Worked hard for Prop. M years ago. Have even put into print a concept that would cut the cost factor down to make it within reason. A must.

f. A proposal to impose higher rates for more than normal water consumption.
Milk: Yes, but this is tricky, as what is normal? What about a man who changes his lifestyle and starts to cook at home

instead of eating out. What about the number of people living in a flat if the number changes?

g. *City investment in corporations which support racist regimes such as S. Africa and Rhodesia.*
Milk: Very much against allowing this to take place. We must use city resources (including money) to awake people's consciences to this problem of society.

9. *How would you involve District 5 residents in city government?*
Milk: Storefront meetings, block clubs, picnics on issues, door-to-door meetings.

10. *Give your Number One priority if elected supervisor.*
Milk: Jobs—It affects taxes, welfare, crime, attitudes and the spirit of the city. Most problems are due to lack of money, both to the individual and to the city.

11. *If you had to be a card-carrying anything, would you characterize yourself as a radical, progressive, liberal, moderate or conservative?*
Milk: Depends on what those terms mean. In most cases, district election of supervisors (which I have fought for for 5 years) is a conservative and Republican issue. In S.F. it became a liberal and progressive issue. So am I progressive? I don't think in terms of labels. I only think in terms of issues.

[121]

18.

"If I become a supervisor, then they'll talk to me."

One of the most interesting interviews of Milk was con-
ducted by *San Francisco Chronicle* reporter Paul Avery in
October, 1977. A top crime reporter, Avery was portrayed
in the movie *Zodiac* by Robert Downey, Jr. His fellow
Chronicle reporter Joel Selvin said compared to the actor,
"the real Paul Avery was scarier, twice as deranged, and
three times uglier." Avery later married a friend of Milk's,
Margo St. James, who founded the prostitutes' rights orga-
nization COYOTE.

Avery knew Milk. Their interview may have been held
late at night; Milk and Avery sound tired, and Milk rambles.

The "Bob Mendelsohn" Milk mentions is a real estate
developer who was a member of the Board of Supervisors
from 1968 until May 5, 1977, when President Jimmy Carter
nominated him to be Assistant Secretary of the Interior.
Mendelsohn was later instrumental in creating the Holo-
caust Museum in Washington, D.C., and the San Francisco
History Museum in San Francisco's Old Mint.

The beginning of this interview is missing, so it starts
abruptly. My comments are indicated by [square brackets].

Milk: Is there a master plan by the Chamber of Commerce? You
know—or, you know, some people in the back room? Ah—the blue-
collar jobs, which were stepping stones for the ethnic minorities and
economically deprived people to move up, are gone. Playland is
gone. Fleishhacker Pool is gone. And it's been replaced by—

Avery: *Are you saying if Fleishhacker and* [pauses, looking for a
name].

Milk: Playland.

Avery: *Playland magically were here today that there would be a significant drop in crime, or do you . . . ?*

Milk: I don't say there's a *significant* drop. But I say there'd be a *drop*, and I say it would be a turning in the *trend*, turning—you know, giving them an alternative. Right now, young kids, "What have I got to *do* on a Saturday night? Where can I go? I can't go to a movie—it's five dollars!"

You know—got no place to go. You go—for two dollars, you can at least get something. It would be a *trend*. In other words, you've got to start the fire someplace. Nothing's gonna be if you make it significant.

But—but you have replacing all the blue-collar jobs and all that, you have Walnut Creek jobs. You know. You have all the office workers. And they all get on BART or whatever, and they go home at night. And you have a desert down there [in downtown]. And—you know—those people, they aren't into crime, some crime; they are not affected. They're not affected by jobs. But the people in Hunter's Point and the Mission and Chinatown and other areas of the city, where they are out of work, and no place to go, no jobs; so, you need money.

I mean, but [mayoral candidate John] Barbagelata gets up there and says, "Crime is *not* a socio-economic thing," and he quotes statistics from one or two cities.

You know, I don't think any of the supervisors—or there's eleven, so I may be wrong, but I'll bet *ten* of them—and that's pretty good odds—have never been to the city *prison*. Down in San Bruno. And walked through and talked to those people. You know, just go through. I worked in the prison system, too. Just go through the city prison, and visually something's going to tell you—it's going to tell you something.

And, so they use a *scapegoat*, and it's the same thing we had when I went down to testify against the police budget, at the police commission. One of the police commissioners said, "Wow! You talk about the narcotics thing. You know that six of the first seven murders this year were related to drugs?"

I said, "What *kind* of drugs? Heroin, cocaine, or marijuana?"

[123]

"Well, I don't know."

And so you just—Joe McCarthy: "Drugs!" You know, and throw it all together. And *why* are they on drugs? Did you ever go [to] that step? If *so many* are related to drugs, doesn't the question ever come to your mind is: Why?

You know? And what are you going to do about it? It's the same thing, you know. It's the double standard we have over and over again. Last year at the Hilton Hotel, we had the photography convention: Eastman Kodak, Polaroid, Nikon, Canon, you *name* it. The whole world was there, you know. In the Hilton Hotel, the ballroom was *massive*, you know with millions of dollars worth of equipment. The center attraction was a hologram of two people having sex. Oh, it [the hologram exhibit] was *packed*. If that was around the corner in one of these adult bookstores, it'd be *filthy* and should be closed *down*. But because the *convention* was doing it, 'cause Kodak was putting money into that convention, it was okay.

We talk about the prostitutes in this city. What about the prostitutes who, you know—and I know there *are*—who play with the—with the wealthy people? It's the whole double standard! And, okay, well, the young people see it, because the young people *know* it. Young people are not dumb. The young people know that President Nixon was on the take. They know their father can't get a decent job because he's an ethnic minority, or he's poor. They know that if a black person kills somebody he gets the electric chair, and they say, "Why should they work through the system?"

Okay, there's an easier way to make the same kind of money, and you don't have to worry about getting laid off. The father works for thirty years and gets a watch, you know. In the meantime, the government inflation kills everything he has. The mother has to go out work, and the kid can go out and make the same thing in a day that the father makes in a week. Well, there are a few things you can do about it. One is, as I say, you could change the police budget. Two, a sense of priorities. It's like the same thing. They're spending—they have a head of the vice squad who's worried about nudity and everything else. Did he arrest everybody on [the] TV show *Roots*, you know? [Chuckles] Right?

I mean, let's face it. A) He's not going to get rid of prostitutes, you know. If he does, even—even Christ accepted the fact that

there's prostitutes, you know. So if they—if they stop this whole thing that sex is the reason for crime, and take that—that money and those people and put them out on the beat, that *immediately* will have some deterrent. Two, to give the alternative to the children. Because the children have to have it, and that is again, I'm going back to the Playland concept. You've *got* to give them someplace for their energy. Children have energy. It's gotta be—there's gotta be an outlet for it. They've got to *get out*. I mean, who—we have to be *kidding* to say that children don't have energy that has to be—they're thrill-seekers. Go to *any* amusement park. They have to have an alternative.

Three, there has to be a real, concerted effort to get jobs—blue-collar jobs—back in the city. They are not doing it. They wanted to keep—instead of a—they want to build a convention center, which is nice and everything else, but that doesn't give the jobs to the right people. Oh, custodians and ticket takers and stuff like that, but, you know, what did that *do*? It's not giving the right type of jobs, long-range jobs. It's not giving enough jobs to the right types of people.

They should bring industry, they should say to—I would—I were—do I be God, I would go to Levi Strauss tomorrow morning, and I would say—who is it? Haas? [Peter E. Haas, Senior, then chief executive officer of Levi Strauss] I'd say, "Look, you made your fortune in this city from Levis, and now economically you can't. You have to make it in Mexico or wherever. And you have an obligation and debt to your stockholders to do that. But do you have an obligation and debt to the city that made you?" And maybe we have to change the consciousness or whatever of what industry is about. And I would like Levi Strauss to be the beginning of a textile industry in the city. And we will put it out on Third Street, where there is *thousands* of acres of land and desolate buildings." Like that. "One stipulation: You have to hire people from Zip code 94107, 94124." [chuckles] "I'm not talking about *affirmative* action, I'm not talking about—but you'd have to hire people from *Zip codes*, so we know where they're coming from. So, jobs. And *if* you build a factory there, and if you go with me to New York and lobby to get more textile industry to come out here, forgetting about economics, so we have a social thing. Because if you're worried about your shareholders, soon there will be nobody in San Francisco [who] has

[125]

money to buy Levis. And then you have that long-range debt to your stockholders, that you have to keep your *market*. Then if you build your factory, and next to it you build a school, or hospital, or homes. Or a park. You will get certain tax incentives; write-offs. Like they did in Operation Bootstrap. You know, in Puerto Rico.

Avery: *What's that?*

Milk: Bootstrap, Bootstrap in Puerto Rico and Cos[ta Rica]—there they had—it was completely misused there, I think. 'Cause they really screwed over the workers there. You know. But, in other words, *somebody's* got to present the argument to—to the Levi Strausses that while there's a debt and obligation to the stockholders, there's gotta be a debt and obligation to the *city*, to the *people*, to the *nation*, or soon there will *be* no market. And then who will you sell it to? And, what is, you know, like—you see.

Okay, I mean, that's not an immediate solution. But it gives hope. And if there's hope, then there's the incentive to school, we have to keep going back to school again, the kids. Because, let's face it, the person who is out on the street, who is twenty-three years old, and illiterate and into robbing, you know, he's a difficult problem. That's the problem.

Avery: *Yeah.*

Milk: That person. But while we're working on that, it'll allow the next generation to come up and fall into that, so it's a double battle. One, get enough people out on the streets from the vice squad and those squads to—to try to check that twenty-three-year-old. At the same time, try to give hope to the sixteen-year-old. And tell the fifteen-year-old, "You've gotta be in school so you *can* get a job at Levi Strauss in the new plant that's opened up." And by hiring people from Zip code, you're also telling *who's* gonna get the first crack. And that's in building and everything else.

So you've gotta give *hope* to the new generation, and you've gotta—you've *gotta* have the army out there to stop today's problem. The citizens are doing it themselves. They're organizing. They *have* to. So you have that problem.

But nothing will take place until the mayor—and I mean the Mayor Moscone and the Board of Supervisors—accept the fact that,

um, "if you do away with sex—when you do away with sex [then] crime goes away"—accept that as a phony, as a—as a subterfuge—accept the fact that adult bookstores—you know, it's the same thing, you know.

I have to—Lenny Bruce was prosecuted and put in jail for saying the word "cocksucker." In a nightclub, which you had to pay [for admission]. Now, in—in—in [the movie] *Network*, which is winning all kinds of awards, they say "cocksman," "asshole," and everything else, and everybody laughs at it. The same people who said "Lenny Bruce is so awful" are now laughing. You know. The same people who said that Abbie Hoffman was wrong by wearing a shirt of an American flag are now selling fire hydrants of American flags. And these people are now saying that it's the porno shows and shops that are causing the crime wave. And someone's gotta get up and say, "Oh, you've been wrong all your goddamn life. Shut up once." You know.

So the people are organizing because the people have asked—the police won't do it. And the reason the police won't do it is because the chief of police and the politicians are saying, "Go after the dirty bookstores. Go after the porno houses. Go after the dope smoker." That gives you a lot of arrest records. "Oh, we have fourteen arrests this year." You know. Well, what kind are they? You know. We know what the *real* arrests are. So as long as they—the—the people are so worried about politics and everything else, we're not gonna get these solutions. Unless citizens just get up and *scream*. And say "I had enough." So there *are* solutions.

[127]

Avery: *Do you think that there's—there's a problem that arises with—with cities now being so dependent on federal funding that they don't go out and try to solve the problems themselves?*

Milk: We have, we have a series of—of—of legislative and executive leaders throughout the nation who are using Band-Aids to try to stop cancer. And what happens when those programs end? Or there's no money for it? There—there's no long-range planning. There's *absolutely* no planning by anybody in this city. I mean, *absolutely* no long-range planning except to turn it into a Walnut Creek, maybe. But they will *grab* at anything the federal government puts out. And then they *never* stop and say, "What happens when that

runs out? What do we—what's the alternative?" They've done nothing. The last ten years, fifteen years, they've done nothing to prepare for that. Yeah, it's easy. And it looks good. And then they get up in front of the voters and say, "I was able to get fifteen million dollars from the federal government for this, and thirty million dollars from the federal government. You didn't have to pay for that."

What do you mean, we didn't have to pay for that? Who's paying for it? You know? It's—it's doubletalk. They are—and I have to blame you people, the media—because *you're* the ones who allow them to get away with it; in essence, the media. The media now doesn't cover [political news in the state capital] Sacramento. Do you know, like I ran an assembly race? For primary.

But do you know how many billions of dollars this—what is it, a twenty-billion-dollar budget, state budget? More now? I don't know. Passes laws that affect peoples' lives? The *Examiner* never did one article on the race? Didn't care. [chuckles ironically]

"But the public doesn't want it." The reason the public doesn't want it is you won't tell them about it.

"Well, this was a dull campaign." It was dull because nobody covered it. If you covered it, it would be a [unintelligible], you know. It's up to you. The media is responsible. The media says, "What're we gonna do?" What'll you do? Tell people what the government's *about*. You know? It's the same thing, we get back to the, you know, the media is very guilty of a lot of this. The presidential debates: "Boring." "Dull." "Awful." Bullshit! They were exciting. I mean, there was no slugfest. Carter didn't hit Ford in the face. Ford didn't kick him.

Avery: *Nobody said "cocksucker."*

Milk: [agreeing] Nobody said "cocksucker." But they delineated the issues. But you know why they were dull and boring? Because up until now, who decided who was the best-dressed candidate? The media. Through a headline, through a news article, through one quote from one person's speech, a thirty-second TV shot. And for the first time since the Nixon-Kennedy debate, you have a hundred million Americans watching both people answering the same question. Right? And the American people make up their mind, not telling [corrects himself] being *told* who to vote for. They're

making their own decision, you see? Up until now, I might have heard Carter making a speech. I might have heard Ford. Might have heard *both* if I'd gone out of my way. And in both cases, I couldn't ask them questions, but I heard their propaganda. *Now* I can sit and hear both men answer the same question—even the *lousy* question—but answer the question, respond, and make up my own mind, not reading the headline. So the media has to say "dull and boring" because the power to make the decision goes from the media to the people.

Okay. Well, the same thing with the crime. The same thing with the government. The media does *not* tell about the government. The media *doesn't* print the police budget. "Well, nobody wants to read that." *Make* it readable. *Make* it exciting. You know. And so I'd put some of the blame onto the media, and then the politician comes along and says, "Well, the media's not going to cover that. The only thing the media's going to cover is my porno bookstore thing, or this kind of noise, so that's what I'm going to talk about. And I'm not going to talk about the crime. And if the media's going to pick up a big article on how I got fifteen million dollars..."

It's the same thing Bob Mendelsohn went around this last campaign, talking about he's gonna raise—and Moscone—business tax. "Gonna *sock* it to the big business!"

And everybody in the streets said, "Yaaaaay!"

Okay, so I'm a businessman. If you raise my taxes, I have an option: move, take a smaller profit, or pass it back to you. Okay, so I'm gonna pass it back to you. And who's gonna pay the most? The poor people. The people who said, "Yay, he's socking it to big business" are paying for it. And—and—and Moscone and Mendelsohn went away looking like heroes; in essence, they were the evil villains. And the people didn't know, and that's the media's fault.

So we get into the whole crime thing, the media doesn't get into crime. They just [unintelligible] the sensationalism of it. They don't go, "What caused this guy to do it?" I mean, why did this guy commit a crime? Gary Gilmore was big. Who ever heard of *why he committed the murder?* [chuckles] Right? The whole—I mean, where did they go into it? Why he committed the murder? Why he did it? Why these people? Instead of "Who did it?," why? And the media: "Well, people don't want to read [that]?" How do you know

they don't want to read? You know. So you have the media setting the ground rules, and the politicians picking up on it and running with the ball.

Avery: *Do you think there is something called "San Francisco violence" due to the makeup of the city, the kind of people that come here? Do we have—is that a special case in the country—*

Milk: No.

Avery: *—because of our tolerance? You don't agree.*

Milk: No way. In that case, most mass murders that I can remember—I'm trying to go through them—well, let's see. There's the Chicago nurses, the guy in—in—in—

Avery: [inaudible] *Texas.*

Milk: —Texas. Then there was, in Houston there was the gay ones. Then there was the guy upstate in the hotel, motel—

Avery: [inaudible]

Milk: —killed about five or six people. Based on that, mass murderers are basically west of the Mississippi. So there's something to say about that here. You can make a case.

Avery: *Yeah.*

Milk: What I'm saying is—what I'm saying is, a statistician could prove that Methuselah was stillborn. I can *make* a case out of anything. There are how many automobiles stolen in San Francisco compared to any other major city? You know, percentage by population? [unintelligible] population? I doubt that—that there's much variance. How many homes are broken into in other cities that have as many homes? See, when you have apartment buildings you have a different type of strata. Which has also a very high rate of unemployment and a high ethnic group. When you have a high rate of unemployment, you probably have more homes broken into.

Well, maybe we have more prostitutes than Des Moines. Or in Dallas—I lived in Dallas in '67, and they didn't have any "Negro problem." Because there was never mentioned any "Negro problem." And there was no statistics or figures or articles in newspapers.

[130]

And there could have been tons of murders and rapes and robberies committed by and of—among the—the blacks. But we didn't know about it.

"San Francisco has a lot of prostitutes." Maybe we do. Maybe Des Moines has more. I don't know. They may not talk about it. [laughs] Maybe Las Vegas has more.

Avery: *If we have more prostitutes than Des Moines, our crime rate—prostitute-related crime rate—is going to be higher.*

Milk: Bound to be. But I don't think that there's anything really unique about this city in that sense. Except that the city is a very large city of ethnic minorities. When you add the Asian and the black, the—the Spanish together, you have a *huge* percent of the city. You throw in the elderly population and the gay population, you have probably over fifty percent of the city. Well, that is unique, naturally, and we *do* know, unfortunately, that a lot of crimes are committed within the ethnic groups, within the blacks. Blacks among blacks. We do know that. I mean, that's statistically. So if you have a large amount of minorities, you may have a lot of internal crime.

Avery: *What about gay against gay?*

Milk: Very little gay against gay. Most of the gays [are] victimized. Most of the "gay murders" are gays being murdered. I mean, there are some of the murderers are gay, but I would say that that's more lovers' quarrels, just like any other murder.

[131]

You see, one thing about gay people is very interesting. Two aspects. One: How many, first of all, we have [an] assistant district attorney now saying that gay people are responsible for crime. [laughs]

Avery: [unintelligible]

Milk: I asked him, "How many rapes were committed by gay people?" [laughs] "How many automobile thefts were committed by gay people? How many banks were robbed by gay people? How many homes are broken into by gay people, you know?" I work in the jail system, and the percentage of gay people there are quite low, you know.

Child molestation are, what, eighty percent of child molestation is heterosexual. The papers don't say that. But it's very interesting.

On top of that is the fact that the lifestyle [of] gay people, because we are not family-oriented, we go to bed with multiple persons. A gay person comes in from out of town, he has no trouble finding a place. He has no trouble finding someone to spend the night with. Or you go to a bar, you meet somebody, you take them home; you don't know who they are. I mean, they could rob you, murder you, like that. And every night in this city I would say a huge percent of the gay population is in bed with somebody who they don't know, who they just met. And yet, the—not—I don't know anybody who's been robbed. I'm sure there's been some, yeah. I have never been, and I'm somewhat promiscuous. I used to be very promiscuous, and I never was robbed; and I used to go to bed with strangers—you know, *complete* strangers you would see on the street. You cruise somebody, pick them up, go home. And there's all the *opportunity*, you know—especially those who drink heavy. They're half-drunk, they go to bed, they have sex, you fall asleep. The guy can get up and walk out and take your everything. It happens—insignificantly. So gays among gay crime, those—those kind of thing, the opportunity is *enormous.* And yet, the *fact* is very low. And that's kind of a certain lifestyle, a certain *trust.* And yet, we have an assistant district attorney blaming crime on homosexuals. [laughs]

Avery: *What's the—what's the estimated gay population?*

[132]

Milk: I hear all kinds of figures. My own feeling is around 70,000 maximum. That's my own. Mine is the lowest figure I've seen. And I based it on, again on—that I used statistics, you know.

Avery: *About ten per cent.*

Milk: Well, I—about ten per cent, maybe a little higher because we are a magnet, and people do come here from other areas. So I say slightly better than ten per cent. But these people saying 100,000, [or] 150,000, they're crazy.

Avery: *A year or two ago, wasn't there a rash of violence in the so-called leather bars south of Market [Street]?*

Milk: Right. This whole past year, there was a lot of gay murders.

Avery: *Is that* [unintelligible], *gay amongst gay?*

Milk: Unfortunately, the police had one—I think, one part-time inspector out working on twenty-three murders. A golden[?] gets killed, and you have ten inspectors working on it. You know? And they got a tip, and that's how they got that one. Most of them are unsolved. Based on what we can find out, and what we have done ourselves, it looks like most of it is outsiders.

There were some people—there was one person in particular—who had been seen in several [inaudible], and he might himself have been a repressed gay. You know, he may—he wasn't, from what we gather, he was not [an] active gay. Might have been repressed. And so when, in essence, you can say, "Well, it's repressed gay. It's a gay-gay murder," but because society keeps him repressed, it's probably the reason he kills. In other words, like he knows society will not accept him as a gay person, so he has to repress it and therefore kill all the gay people, to show that he's *not* gay. And so in essence society is responsible for that, if that's the case.

Avery: [unintelligible]

Milk: That's all any of it is, because we don't know who these people *are*.

Avery: *As many as twenty-three?*

Milk: I think—I think there was twenty-three in one year. And— and the police could care less, you know. I—you know, it's—it's amazing. I could show you sick letters that I get, you know. I don't even bother sending them down to the police anymore. I don't even open them up. But yet a wealthy white person gets murdered and you have the whole force on the case.

And, you know, then the [unintelligible], that tells the—the murderer, "Yeah. I can go murder any ethnic person I want. Might get caught, might not, but they're not going to kill themselves trying to track me down."

In other words, the police—the government is telling criminals which ones they're going to go after, which ones they're not. "You rob somebody in Pacific Heights. You kill somebody in Pacific Heights or Saint Francis Woods, you're gonna—we're gonna put everything

[133]

to getcha. But if you do it in Hunter's Point, or the Mission, or Eureka Valley, or Tenderloin, well, we'll make a token effort."

Avery: *Eureka Valley is middle class.*

Milk: Very. Very. Very. There is some wealth, and there's some poverty, but it's middle class. And it, you know—so I say the *crime*—again, going back to answer "What can be done?" Immediately, there must be established by the government in whatever way possible that we will go after crime where *ever* it exists, not just in the wealthy areas. The government won't do it! "I don't have enough men." You know, that's the—three years ago, two years ago, one year ago, when we asked for beat patrolmen, there wasn't enough men. Now there's enough for a beat patrol, with a smaller force. So they're *lying!* Blank. Period. Exclamation point. They lie. They lie through their *teeth.*

And until they *stop* that, they can't build up the trust. And you've gotta have *trust.* Among other things. So the government has to, you know, go after crime. They have to declare war on crime. And again, not on the prostitute, not on the bookstore, not on the—the guys pushing on the street corner, but after the big crime. If you go after the big crime, that's gonna, you know, filter down. The message should be clear. Then there are other things you can do, you know. The show of force, the deterrent, is very vital. Get those people out, out in the police cars. They keep telling me, "The most effective thing is in a police car." Well, *that's* effective! We know. [chuckles] Their record is effective, and let's try it the other way for a while. Maybe we *are* right. You know.

[134]

Avery: *Would this take a concerted effort of all of government and the community?*

Milk: Sure!

Avery: [unintelligible] *are going to tolerate this, and the judges, you know, are just going to flat-out give the top sentence—*

Milk: Right.

Avery: *—as a matter of San Francisco's position? Isn't that going to be—*

Milk: It takes a concerted effort.

Avery: [unintelligible] *little old lady who's seventy and you're going to—*

Milk: Okay. We have—you know, like we have the death penalty. We *must* put the death penalty back for anybody who kills a cop. Why? The cop knows when he becomes a policeman his life's endangered. He's *trained* for it. He is *armed* to protect it. I think if we *are* to put the death penalty back—which I'm against—it should be for the guy who kills a little old lady, who is *not* prepared for it, who is *not* trained, and who is not *armed*. Like anybody who murders a soldier is guilty of a cr—you know, in war. [chuckles] You know? You know? It's, it's, it's *phoniness!* You know, sure, I—I think anybody who kills a cop should be put away and all that stuff.

I think anybody who commits any kind of crime with a gun should get a hard penalty: ten years, fifteen years, twenty years, whatever. Lock them up. Let 'em know. Any crime with a gun—no ifs, ands, buts about it—no parole, no extenuating, mitigating circumstances. You commit a crime with a gun, any kind of crime, into the slammer. Bang! Hard-nosed. 'Cause, you know, you could kill somebody with that, or the person can't defend themselves. But to say that if you kill a police officer with a gun, you know, and it's—it's a more serious offense than to kill a little old lady on the street who can't defend themself and has no protection—

Avery: *Do you think that rehabilitation as a goal is just a farce?*

Milk: Rehabilitation the way it exists is a farce. The way it exists. Rehabilitation, people say it's been a failure. Sure, it's a failure, because they never put any effort or money into it. If you have hundreds of people in jail and you have a couple of volunteers as rehabilitation, then what—I think they have *one* salaried person in San Francisco last year, two years ago. And volunteers. Well, then, it's a *farce*. So we don't know.

Avery: *In the county jail system.*

Milk: Right. So rehabilitation, we don't know. We know punishment doesn't work. You see, the thing is, like they say, "Well, rehabilitation doesn't work." Well, punishment doesn't work *either.*

'Cause we've *had,* in this country, two hundred years of punishment. It doesn't work! Hasn't stopped crime. Now, as long as President Nixon goes free, as long as the chairmen of the boards of Westinghouse and G.E. can get together and price-fix and screw the people, you know; punishment doesn't work. Because people say, "Yeah, it's—you know—how many black—you know, look at *death row.* How many of them are black?" It's about the nation. And punishment doesn't work. Rehabilitation doesn't work, 'cause rehabilitation has no funds there, and punishment is strictly a one-sided punishment. And—

Avery: *Why shouldn't there be a—a—a broad coalition of—of the community that—that acts in concert to say, "Hey, San Francisco has the opportunity to really do something revolutionary in the way of—of—of approaching this. And we're gonna—we're gonna set the model for the nation?"*

Milk: Because of politics. Because everybody wants to be mayor. 'Cause everybody wants to be the messiah. And when one person suggested the—the person who sees "Well, that's guy's got the right idea. But if I'm sure he's gonna be the next mayor, and I wanna be the mayor, so I have to shoot him down."

I don't—Barbagelata gets up there in front of three hundred people and in front of everybody else says, "I wanna learn about crime," then walks out. He wants to be mayor! He doesn't want the idea to come from the "opposing force." The *mayor* gets up there and makes a P.R. speech and says "We need input" and then doesn't stay around to hear input and walks out on it.

[136]

How there be a—how can you sit down and *talk* to these people? The people who are a position to make decisions, to *lead*—to *lead*—show no leadership. Absolutely none in this way, except it's gotta be *their* way or no way at all. And we are do—and they get up there, and they quote statistics to show what they are doing. Your house has just been broken into. What do you care about statistics? What should you be doing about that? Well …

You know, how do you say we should spend money on a—with the budget—on gambling? [unintelligible] that's all part of the vice, but it's part of the thing. This is interesting. They said, "spend money on doing gambling," but during the police strike—during

the last police strike—on the front page of the paper there's a picture of the mayor in City Hall playing cards and gambling. You know?

Avery: *I remember that.*

Milk: Right. Okay. Who arrested him?

And if the *mayor* can do it, why can't *I* do it? So in essence it's saying, "Go ahead and gamble." So then why spend all that money on [prosecution of] gambling? It's—it's—it's Catch 22.

The mayor says, "You can't do this," but I can do it, you know. And the young people see this and the young people say, "The hell with it all." So what you need, besides all those other things we talked about, I think the vital thing is leadership. The vital key to it all is leadership. And the—the—the media won't allow that to develop.

Avery: *I think that you* gotta *do something about this, the narc— you know, the heroin. Take the profit out of heroin. I mean, you just serve—*

Milk: Do you know who's stopping it?

Avery: *Who?*

Milk: People who don't care, but are trying to get votes from the little old lady around the corner or the old-type religious fanatic up the street. They want to get their votes, so they have to talk of heroin.

This is the same thing. I go back to the days of Prohibition. Not personally! [chuckles] But I go back to the days of Prohibition, that because of Prohibition the mafia got started. And that every single person who was murdered during Prohibition, the charges should have been brought against the people who put Prohibition on, 'cause they're responsible.

And they tried to legalize that through morals, and now they're trying to do it through heroin and marijuana, and they are just causing the crime syndicates to be wealthier, and I think those little old fanatics are the ones who should be brought in front of the judge on charges. And they are responsible for all this murder and crime. Because their refusal to accept that there is a problem here, that there is a problem here, that it is not a moral problem—a lifestyle

[137]

problem that has to be *solved*. This person is *hooked* on it. And if you're going to bring charges against anybody in this justice system, [I] think *they* have to stand up and take the blame, just as those people who put Prohibition on the ballot have been responsible for all this, in the name of morality and Christianity.

And the *media's* responsibility is to call attention to this. But the media won't, because who buys the papers, and who puts the ads in, but the same old people? And so they're trapped into this game—

Avery: *Yeah.*

Milk: —of not being honest. I don't think I've ever read in print—in—or the TV, or radio, or anything else—that the people responsible for the mafia were the moralists. And the people responsible for the junkie to go—to make that big profit are the moralists. And the politician *plays* for it, because the politician wants to get reelected. And so the politician lets the—the junkie go free, lets the mafia go free, because to go after *that*, they have to go in front of the moralists and say, "Well, I [unintelligible] for free heroin."

Avery: [unintelligible] *consideration of everything we've been talking and thinking about here, where do you see it going? Will it get better or worse or how much worse? How bad do you think it will get?*

Milk: Fabulous—I am now a fabulous, wealthy capitalistic Jew in Germany: "Aw, Hitler's picking up the scum Jew; the socialist, the communist, and things could be worse, you know. They're not gonna be any hassle, let's get rid of them."

Okay. It could become the true *Clockwork Orange*. It could become where you'll have an armed camp; both sides. As long as the government—and that's all branches—refuses to accept the responsibility that they—*they*—are part of the reason there's crime; as long as the *media* refuses to accept responsibility, crime will continue. I mean, nobody is really going after any effort to stop it, except haranguing and Band-Aids. And you don't stop crime with Band-Aids or haranguing.

You may stop *some* of it. You—you may shove it from one area to another area. It's like, "Let's get the drunks off of Market Street." So you put 'em on Mission Street, and get 'em off Mission Street, you

put 'em on Van Ness [Avenue], you know. The question is: Do we go after the alcoholic? How do we solve the problem of alcoholism? So until you *solve* it, it's gonna get worse. As long as the economy in the city, in the big cities, gets worse, there's gonna be crime. As long as you don't offer jobs to the people or an incentive to go to school, crime's gonna get worse. As long as—you know.

Let's look at the movies. We go to the movies a lot; not as much as we used to. Go to the big movies. A *Star Is Born:* cocaine. *Network—Network* is "Screw the people, steal all you can. Tell them anything you want." You know, where are the movies that offer them hope or something else?

So they go to the movies, and they say, "Well, the pusher man gets it. He makes it. He makes it big." So the education process of the young people is, "Crime is the best way." The school education process is a disaster, 'cause [it gives] no incentive. So the young people [are] being educated into crime. But I am not without hope. I am not without hope. I am not without hope.

Avery: [unintelligible]

Milk: I am—because, I *see* it. If I see it, you can see some solutions. Levi Strauss is not going to talk to Harvey Milk, who's trying to making a living on Castro Street and raises hell. But if Harvey Milk is a supervisor, Levi Strauss is going to talk to me.

Avery: *Say that again.*

Milk: If I become a supervisor, then they'll talk to me.

19.

"*Gay rights protect everyone.*"

In the midst of his campaign, Milk was interviewed by
Herbert Gold, one of San Francisco's finest novelists. Gold
enjoyed Milk's sense of humor but couldn't take notes as
fast as Milk dropped ideas and colorful remarks. "I liked
him personally," Gold told me, "but I never thought he'd
be elected supervisor."

Gold included Milk's interview as part of a larger
article called "A Walk on San Francisco's Gay Side" that
appeared in the November 6, 1977 issue of the *New York
Times Magazine*. Gold recalls that his article was supposed
to run as the cover story of the magazine but was demoted
by an editor who said, "I'm not going to put a fairy on the
cover of my magazine."

H ARVEY MILK, owner of a Castro Street camera shop, candi-
date for Board of Supervisors in the coming elections, has a
reputation as a hard-line, right-on gay candidate for both elective
and appointive office. When I visited his shop to sit on a tattered
couch and discuss what it means to be early ("I was *first*," he says) in
this field, he warned that he tends to exhale in words and I should
interrupt if he was talking too much. What follows is an abstract of
the scribbled notes of our conversation.

"I made it respectable. We don't want sympathetic liberals, we
want gays to represent gays. Alice [the Alice. B. Toklas Democratic
Club] is controlled by Jim Foster, but the vote can't be delivered.
There are gay capitalists and gay socialists. I represent the gay street
people, too—the 14-year-old runaway from San Antonio. We have
to make up for hundreds of years of persecution. We have to give
hope to that poor runaway kid from San Antonio. They go to the
bars because the churches are hostile. They need hope! A piece of

the pie! Our share of taxes for our parades! Listen, like the blacks, we got our share of Uncle Toms, too. If you bring the open gays into the political process, you cut the welfare rate, you cut the crime rate—they're willing to work. Gay rights protect everyone. A gay candidate supports *every* gay issue and person. That's my job."

"Doesn't that make you a one-issue candidate?"

"I'm thinking of that poor kid from San Antonio, growing up in bars, hustling, on welfare. He's only got one issue. I'd back the sheriff for anything: he supports us. The mayor, O.K., he appointed some gays, some closet gays, too. I want 'em out of the closet! That 14-year-old from San Antonio needs us! Listen, we do our own get-out-the-vote drive, 30 to 50 gays working out of Castro Camera."

And he offered a political slogan: "Gay for gay!"

With his lean charm, smiles, shining teeth and street smarts, Harvey Milk resembles some of the black *enragés* of the 60s. [District 5] is an area which combines the small-town America of traditional San Francisco neighborhoods with the flashy fern-boutique look of Castro and 24th Streets. Milk, as a small businessman sympathetic to labor, claims support among all groups in the district. He is cautious about his support among gay women. "They don't trust us. They learn not to trust men. They're more interested in feminist issues than gay rights."

Does any homosexual organization bring men and women together effectively?

"Gaypac," he said, "the Gay Political Action Caucus—about 60 people, I guess, but they're growing. Maybe some in the Teddy Roosevelt Rough Riders. The Coalition for Human Rights, too. It's not easy."

Milk walked with me to my automobile, still explaining, greeting his friends and constituents as we strolled down Castro in the summer sun. "I'm a left-winger, a street person," he said. "Most gays are politically conservative; you know, banks, insurance, bureaucrats. So their checkbooks are out of the closet, but they're not. So you try to get something going, and all the gay money is still supporting Republicans, except on this gayness thing, so I say 'Gay for gay.' That's my issue. That's it. That's the big one."

20.

"I can really appreciate what Jackie Robinson was up against."

After four years of hard work and three failed campaigns, on November 8, 1977, Milk defeated sixteen competing candidates and won his fourth campaign. He was elected supervisor for District 5.

Now that Milk was a winner, he became national news. Robert McEwen of Associated Press interviewed him on election night. The resulting story ran in several newspapers across the United States over the next few days, appearing, for example, in the *San Diego Union* on November 18 under the title "S.F.'s first gay supervisor sees self as symbol."

T HE FIRST avowed homosexual to be elected to the Board of Supervisors compared his task Wednesday to the one Jackie Robinson faced as the first black to play major league baseball.

"I can really appreciate what Jackie Robinson was up against," said Harvey Milk, 47, a camera store owner who was booted out of the Navy a quarter-century ago when it was learned he was gay.

"There is a great similarity in our situations," he said. "He had to be as good as possible, and he couldn't blow up out of anger. Every single black youth in the country was looking up to him. He was a symbol to all of them.

"In the same way, I'm a symbol of hope to gays and all minorities. My election, against all the odds, shows that the system can work and that there is hope."

Milk was elected Tuesday, drawing 5,922 votes and defeating a field of 17 candidates which included several other gays and former San Francisco 49ers football player Bob St. Clair. Two years ago,

under the old citywide elections, Milk received more than 50,000 votes and was runnerup to a board seat.

Asked whether a "gay bloc" in his district was instrumental in putting him in office, Milk replied, "I don't think so. Maybe if it had been a closer election, that would have helped. But it was an issue-oriented campaign . . . I think the gay vote was pretty well diffused."

San Francisco, choosing supervisors by district for the first time in more than 80 years, also elected its first black woman supervisor, Ella Hill Hutch, 54, a director of the Bay Area Rapid Transit system.

All six incumbents who sought reelection to the 11-member board won along with three other newcomers.

Opponents of district election of supervisors had argued that board members would be concerned only about their own districts, and the welfare of the city as a whole would suffer.

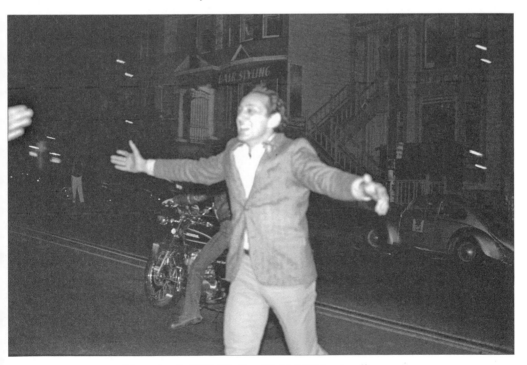

November 8, 1977, Election Night: Milk jumps off a motorcycle on Castro Street and runs to hug . . .

. . . his well-wishers celebrating at Castro Camera.

But Milk, a two-time loser under the old system, disagreed.
"I think it will function well. A well-balanced, right-to-left spec-
trum came out of the district elections and I think we have a board
who knows what the concept is all about. I think we'll work very
well together," he said.

21.

An "unofficial supervisor" gets a shot at real power

Later that month, on November 30, the *San Francisco Examiner* printed this longer interview by W.E. Barnes.

HARVEY MILK is laughing.

He is leaning back on the battered red couch in the back room of his camera shop on Castro Street, a place cluttered with shaded precinct maps, stacks of incoming and outgoing mail and other evidence of recent campaign activity, and he is chuckling as he describes to a visitor one of the perquisites of victory.

"After the election night party, this place was ankle deep in crushed beer cans and styrofoam cups, so we decided to get a debris box for the cleanup," he is saying. "I called a scavenger company and said, 'This is Castro Camera,' and they told me there wouldn't be one available for a week.

"Five minutes later, I called back and said, "This is Supervisor-Elect Harvey Milk's office," and they said they'd have one over first thing in the morning."

Milk grins, savoring the transition from outsider to insider, from neighborhood advocate to city official, and from gay activist to the first openly gay individual elected to the San Francisco Board of Supervisors. "But that's it," he says, changing to a tone of mock seriousness. "I've had my taste of power. I'm quitting tomorrow."

After two unsuccessful campaigns for supervisor (1973 and 1975) and one for the Assembly (1976), there is little chance of Milk's resigning from the board, where he is expected to be a pro-neighborhood liberal with a deep commitment to civil liberties.

But a warm laugh and subtle humor are very much a part of Milk's style and personality: "You're in trouble if you take this whole

Milk in the kitchen of his apartment above the camera store.

business too seriously," he said often during the intense campaign in District 5.

"After I ran the first time," he says, "the phone began to ring. It was not just gays, but all kinds of people who needed help. Before long, the store became a political hangout for people with problems who kept getting the runaround from city officials. It's been that way ever since.

"If there is a single reason why I won, it is because, in a very real sense, I've been an unofficial district supervisor for five years and this has been my district office. If Phil Burton had just spent an afternoon here he would have realized that."

Almost as if to prove the point, a woman walks in and interrupts the conversation to inform Milk that a shop down the street has just been robbed and the elderly proprietor is very upset. "I just thought you'd want to know," she says. Milk thanks her, saying he knows the victim and will stop by to offer his help in a few minutes.

"That's the kind of thing I'm talking about," he says when the woman leaves. "I think I know of just about every robbery in the district within an hour after it happens. Usually, there's not much I can do to help, but people have gotten the message that I care. I believe that's important to them."

A combined camera store-district office on busy Castro Street is a far cry from the sleepy Long Island village of Woodmere, where

Milk was born 47 years ago, the second of two brothers. His grandfather was a dairy farmer. His father was in the clothing retail business.

In 1951, he graduated from Albany (N.Y.) Teachers College, with the Korean War in full swing. He joined the Navy.

Commissioned an ensign, Milk attended deep-sea diving school and was made diving officer on a submarine rescue ship on patrol in the Pacific. During high school and college, he had kept his homosexuality a well-guarded secret, a feat that proved more difficult in the confines of a warship. In 1953, he was dishonorably discharged for being gay.

"That was a difficult time," he says. "Teaching was out because of the discharge. [In reality Milk did teach high school after his Navy service.] I knocked around at a series of odd jobs before taking one as a statistician with an insurance firm in New York City. From there he shifted to a brokerage, a move that eventually brought him to San Francisco as a securities analyst with J. Barth & Co.

In the barber's chair in the front room of Castro Camera, Milk pets The Kid.

[147]

The early 1970s brought more change. Milk found himself increasingly outraged by first the war in Vietnam and later by the evolving Watergate scandal. During this period, Barth merged with another firm and Milk's job was eliminated.

"I had been thinking about changing my lifestyle," he says. "One day I realized I couldn't remain silent about Vietnam any longer, and since that was the case, I obviously couldn't remain silent about my life."

After leaving Barth, he came out of the closet. "It wasn't a difficult transition. In fact, it was easier than I expected, almost like a weight had been lifted off my back. I realized I no longer had to lead a double life with double standards," says Milk, who shares a flat with his lover.

Milk credits Richard Nixon and Watergate with pushing him into politics. "During the hearings, I found myself shouting at the television, I was so angry. I finally reached the point where I knew I had to become involved or shut up."

Gay leaders in The City warned him that the climate wasn't right for an up-front gay to run for supervisor, but he made the race anyway, polling an impressive 17,000 votes citywide.

As The City's first avowedly gay supervisor, Milk already has received nationwide attention and is well aware that he will be judged by more harsh standards than are his board colleagues. As a result, he says earnestly, "I'm going to drive myself to do a good job.

"I understand the responsibility of being gay. I was elected by the people of this district to represent the district, but I also have a responsibility to gays, not just in The City but elsewhere. Last night, for example, I received a call from a gay college student in Pennsylvania. He just wanted to say, 'Thank you.'

"Knowing and understanding that responsibility will make me work twice as hard to show there is no difference between gays and anyone else as far as doing my job on the board. I know the bigots will be watching, hoping that I fail, and because of this I think I'll be putting in more time than anyone else."

As Milk talks, Anne Kronenberg, his campaign coordinator and soon-to-be administrative aide, arrives and the conversation turns to the campaign. Both describe it as "a madhouse."

"We had the most disorganized campaign in the district," Milk says.

[148]

"I'll say," Kronenberg confirms with mock disapproval. And then Milk laughs again.

"Did I tell you my plan for selecting the next board president?" he asks. "I'm suggesting it be the non-incumbent who received the highest percentage of votes in his or her district." That, of course, would be Milk, who readily admits he's the last person his colleagues would turn to for the job.

"Just want to keep them on their toes," he says, enjoying the joke. Then he is off to visit the elderly owner of the store that was held up. "You know, this is the third time in a year the store has been robbed, all during the daytime," he says, concerned. The now-official supervisor from District 5 is back on the job.

1978,
Supervisor Milk
Raises Hell

Supervisor Milk.

22.

Harvey Milk talks about politicians and lying

On its *Closet Space* radio program, WCAS in Cambridge, Massachusetts aired Joe Martin's interview with the not-yet-sworn-in Supervisor Milk, conducted in the first week of January 1978. That lengthy interview has been lost, but fortunately the February 25 issue of *Gay Community News* printed this condensed version under the title "Harvey Milk talks about politicians and lying." My comments are in [square brackets].

L AST NOVEMBER, *Harvey Milk was elected to a seat on the San Francisco Board of Supervisors (city council). His campaign victory marked Milk as the third openly gay person to win public office in the United States.*

Milk's victory followed a tough political battle that included another openly gay man, Richard Stokes. The fight between Milk and Stokes characterized a classic struggle within the gay movement. Stokes, an attorney, was backed by The Advocate *and many controversial "professional" gays. The Stokes campaign was one of the most highly-financed campaigns ever in San Francisco politics—spending some $35 per vote cast for the candidate.*

Critics and supporters alike describe Harvey Milk as being "emotional" and sometimes "too direct." His no-holds-barred attack on gay movement colleagues disturbs even some of Milk's strongest advocates.

His flamboyance never fails to attract attention, however. On January 9, 1978, Harvey Milk marched a mile to City Hall for his swearing-in ceremony. Television cameras swarmed the newly-elected supervisor who walked with his arm around his lover.

[151]

The following interview, conducted by Joe Martin, took place a few days before the swearing-in. The interview, in its entirety, was recently broadcast on the WCAS program Closet Space.

Martin: *What makes Harvey Milk run?*

Milk: (laughter) I've told this story before. It'll be a five-minute story—or three. I remember what it was like to be fourteen and to be coming out. In some ways, today, I know that there's a fourteen-year-old child (and I always pick San Antonio or Des Moines) who discovers that he or she is gay. The parents of that child throw the child out of the house, in one way or another. The child knows that he or she will be tormented by his or her classmates. That child will be harassed by the local police officer. That child is a criminal under state law. That child hears from the pulpit of churches that he or she is sinful. And finally, the child now turns on TV and hears Anita Bryant saying "how wrong."

That child has several options in life: to remain closeted, to become an alcoholic, suicidal, or depressed, or whatever. Then, one day, that child picks up a newspaper that says "Homosexual Elected in San Francisco." Then there are two options for that child: to come to San Francisco, where it's accepted, or to stay in Des Moines or San Antonio and *fight*.

I've always said that. Upon my election, we got newspaper clippings from all over the country with the story "Homosexual Elected." The day after these stories appeared, I got a phone call— and it wasn't from San Antonio and it wasn't from Des Moines. It was from Altoona, Pennsylvania. There was a young voice saying, "Is this Harvey? Thank you very much, Harvey."

Martin: *So you're very much a gay liberationist.*

Milk: That's right. Subsequent to that, there have been many other phone calls. From Richmond, Minnesota, there was one from a guy who's seventeen years old. His family wanted to put him in an asylum.

Martin: *What do you say to people like that?*

Milk: Pack your bag. I give them directions to the nearest major city. Maybe I'll tell them to go to the nearest gay community center.

Find a cab. Ask the cab driver to take them to a gay community center. Talk to people at the nearest center. Find help there. Use that as a transitory step to . . . wherever: California, New York, Boston, Miami.

Martin: *Do you worry that the pressures placed on you by the new change in your life will affect you adversely?*

Milk: The workload—between filling the potholes in the street—the budget—major city problems—you must understand I did not run as a gay liberationist. I *am* a gay liberationist. I *ran* as an issue-oriented person. Of the seventeen candidates running in [District 5 of] the city, I was probably the most issue-oriented one. I am incredibly issue-oriented.

The workload on issues is incredible. The workload on the city is incredible. The responsibility, as a gay liberationist, is incredible. I knew it. I knew what I was getting into. I accepted it, and I feel I'll be able to do it. I won't be able to do as much as I would want. But you can be sure, I'll be setting styles and tones that this city has never seen before.

Martin: *Before I ask you how you'll accomplish that, describe the issues of the district. Describe the district. Were you elected by mostly gay people? And who are your constituents?*

Milk: First of all, District 5 is the central core of San Francisco. It covers the Haight [Haight Asbury neighborhood]. It covers Eureka Valley, the Castro area. It covers an area called 24th Street, Noe Valley, and part of Diamond Heights. It covers a very poor welfare area close to the Fillmore area, highly black. It covers Diamond Heights, which is almost suburbia within the city. It cuts across everything. It is a very high . . . workingly-class neighborhood.

My constituents are . . . There are 98 precincts within the district. I was the first-place vote in 60-odd precincts. I was the second-place vote in some 30-odd precincts. There were six precincts in which I came in third or fourth of seventeen candidates. My support cut across everything. I would say the district is no more than fifteen to twenty percent gay, at the very most. To get elected, you have to have a lot of other votes.

I had strong support by some unions. Some traditionally stereotyped anti-gay unions like the firefighters supported me. The Teamsters—and the Teamsters in San Francisco are the antithesis of the national Teamsters—they supported me.

I was supported by the *Bay Guardian*, which is our alternative newspaper. It's been fighting against the trend of this city of the last ten years. And I was supported by the *Chronicle*, which is the most conservative paper of this city. Also, I was supported by the *Berkeley Barb*, which is . . . "big stream."

So, what I am trying to say is that my support is broad-based.

Martin: *When you referred to the* Bay Guardian, *you asserted that it opposes recent trends in San Francisco. What are these trends?*

Milk: Well, we call it the Manhattanization: the building for building's sake; the driving out of light industry, blue collar jobs, and turning it over to a white collar city; the putting all the eggs in the tourist basket and not having anything to fall back on; the destruction of the neighborhoods; the encroachment of downtown into the neighborhoods; the disregard for the needs of the neighborhoods; and in turn, giving everything to whatever the Chamber of Commerce has wanted. That's been the trend for about ten years, and the *Bay Guardian* has been fighting that.

Martin: *You won by a substantial margin this time. When you ran for a state assembly seat in 1976, you did not win. Why?*

[154]

Milk: There was a combination of factors. The state assembly big was during the Democratic primary, and only Democrats could vote. A lot of people in this area are registered as independents. They couldn't vote. That's one part.

There were some strange influences, which you could pin down to one. [California governor] Jerry Brown was running for president at the same time in the same primary. Jerry Brown had given his promise to everybody in the state that he wouldn't intervene in any primary election in the state. [Milk's opponent Art] Agnos won the assembly primary the weekend after Jerry Brown endorsed him. All Jerry Brown had to do was to swing five votes per precinct to my opponent away from me. That was the crucial thing.

The reason he did that: Brown broke his promise, his pledge, because of the fact that his campaign manager was [Leo McCarthy,] the speaker of the state assembly. The speaker's aide was the one I was running against. So I was running against that power.

There were a lot of other things that chipped away. I don't think they would have made the difference between winning and losing unless you added them all up. But the Brown endorsement was the major thing.

There was the intervention in our local election of people from your city, like Elaine Noble, coming 3,000 miles to California to campaign against a gay person for a straight person—both of whom she had never met. Then she would not meet me. She put out a lot of information, a lot of photographs, a lot of endorsements, a lot of statements . . . erroneous. I could use the word "lies," because they were lies. She actually spread lies about me that she had met with me and said I was weak on issues and so forth. It was total fabrication. That hurt. It didn't cost so many votes *per se* because most people understood. But it meant devoting time and energy to counter that, where it should have been going to a positive means. That hurt.

And there were some little other factors. We feel it was the governor's coming in at the last minute that, we feel, made the difference between winning and losing.

Martin: *Gay people in this city make up a substantial portion of the population. I understand that no openly gay person has been elected to city-wide office in San Francisco before. I'm a little surprised that Boston beat San Francisco in electing an openly-gay person to public office.*

[155]

Milk: Part of the reason for this is size. Until we had district elections, you had to run for city office city-wide. You're talking about 250,000 people who actually vote in a city of 600,000. Plus, city-wide, you need a lot of money. I almost got elected two years ago in a city-wide race for supervisor. The six incumbents were reelected. There were twenty-three other challengers, and I was next. I was the best loser. What kept me from getting elected was lack of sufficient money.

Also, there was a police and fireman's strike. The weakest incumbents came out looking good, and the media gave them good press. I could have done it then.

On top of that, we've had quote so-called "gay leaders" . . . people who have passed themselves as spokespeople for the gay movement based upon the fact that they've been able to pass themselves off on it. They have always opposed me. *The Advocate*, Jim Foster, Jo Daly have always opposed me. They have always opposed any gay person who was trying to get up ahead, if they can't control that person. All movements go through this—the internal bickering and fighting. They opposed me with smears, lies . . . They were worse than the legitimate people who opposed me.

Martin: *Who are these people you're talking about? You mentioned* The Advocate. *People in Boston are familiar with* The Advocate.

Milk: Well . . . yes, [*Advocate* publisher] David Goodstein has always opposed me. His top aides in San Francisco have always opposed me . . . for no reason, never on an issue. They have never said, "Well, Harvey's too close to unions and thinks like a union person and we don't need that." Or "Harvey's too much of an environmentalist and we don't need that." They've done it on phony reasons . . . to actually lie because they don't want anybody else to get to the top of the mountain.

I think that's how Elaine Noble got out here. They paid for Elaine's trip out here. Who knows how much money they gave her under the table, above the table, whatever, aid or promises to help her so that she could oppose me? And she never opposed me on any issues—except lies.

[156]

They felt there could only be one person on top of the mountain. These are the type of people I always say who *use* the movement, rather than are *for* the movement. I recognize that there's plenty of room for a lot of gay people at the top of the mountain . . . that we're going to need them . . . we desperately need them.

That's why I keep encouraging more and more people to get involved . . . more and more people to run for different offices. We may have a gay person running for judge next year. We'll have people for the Democratic Central Committee. I'm encouraging it because we need that multitude. I think that's the difference between myself and some of these so-called gay leaders who've never done anything except speak up.

And they're being pushed aside. My election says, "Elaine Noble, you were wrong. You were rotten to come out here 3,000 miles to get involved against a gay person for a straight person."

We don't need "friends" to help the gay movement. We can do it ourselves. You don't find blacks any longer electing "friends" of the black community. You find blacks electing blacks. You find Latinos electing Latinos. You find Asians electing Asians.

If Elaine Noble doesn't understand that, it tells me she's either dumb or she was using the gay movement for her own personal reasons. We had gay persons in San Francisco the same way. My election tells them, "You were wrong. We don't want that concept. We want to get gay people who are qualified, who understand what the city's about, what the state's about, elected. Let them help us."

If Elaine Noble had not fought me last time and had come out here and helped me, it's conceivable that I could have been elected. Then we would have had a state legislator here and a supervisor. And we would have had somebody to fight Senator Briggs and his initiative. We would have had a gay legislator who could have gone from California to Miami [to fight against Anita Bryant's repeal of gay rights]—instead of having "friends" go to Miami.

That kind of leadership, this Uncle Tomism, is finished in San Francisco. There will still be those few people who will fight for Uncle Tomism. We will do our best to prevent it.

Martin: *Your election last November was probably the only positive major event in the gay movement in 1977.*

[157]

Milk: No.

Martin: *Okay, what other things have you noticed?*

Milk: I don't know what the others are. I do know of . . . two others. One is in Los Angeles. There's a gay person down there by the name of Don Amador. He teaches a university gay studies course . . . for the gay movement. He was just recently—about two months ago—appointed by the mayor as a liaison to the gay community. It is not a token position. It is a paid salaried position as staff liaison.

From the point of gay history, that is important. From the point of the movement, it's important that Mayor Bradley would issue Don Amador his calling cards. There's the seal of the city of

Los Angeles, the major's name, Don Amador's name, and under it "Gay Liaison;" coming out of city hall, the word "gay" printed with official recognition.

That is important. It may sound menial. It may sound small, but it's important. It breaks the barrier. It breaks the precedent. So that's important. Now, because of that, Don and I are working very close together to try to tie together a real gay movement in this state . . . to have a state-wide impact.

The other very positive thing that happened is Miami. My strongest thing is registering gay people to vote. Anybody, but mainly gay people. Out of my store over the last few years we registered a good 5,000 people . . . not all gay. We always had trouble getting [a registration drive] going. Subsequent to Miami, the next day, we set up card tables outside with signs saying "Don't let it happen here." And we had no gay issues on the ballot. But we registered 800 people . . . in twenty-four hours.

Subsequent to that, we registered many, many gay people. Many, many gay people got into political organizations. We formed more political and powerful on-going organizations since Miami than in the last several years before that. So, out of Miami, something very positive happened.

23.

"You can throw bricks at City Hall or you can take it over."

Even before his first month in office was complete, the new supervisor bragged "I've begun raising hell already" to John Bryan of the *Berkeley Barb*. This interview appeared in the January 27 *Barb* under the title "S.F. Supervisor Harvey Milk: "You can throw bricks at City Hall or you can take it over." The article briefly reviews some of Milk's activities during his first two Board meetings, and lets Milk describe what he wanted to accomplish.

I T'S GREAT to be here!" said San Francisco Supervisor Harvey Milk as he strode briskly to the top of the grand staircase in the big-domed edifice he likes to call "Silly Hall."

"Of course, I'm not happy with the system," he added. "I'm not happy with the economic system. I'm not happy with the political system. I mean, you can stand on the outside and throw bricks at Silly Hall or you can take it over. Well, here we are."

As San Francisco's first self-acknowledged gay elected official and a longtime demonstrator, organizer, candidate, and general critic of the city's politics, Milk has every reason to look upon his election (representing the heavily gay District 5) as a highly encouraging step forward.

Milk, who took office earlier this month, is full of ideas, plans, and dreams. He now has a significant public forum from which to air them, and he's made it plain during his very first month in office that he's going to be heard. No nice-guy, quiet-gentleman role playing for Milk.

"I've begun raising hell already," he told the *Barb* during an exclusive interview recently. "I raised it during the first meeting.

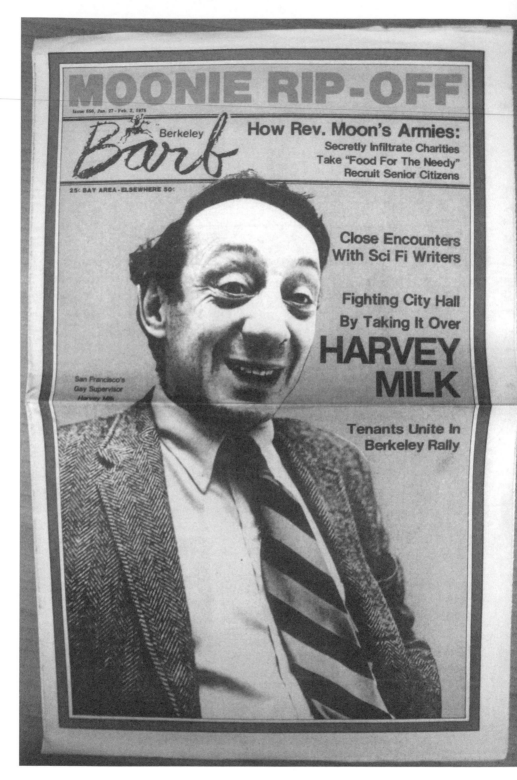

An unattractive photo of Milk dominates the front page of the January 27, 1978, Berkeley Barb

The first speech I made was symbolic of what I'm going to be like, that I will not be taken for granted, that I will not go along because it's the 'right' thing to do. That I will stay with the issues and principles and will fight for them even if it upsets people.

"I'm not concerned about the Emily Post attitude of life. Emily Post kept the blacks suppressed for hundreds of years. Emily Post kept the Jews out of the boardrooms of the major corporations for hundreds of years. Emily Post kept the gay people where they are."

Harvey has seen enough of politics to know that it will be impossible to please everyone, that he will often anger his longtime supporters and surprise his adversaries by agreeing on issues where their interests intersect. He knows that staying in "Silly Hall" may be more difficult than getting there in the first place. (He's up for reelection in only two years.) But he feels that he'll perform a valuable function by "opening the dialogue" on issues supervisors have ducked for decades.

At his first board meeting, Milk took on the "airport lobby" by questioning their right to uncontrolled expansion and challenged the Muni transportation system on several crucial issues.

"Even though we lost the votes in the end," he explained, "the dialogue was opened and everyone realized that they're going to have to prove their case from now on. What I was telling them was that I'm going to tackle them on everything—even airport expansion. Last year, only (Supervisor John) Molinari voted against it. Now we have four votes—what you could call the 'progressive minority' on the present board. But definitely a minority, since there are seven votes against us on most things.

"But now they realize they no longer can ram airport expansion down the public's throat. They have to prove their case and they have to be more careful. They just can't get anything at all through anymore. If I accomplish nothing else on the board except forcing them to stand up and be true, that's a major accomplishment."

At his second meeting a few days later, Milk expanded the "dialogue" even further. At issue was supervisorial approval of a federally-funded drug rehabilitation center to be located in a residential part of the Mission District. Milk and three other "progressives"

managed to overcome the reluctant conservative majority and won the day.

Even more interesting, from Milk's point of view, was the "dialogue" which developed between himself and a horrified Board president, the arch-conservative Dianne Feinstein, who lives in posh Pacific Heights and could not understand "squalid" conditions that might exist in the new drug center.

"It was the first time that old guard members like Feinstein heard the 'other side' from another supervisor instead of from public testimony," Milk explained. I got up and told her, 'Don't judge the standard of living of these people by your own standard of living up in Pacific Heights.' Sometimes we'll win the votes, and sometimes we'll lose, but the dialogue will remain open."

Needless to say, the Feinstein-led "old guard" does not much like the 47-year-old Milk, who, to their way of thinking, is simply not a gentleman.

Nor does he intend to be. Born in New York City, Milk is the son of Russian Jewish immigrants, both radicals. He learned the realities of city life the hard way, moved to San Francisco in 1969 to open a camera store in the increasingly-gay Castro-Market area where he still operates.

During the 1960s, Milk says he was an activist "like everybody else—demonstrations, marches, yelling, mostly against the Vietnam War. Actually, it was Richard Nixon who made a politician out of me. It was watching the Watergate hearings in 1973 that made me so angry it politicized me. I decided to run for office rather than throwing bricks from the outside.

"A lot of people throw bricks and vent their frustrations. They throw pies in the face of authority and kick the stone walls, and I guess all of that is needed. But if you really want to put long-term energies into changing things, do it through the system. Beat the system, as I did against tremendous odds.

"I ran for office three times before I finally won. I ran for supervisor in 1973 at the last moment and lost. In '75, I ran again and almost made it. In '76, I ran in the Democratic primary for an assembly seat and was beaten by the Democratic machine. Even the governor got into that one.

"I fought last year against the entire Democratic machine, against the Labor Council, against the money interest and most politicians. I won. That shows it can be done if you really mean it."

Needless to say, Milk was helped considerably by the division of the city into eleven electoral districts—a reform he'd campaigned long and hard for. And by the fact that he then had only to get approval from residents of his own District 5, where there's a gay majority. [District 5 did not have a gay majority.] Harvey has long been totally upfront about his own sexual orientation and he promised to fight hard for gay interests. (He estimates San Francisco's present homosexual population at about 70,000—considerably less than the 150,000 some gay activists claim.)

"Speaking up for gays is certainly one of my responsibilities," he told the *Barb*. "Not to be the main spokesperson, but to be a strong spokesperson. Nobody can speak for the entire gay community—it's too diverse. But I certainly will express the views of a large number of people.

"I seem to have become something of a gay leader on a state and national level as well. I've been speaking all over California since the election, helping to organize gay communities in other cities. I've also gotten speaking requests from Chicago, Phoenix, Kansas— other parts of America. But I'm not going out of the state yet."

Milk expects to stand up for gays on at least two major issues that are bound to come before the board in the near future—police harassment and plans to tear down the badly-needed Gay Community Center near City Hall.

[163]

"Police harassment of gays has existed as long as history," said Milk. "Unfortunately, it will probably exist for some time to come even with a sympathetic mayor, police chief, and sympathetic captains. There will always be some policeman who lets his own bigotry and prejudice come out—not just against gays, but against blacks, Latinos, Chinese, all of us.

"I'm more aware of gay harassment because I'm gay, but I'm equally aware of what the other minorities suffer. There's no way I can put a button in each policeman's head and push it to make him think the right way. So the only option is for me to go to the police and raise hell and let them know harassment will not be tolerated."

The Gay Community Center, said Milk, will probably have to move, but he's holding Mayor George Moscone to a promise that city funding will be provided for a new center "just as soon as the site is found.

"We need the center badly," he explained. "The reason so many young gay people are into drugs and prostitution is that they come here and cannot find advice and jobs. The center can provide both."

Harvey was busy. His phone was ringing and a big stack of letters awaited his signature. We had time for one more question.

"What would you do in San Francisco if you had the right to do whatever you wanted to?" I asked.

"Do I be God, you mean?" he asked. "Do I be God, I'd take the whole South of Market area and not just build business and industrial sites but whole neighborhoods where people can work and shop and live without cars. A place to enjoy freedom and the quality of life, a living neighborhood so that at six o'clock each night they wouldn't throw a switch and turn off a section of the city making it dark and cold and unlivable. I'd build a city of the future.

"The second day, do I be God, I'd take all the battered, boarded-up storefronts in the Tenderloin and make them into child-care centers and take the senior citizens out of all those crummy hotels and put them in charge of the children, giving them jobs and a reason to live.

"Then I would rest. But only after I'd done something about the dogshit. Dogshit is a very important San Francisco issue. I'm tired of stepping in it. It's a health hazard. Kids play in it, and blind people slip and fall. It's symbolic of all the problems of irresponsibility we face in big, depersonalized, alienated urban societies. It's not the fault of the dogs. I wouldn't plug the dogs; I'd plug the minds of their owners who let them run loose.

"But of course I'm not God," said Harvey with a whimsical smile. "I will not accomplish all I want to accomplish. I will make mistakes. I'm human. I hope I can give a bit of leadership. Because—if I do that—it's almost as good as being God."

[164]

24.

"There's got to be a lot more Harvey Milks."

According to Harvey Milk's 1978 appointment book, he was interviewed by Los Angeles-based radio reporter Greg Gordon on Saturday, February 19 in Milk's Castro Camera store. Gordon conducted the half-hour interview for a program produced by the IMRU Radio Collective and broadcast on KPFK radio. The program is now called *This Way Out,* and Gordon has been its executive producer since 1974, making it the oldest GLBT-focused radio program in the country.

This Way Out is a nonprofit program. As a fundraiser, it offers an audio CD of this interview with Greg Gordon and Harvey Milk to anyone who makes a donation of $25 or more. If you would like a copy you can make a payment online at **thiswayout.org**, or mail a check for $25.00 or more payable to This Way Out to this address:

This Way Out
P.O. Box 38327
Los Angeles, CA 90038

In the text below, my comments are in [square brackets].

Milk: I'm Harvey Milk. I'm a supervisor in San Francisco.

Gordon: *And I'm Greg Gordon from IMRU for—*

Milk: And I'm *gay.* [He laughs.]

Gordon: *And so am I. And we're up in San Francisco, in Harvey's office at Castro Camera. And Harvey's graciously taken a few minutes out of his very busy schedule* [Milk laughs] *to talk with us about*

politics in San Francisco, and how he got elected; the first openly gay person to be elected to public office in California history.

Milk: I'd like also to talk about politics in California, rather than in San Francisco.

Gordon: *That's fine.*

Milk: Because I don't think there's a delineation.

Gordon: *You don't think that there's a difference between politics in San Francisco and—let's say—politics in Los Angeles?*

Milk: It's a matter of degree. There's no moat built around the city of San Francisco that separates us from the rest. Sometimes we wish there were. [Both men laugh.]

But I think what takes place in San Francisco, for whatever reasons, can take place anyplace. And it's just a matter of understanding what it's all about. And San Francisco—it's very interesting that because of the fact that I'm gay, that becomes the media event. That sells the newspapers. But it's very important that we realize that I was elected as a candidate who was gay, rather than a gay candidate.

I did not run on a gay issue. In San Francisco, the difference from L.A. is that we [in San Francisco] are both county supervisors and city council people; one and the same. Our city is divided into eleven districts. Since we are city and county [combined], it's one *powerful,* very powerful legislative group. You have to picture if your L.A. City Council and your L.A. Board of Supervisors were one and the same. That's what we are. And we are an *activist* group, rather than puppets of a strong mayor or something like that.

Gordon: *Or a strong police chief.*

Milk: Or a strong police chief. We are very, very strong in the city. Of the eleven districts that were up for election in this past year, there were a total of something like 162 candidates altogether. Of the 162 candidates for the Board, there were eleven—not even eleven, but about seven or eight who were incumbents who ran—six, I guess. And exing those out, because they have a record of voting on issues, of all the other 150-some-odd people, I was probably

the most *issue-oriented* person running. Probably have taken more strong, *definitive* stands—not, "Yes, I'm for that," "No, I'm not for that," but *why*; and I've been in [more] battles than *all* of the other candidates running. Probably more issue-oriented than some of the supervisors who ran for reelection. At least I'm more [unintelligible]. It's vital to know that it took four years—or five years, or whatever it was—to build up that kind of a reputation.

Gordon: *Yes, because you had run for office in the past.*

Milk: It has nothing to do with running for offices. The reason I run for office is because I was *issue-oriented*. People say, "Oh, you ran for office, name recognition." No.

In my particular district, we've had about five or six major *district* battles versus city-wide problems. In every one, I was *involved* in them—on one side or the other. There wasn't one other candidate—there were seventeen people running in this district—there wasn't one other candidate had been involved in every single district problem. I was *there*. People on the streets would say to me, "Harvey, I don't agree with your issue, but I know you're a fighter. I know you're there. I know you will be there when we need you."

Let me give you a classic case of this, going to be controversial right now. We have a statewide primary coming up: attorney general. One of the people running for statewide [office] in the Democratic primary is [Congresswoman] Yvonne [Brathwaite] Burke. My heart goes there—she's black, she's a woman, wham! There I go.

But—but—I go in Orange County, at the Democratic statewide meeting a couple of months ago, where they all spoke. Orange County. *conservative*. Orange County, most of the people there— in fact, I was the only elected official outside of the L.A.-Orange County area. So basically, you had the conservative wing of the Democratic Party. Yvonne Burke got up and talked about the black people, talked about women. Great. She sat down. [Los Angeles City Attorney] Bert Pines got up and talked about battered wives, what he's done for them, the Latinos, what he's done for them, the blacks, what he's done for them, abused children, what he's done for them, and the gay community, what he's done for them. *Three times* in his speech he talked about what he's done for the gay people, in front of a very conservative audience.

[167]

Three months later, after the campaign trail—and these [two] people have heard each other, back and forth—in Sacramento, before the Democratic Minority Coalition, which is the traditional minorities, the feminists, and the gay people—they're speaking, knowing who the audience they're speaking to—this is now not the *conservative* wing of the Democratic Party, but the *liberal* wing of the Democratic Party—they got up. Yvonne gets up and talks about the black issue, about women. Sits down. Bert gets up and talks about the same thing.

That's the difference. He's done his work, he's *paid his dues.* He's willing to talk about it. He's an activist. He was *involved*, doing things. She will vote right, but he's been there.

A lot of candidates I ran against would vote right—the same as I do—but they wouldn't be the activist, they wouldn't be the advocate, they wouldn't be the leader.

Gordon: *I think that's what people are looking for these days, is somebody who will—you know, that's what we're crying out for, up even to the federal government, you know.*

Milk: Okay, statewide—let's get together statewide. May fifth—I think it's May fifth or May sixth—Sunday—[rustles papers]. May sixth, I guess it is. Sunday, L.A. We're calling together a statewide caucus of gay people. [The California Gay Caucus was held on Saturday, May 6, 1978.] A convention. But *not* an endorsement. And we are inviting all the candidates for statewide offices: governor, lieutenant governor, attorney general, and I guess, secretary of state.

Gordon: *It's nonpartisan, or . . . ?*

Milk: Nonpartisan! Democrat, Republican, Peace and Freedom, American Independent. We want gay people from *all* the state to come. We're sending the letters to these people, we would have this caucus. We're gonna say that you have ten-fifteen minutes to present your case, and then questioning. And we don't wanna hear about dams. We don't wanna hear about redwood trees. We want to hear about what you think about the gay issues. What you think about that. And then we'll accept questions from the audience, filter them through a panel of gay newspaper people, so that

someone doesn't get up and do a ten-minute tirade. [Both men chuckle.] Right?

Gordon: *Yeah.*

Milk: Like I do. [Gordon chuckles.] And they'll be asked questions. And if [governor] Jerry Brown does not show up, that will be published. If he shows up, what he says will be published. There will be *no endorsements*, but we will disseminate the information.

Gordon: *It's a forum, basically.*

Milk: It's a forum. It's like the black community does. We *must* follow what the black community does. The black community does this on a *national* level. All the candidates for the Democratic primary for president met before the Black Leadership Forum—or whatever it was called—in North Carolina and talked about black issues. We must do the *same thing*, the gay community. We must move *out* of San Francisco, *out* of L.A. We must move to California. If you add the gay community with the other traditional minorities, we should have control of the state. But we cannot sit in the back of the bus and let the other minorities lead. *We should show the leadership.* In fact, in the incredible position, you see—

Gordon: *Well, let me ask you: Are other minorities coming around to realizing that they can and should work with the gay community?*

Milk: Oh, yeah. Lieutenant Governor [Mervyn] Dymally has stuck his neck out for the gay community over and over again. When Willie Brown's sexual bill was before the senate, he flew in from Denver to cast that vote, in front of the eyes of the world. So he stuck his neck out there. And he understands working together. He understands the importance of gay people in there. So it's very interesting.

Take San Francisco, which is a very heavy minority city. Over fifty percent of the population is minority. Because of the fighting for those crumbs, sometimes the black community doesn't talk to the Filipino, won't talk to the Asians, the Asians won't talk to anybody. You know, nevertheless: They all talk to me. A gay person.

Partly for two reasons. One, because within the gay community we have gay Asians, gay blacks, gay—we are infiltrated. That's part

[169]

of the reason. We cut across lines. Second of all, for whatever reasons, I'm the one that can pull it together.

So we are trying strongly to pull together that coalition. In view of that, we realized—at least, *I* have always realized—is the voter registration. We are kicking off a massive voter registration drive within the Chinese and gay community together *soon*. You know. There's many reasons for that. Working very tight with the Asian community, very tight. And if we can pull it off here, and if L.A. pulls it off, we pull it off statewide, that in—in—within ten years, the minorities will be running the state. And when [I say] "minorities," I'm talking about the feminists, I'm talking about the gays included with that. And so we have to fight that, we have to fight with our natural allies, but it can't be just because a person is black, or green, or gay, or orange, or whatever may be. They have to be *issue-oriented*. We cannot expect somebody to get up there and say, "I'm gay, therefore vote for me."

Gordon: *How do you motivate people to register? Because this is a fundamental problem that we've always had.*

Milk: Motivate 'em? Say, "Do you like [Los Angeles Chief of Police Ed] Davis? Do you like Senator Briggs? Do you like Anita Bryant?" You motivate 'em because you tell them that the *legislators* and the *executive officers*—be they the local supervisors, be they statewide—*run your life.*

They run your life and they spend your money. When they collect tax money from gay people, and don't give us anything back in return—take it for *their* golf courses, take *our* tax money for *their* pet projects—and give us—and on top of it, *insult* us by not giving us our rights. If that's not motivation: If you like being *harassed* by the police; if you like being a *third-class* citizen; if you like being *beat up* by punks; if you like the *church* yelling at you: Don't register, don't vote. But don't complain. If you want to be shoved back into your closet, if you want to be the traditional gay person who gets beat up and whimpers home and says, "Well, I'm gay, and I deserve to get beat up," fine. Otherwise, the *only* thing you can do is *register* to vote.

Gordon: *What about the reasonably well-off gay couples or gay singles in the hills somewhere, who never have any trouble with the police,*

who—you know—they can say "That's never happened to me—"

Milk: Right!

Gordon: *—You know, "Why should I get involved? My life is beautiful?"*

Milk: Right, i.e., that reminds me of the wealthy Jews in Nazi Germany, when Hitler was first pickin' up the Jewish Communists and Jewish socialists. They went, "They were *scum*. That's not us. We are *accepted*." You know, "We've been the accepted. We ride on the back of the bus." It's like the Uncle Tom. And believe me, when Hitler started in having the concentration camp[s], he didn't care whether you were Jewish socialist or Jewish fascist. If you were Jewish, you went.

When the Briggs and Anita Bryant take over, they don't care if you are the accepted hairdresser or the gay doctor or the gay lawyer or the gay society person. You are gay, you will go off. And if you don't—if that sounds like a stereotype thing, stop and think: Nazi Germany—what it did to the gay people. There were 600,000 gay people killed. Prior to Hitler's taking over, in the twenties, the gay movement in Germany was more advanced than the gay movement in San Francisco in 1978. There was a statewide—a *nationwide*—convention of gay people in Germany: 8,000 gay people. We've never had anything like that here. There were letters written to the Reichstag to tell them to throw out the anti-gay laws. Scientists, doctors, everybody was preaching for gayness and acceptability.

In Russia, 1917: They threw out the anti-gay laws. And then Stalin took over and that was the end of the gay movement.

Hitler took over, the end of the gay movement.

And if you think history doesn't repeat itself, you're *crazy*. And the only defense about that is not just to be organized, but to get involved, and to realize who the common enemy is.

Unfortunately, within the gay community we have such a class distinction, and *racism* within the gay community, and *sexism* within the gay community. Because some people think they are better than the others. When it comes down to it, we all do the same thing. And the elitists in the gay community—those who are "accepted;" those who are the Uncle Toms; those who have sold

[171]

out, must realize that when the push comes to shove, that if Senator Briggs wins against the gay schoolteachers, the next thing he may say is, "We don't want gay people to vote." And when my gay, elitist, wealthy brother or sister says, "I don't have to worry. I don't get into trouble with the police. I don't go to the bars. I don't go this"—okay. It's that old story in Germany. First it was the gays and the gypsies, and then the Jews, and they kept going. Finally there was nobody to protest.

You've *got* to stop them at the beginning! They've *got* to get involved. The gay elitists, the gay wealthy people, the gay society people, the gay people who have made it: They have to fight the battle *now*.

Gordon: *In many cases, they're in the better positions to be able to do it.*

Milk: And they're also in the position to *lose* more. 'Cause the gay street person (i.e. whatever that means); what has that person got to lose? By fighting the battle?

Gordon: *Why, that's why they were out in front in the beginning.*

Milk: Right, right. But the well-to-do, those who have made it, they've got a *lot* to lose. They've got to lose what they're worried about. And they're the ones who will have to come through. And if they want to stay in their closets and so forth, that's fine—but get their checkbooks out of the closet! It's *needed!* It's desperately needed, that their checkbooks come out of the closet.

The only—I know the *power* I have as an elected official in this city. It's incredible. I mean, I'm restricted by the charter of what I can do or I can't do. But, boy, can I do it! [Gordon chuckles] And I *know* that when I speak out in this city—I mean, the police department is nervous, the Chamber of Commerce is nervous. I know the power I have.

And if you don't start—whoever's listening, if you don't start helping electing gay people—and not just gay people, but gay *fighters*—who will get up, and not take it and sit back, who'll fight for the—if you don't start electing them, we're going to be in trouble. So people who—gay street people have to register and vote, and

they have to realize that it cannot be only voting for the people who believe in every single thing they do. No such thing! There's no such perfect candidate!—you know.

[What they need to understand] is *they* have to compromise, and then to realize the gay person who is living in the hills has to realize that he or she can't only support the "conservative"-type people, or the "respectable"-type people, that they both have to lose—both will lose and if you don't get together. And you've got to join hands now. It's—it's desperate. It's desperate.

Gordon: *We have a couple of gay candidates running for assembly in Los Angeles, in Los Angeles districts 44 and 46. Some political gay—gay political clubs did not endorse them. I'm not going to be critical—I don't want to get into that issue. But what I want to ask you is: What happens when you have two or three or four gay political groups or gay organizations that are in a position to help, but who cannot seem to get together? Because obviously, you've gotta have a coalesced movement in order to elect somebody. What can you say to these people?*

Milk: In my first three attempts to run—I've run four times before I win—I was never supported by the gay establishment, I was never supported by the gay political leaders, I was never supported by the gay clubs. And the reason why, is if I won, I would have been what I am now that I won. And they would no longer be the top of the hill. They don't realize that there's room at the top for a lotta people. They wanted to be—they would rather have been the Uncle Tom at the back of the bus—or the "Aunt Mary," as I call them—and be the token, be the first to discover Barbra Streisand, to be—you know, the token fag—rather than see a gay person elected and the power go that way. They didn't realize there's room for plenty.

And I have found out in San Francisco, the so-called "gay leaders" of the time—the Jim Fosters and all those people—they were for themselves. They were not for the gay movement. Their attitude was so offensive that they would back straight people. I found that their influence was such that they brought Elaine Noble three thousand miles cross-country to campaign for a straight person against me, a gay person—both of whom she had never met. And even *this*

[173]

year [the] Alice B. Toklas [gay Democrats club] would never support me. Some of the other gay candidates—

Gordon: *You're referring—for those of you who don't know—to the Alice B. Toklas Democratic Club—*

Milk: That's right.

Gordon: *Which is the* [San Francisco] *version of the Stonewall Democratic Club in Los Angeles.*

Milk: Right. Some of the other Democratic clubs this time *did*. They finally realized what it was all about. And *finally* I was able to break [through]. It took me *four times* to convince them, and the thing is that I've always done well, even those these people were *knifing* me, lying, smearing, and everything else about me. Because the people in the streets understood. The people in the battles understood what I meant.

And so my answer is to L.A. is, "Get it together." [I] find it *offensive* that gay leadership is so jealous of somebody else. I find that offensive. I find that people who say, "Oh, well, but we owe this person like that." Bull. The *reason* [for] gay political clubs is the ultimate is to get gays elected. That's why it *exists*, because we've been, you know. And then to walk away from gay candidates—unless they are unqualified, that's a different story—when I say "unqualified," I mean when they are really ass—er, ex beep beep beep beep [chuckles].

[174]

Gordon: [laughs]

Milk: X-rated! Beep. If they're no good, if they're turkeys, it's a different story.

Gordon: *Well, if they're turkeys, they probably should never have gotten to the point where they're running in the first place.*

Milk: Well, no. Turkeys can run. Anybody can run.

Gordon: *That's true. Well, I have seen that.*

Milk: Turkeys get elected.

Gordon: [chuckles] *God knows.*

Milk: But when you're faced with a—even if you're faced with a gay turkey and a straight turkey, you know, you go to the gay. And show me how many great non-gay candidates there really are.

But to come up with these reasons that I read about, I just— well. I know there are gay candidates in L.A. who are faced with the same things I did. My advice to them is: then work that much harder, and *throw out* those so-called "gay leaders" who are not gay leaders, but self-perpetuating self-leaders—self-appointed, have never done anything to get broad-based support. Elitist support, yes. Or groups, yes.

Gordon: *Sounding very much like David Goodstein. And yet I understand his magazine did not support you.*

Milk: Oh, Goodstein fought against me bitterly. Bitterly. For the same reasons.

Gordon: *And then he threw a victory party for you.*

Milk: Well, he lost. You know, and at least he's smart enough to realize who won. He lost. And he understands it. 'Cause he was always against me, used everything he could against me. And—'cause he never met with me. Never understood what it was about. But if the gay establishment doesn't understand what the gay movement's all about—gotta get rid of 'em. And I'm not talking that they're nice guys! Not nice, wonderful people! I'm not talking about, "Are they fun people to be with?" But if they don't understand what the gay movement's about, you gotta get rid of 'em.

And I'll tell you what the gay movement's about. After I got elected, I got the phone call I knew I'd eventually get. Got quite a few of them. One was from a seventeen-year-old child in a small town in Minnesota. And the boy is handicapped. And the boy's parents found out he's gay. And they want to put him in an insane asylum. And that boy needs help.

And the gay movement is about the letter I got from Southwest Africa. When he read about a gay person getting elected here, and that person has *hope*. And that seventeen-year-old kid in Minnesota has hope. And when we have gay leaders, not understanding *that*, and more worried about their own personal power, they're not gay leaders. They're offensive.

Gordon: *Another reason that some people don't register or don't want to get involved in what they will call, quote, "establishment politics," is that they are just anti-establishment politics period, you know; that, "the way to change the system is revolution, blah," et cetera, et cetera, et cetera. What can you say to these people who don't want to get involved, who don't want to register, who feel like voting and the whole establishment political process is a waste of time and not the way to do it?*

Milk: Okay, the establishment political process *stinks.* I, too, would prefer to throw a bomb. Except the establishment has more bombs than I have. So the option is something that I told—oh, about three years ago—three years ago, they were a group of three—or maybe it was four years ago—three gay socialists came in who I know, and we had a nice long talk. And we talked about how bad the system was—"The system has to be overthrown." Then we got talking about police brutality, harassment. And I said after a while, "What if you, you, and you were the three police commissioners, and I was the chief of police?"

And they said, "Great!"

And I said, "I thought the system stinks?" [Someone laughs.] It's not the *system* that stinks, it's the people who're *running* the system stinks. If *anybody* out there who thought the establishment and system were rotten were *running* it; if the most radical, liberal person—revolutionary person—was the mayor of L.A., and the next one was the chief of police, and the next group were the city council, and the next group were the board of supervisors, they would be able to *change* the system.

[176]

You have two ways of changing the system: revolution, or getting in and bending it from within. Unfortunately, revolution will not work. I mean, it ain't gonna happen. As long as there's two cars in every garage, and a drop of gasoline and a TV set, and you can wash your glasses and not get spots on it, the revolution is not gonna exist. Because people are afraid of the unknown, and so they'd rather have the awful conditions that exist rather than the unknown. "The revolution will *not* be televised." But rapid evolution *can* take place. Already, on the board of San Francisco supervisors, in six weeks, things that were never discussed before have been discussed. The

dialogue has been opened which was never there before. And we won a lot of their votes.

The very first major battle—and it doesn't sound like a major battle, but it *is* a major battle—was the location of a drug rehabilitation center—a Latino drug rehabilitation center—in a white neighborhood. And the conservatives just went at it. And I *battled* them. I really battled them on it. And we won! We won the vote. A, that dialogue never would have taken under the old board. Seven weeks ago, that would never even have come up for vote. And B, we *won* it!

So, what is revolution? You know, it's not what I like to see. But we are going to have a rapid evolution. We already *had it* in San Francisco. Just stop and think. The day the Board of Supervisors [of] San Francisco [was] sworn in, the tradition is every supervisor gets up and says a few general words and introduces their family there. And the first words out of my mouth—and the national press was there—was, "As you know, I am gay." That has never been spoken before in any legislative body in this country. And I said that "There's a state law that says gay people cannot legally be married. But there is no state law, or a law anyplace in the universe, that says two people cannot love each other. And I'd like to introduce my lover."

And if that's not a revolution—[Both men laugh.] I don't know what is. Sure, it's not what we want. But, you know, we're battling thousands of years of prejudice and thousands of years of the system. It's got to *change*. It's not going to be easy. I can only do it if I have a lot of support out there. Can't have a lot of support out there if people are not aiding financially or—and—not or, *and*—registering and voting.

And there's got to be a lot more Harvey Milks. There's just *got* to be. There's too many young kids in little towns in Minnesota.

25.

" . . . every time you take a stand you make an enemy. But you also make a friend."

In late February or early March, Geoff Mains interviewed Milk in his City Hall office as the basis for an article in the *Northwest Gay Review*. The text here is based on a typed transcript of Mains' full interview, from an audio cassette tape which starts in mid-sentence. As usual, my comments are in [square brackets].

The publication *The Body Politic* that Milk and Mains discuss was a gay newspaper in Toronto, Canada, which had been raided by police.

Mains: *Northwest Gay Review, which serves Seattle, Portland, and Vancouver, B.C. And I'm with the community organization which handles the publication in Vancouver. So we're interested in talking to you, having an interview with you on several points. First of all, your election as supervisor; secondly, on what you think of the future of the gay community; and thirdly on this boycott against Canada that you're talking about right now, because it will affect a lot of people, you know, in our own country and we're very interested in the boycott.*

Milk: In the essence of time and methodology, I mean, cut through to—the whole boycott is exactly what the election was all about.

Prior to election, Harvey Milk and other people who are committed [went] to the Board of Supervisors hearings, committee hearings, and police commission hearings, and everything else, and sometimes they would listen to us. Sometimes they wouldn't—more often than not. We couldn't get money for the Gay Day parade in this city—it's the biggest parade in the city. All the other parades,

some of them get up to as much as twenty thousand dollars; we got nothing. In fact—basically—and so much, we got not even the crumbs to fight over with the whole community. If I went ahead and called a press conference on any issue, the press might come, may not come. And there's no guarantee that anything will be covered or not or be buried or what.

Okay, Harvey Milk was elected. Okay. Now when Harvey Milk speaks out about a boycott about Canada, all of a sudden Canadian [radio] stations all ask me—

Mains: *You had a very strong reaction, then, from the Canadian press?*

Milk: Forgetting about them at this moment, what I'm trying to say is the power of elected office, especially to a gay person, [is that] all of a sudden the press will listen to you. I have to cut this interview short because I'm having a hearing at my instigation on seeing if we can get the U.S. government to ask South Africa to close their consulate here in San Francisco [in protest of the South African government's policy of apartheid]. So here we're talking about the South African government and we're not too sure of the powers in the city streets.

This is the power of why a gay person—any elected official, but particularly a gay person—has incredible recognition.

This weekend I'm flying to Chicago. [Milk was in Chicago Saturday and Sunday March 4 and 5, 1978.] There's a gay person who's running there [and] has a chance to win, and so I'm breaking my pledge. Not pledge, but I told people I would not go out of state unless I felt it was urgent. This is urgent.

Whenever I say something, the media pick up on it. We got funding for our parade. Gay people are being hired in city programs. The seated jobs of the federal government, we couldn't get any—very few—gay people into it before. Now we're getting lots. So what I'm saying is a gay person elected makes a lot of difference, a powerful difference.

In a city of 675,000 people—San Francisco—the most powerful person is the mayor, then the chief administrative officer (who's like the city manager). Those are the two most powerful people. Then [the] next most powerful people in this city are the supervisors.

There are only ten people—[he corrects himself] there are twelve people in this city—[corrects himself again] there are two people in this city who have more power than me. There's only ten others who have as much power.

That's why it's important for a gay person to be—to answer your three questions—

Mains: *Well, I just wanted to bring out a few details on the election because Vancouver is very like San Francisco. We have ten aldermen and a mayor—elected at large now—, and so—*

Milk: Let me get into that, in the essence of time.

Mains: *Okay, so if you could go into support from the straight community—*

Milk: In the essence of time—I really, you know, I would spend an hour with you, but in the essence of time, I'm going to cut short.

Okay, I think it's clear—I think it's vital—first, that I establish *why* and the importance of getting elected, rather than *how* to get elected or anything else.

And so what I've been dwelling on is the fact [that] when a nation like Canada will quote me; the radio stations in Canada will pick me up and interview me long distance; when Washington is watching what I do; when people running for statewide office here are quoting me to support them for their position; when the chief of police is at my beck and call; when the conservative elements of the city cut Catholic social services and [send] threatening personal letters like that; when the Chamber of Commerce, which is notoriously anti-minority, invites me to be the guest speaker; then it shows the power and the incredible force that comes out of elected office.

When a young boy from Richmond, Minnesota calls me and his parent want to commit him [to an institution] because he's gay, and I am his only hope; when I get letters from the Union of South Africa and Southwest Africa; then you know that it's very important.

Okay, how do you get elected and how do you do it?

You can't get elected just as a gay person unless the [local gay] community is so big. In San Francisco, we have eleven districts now. There was 160-some-odd candidates—only six of whom were incumbents from six different districts. Of the other candidates—the

150-some-odd candidates—without any question, I was the most issue-oriented candidate around. I probably was more issue-oriented than some of the incumbents.

Mains: *In terms of housing,* [unintelligible—both men spoke at the same time].

Milk: Where do you stand? Where do you stand? I'm not saying which way, but you have to have a stand on housing. Yes. What is it? Bang.

Of the last five or six years, there have been in this city many battles, neighborhood battles, institution[al] expansion, freeways, taxicab rate increases, and so forth, union wages. In almost every one, you found Harvey Milk taking a stand. Naturally, every time you take a stand you make an enemy. But you also make a friend.

Over the past five or six years, I cannot think of any major issue I was not involved in, in the city. And in every issue in my district, I was there one way or the other, on one side or the other. Because of that, we had the following thing take place during the campaign.

Let me just digress for a moment. The mayor of New York City has just introduced a gay rights ordinance or proclamation—no, it was a proclamation—where the police and firefighters would have to hire gay people. The firefighters in New York City are fighting this tooth and nail, against it, anti-gay.

In San Francisco, the firefighters not only gave me the maximum amount of financial contributions, but on Election Day, they had men working, knocking on doors getting the vote out for me. And at my victory dinner, they were there, you know.

[181]

How much clearer can I show the difference between being involved in community issues than to show that group, the Teamsters in San Francisco—which are the antithesis of the national Teamsters—who supported me. And the building and construction trade unions, the hard-hats, the plumbers, the electricians, these type people, the Archie Bunkers, they were supporting me.

Mains: *So you got a very large non-gay vote?*

Milk: I got a very large union vote.

The environmentalists [were] behind me almost a hundred percent, except for some political ones who are the wheeler-dealer type

people. But of all the candidates, I was the staunchest one against airport expansion. I was the staunchest one against institution[al] expansion, the staunchest person for the preservation of the neighborhood. Incredible environmentalist.

Because of things like that, and I can list on and on, the largest political force, the Latino community Mexican-American Political Association (MAPA) endorsed me. A Latino group endorsing a gay person. That's wild. It's incredible they were supporting me.

I could go on, list after list after list. It comes in two waves. One, me being in their battles on their side. Two, a lot of people realizing that they may disagree with me on a particular issue, but that I'm a fighter, that I will get up and I will speak out cleanly, clearly for an issue. And they know that when their issue comes up, if I agree I will fight with them, and therefore they can support me; they can lobby me; they explain their position and I'll fight.

I've also proven over the years that I was completely and politically independent, that I'm not a puppet of any of the higher bees who tap the lower people to protect themselves. I was out there. I've had a major battle with the mayor. In fact, we had really a to-do. He was terrified of me as far as where I'm going to be on the Board. And yet we made our peace, because we have to work together. But that doesn't mean I am his puppet or [will always] go his way. I will defend him when I think so. I'll fight him when I think so.

I, probably, of all the people—as far as the activists in the city—the most independent one out there is me. So between being a faggot, issue-oriented, and independent, my support was incredible. The major support funding came in. When you look at the craziness during the campaign, but the most liberal progressive paper is a weekly called the *Bay Guardian*. It's like a counter-culture paper. It's not an underground paper or hippie paper big deal, it's counter culture. And it's very independent. They supported me with an incredible, incredible endorsement. At the same time, the *Chronicle*, the most conservative paper—this is a paper that supported Nixon and Reagan—they supported me, too. So, I mean that shows the dichotomy of the support, the wide spread.

The final vote is interesting from an historical point of view, even if it was boring to some people. In my district there are 98 precincts. I was first place in over sixty of them. I was second place in

another thirty-some-odd. So it was a widespread support throughout the whole community, which means the poor black neighborhoods, and the affluent suburban-type neighborhoods in my district. It was a very wide support.

Against me were the candidates with an incredible amount of money and spending much more than I did. Against me were most of the political leaders. Against me was the organized Democratic Party. Against me were quite a few elected officials. And against me was the massive labor movement, the AFL-CIO, the wheeler-dealer cigar-smoking—all against me. Against me was the—some of our quote "established gay leaders." They even put another major gay candidate [Rick Stokes] up against me to split the vote, hoping a third person [Terence "Kayo" Hallinan] would slip through. And to win overwhelmingly in the face of that means that the people—not the gay people, but the people—in the district understood what I was about.

And that's the only way gay people can get elected: so that people come to them. That doesn't mean you walk away from a gay issue.

Mains: *Right. It points to a new role for the gay community in terms of supporting other communities and other groups and other issues.*

Milk: We must reach out to them. It's like today's hearing in a few minutes is if I—you know, a white person—is bringing legislation to close down—try to close down—the South African consulate. That's [a] black [issue]. I was the one that led the battle for the Latino issue recently before the board for the drug rehabilitation center for the Latino community. I am working very strongly with the Asian community. In fact, I led the battle to try to get an Asian appointed to the presidency of the Board, you know. It was a political battle: who's going to be the next speaker? And I thought the Asian would be the best. I put the coalition [together]; we lost six to five. But they all know that I did that, that I tried to get an Asian in there.

All the other minorities know that I've reached out to them. I'm working within the city to put together a minority coalition. I'm working statewide on a minority coalition, too. And it's important that we realize, not economically who our friends are—because a lot of the gay people, they think of their pocketbook. And my answer

to that is: What good is it having the best country, the most efficient country, economically sound if you're in jail 'cause you're gay?

So our natural allies, whether we like it or not, are the blacks, Latinos, Spanish, feminists, and the rank-and-file union. And we must tie together, because as soon as they realize who their common enemy is, and we realize who our enemy is, it's that common [unintelligible]. And it's hard for the affluent gay person to understand that. And that's my job; it's to put together these coalitions, and tie these people together. And that's what I was doing during my campaign, and you'd be surprised at the little Irish ladies who are supporting me.

Mains: *Could you have done it city-wide?*

Milk: I think so. I came close last time. Two or three years ago when I ran at-large, the six incumbents were reelected. I was seventh. And I had very little money, and there was a police and firemen's strike here—which made the incumbents look good. And the two weakest incumbents got reelected. If it wasn't for that fire and policemen's strike, I don't think they would [have been reelected]. I think I would have been on, 'cause I was building up the police support. I think [that to win] this town city-wide would demand that.

But it takes years of work. It takes dedication. It's a lot of hours. You go to neighborhood meetings. I go to neighborhood meetings—almost every night, I go to meetings, 'cause sitting on your ass [at meetings] is called "ass power." Going to meetings, sitting in there, knowing that you really are concerned—not to walk in and say "hi" and walk out. Take part in the battle.

Take part in the fight and [also] not to walk away from the gay issues. Fight for that just as hard.

I also, over the years, belonged to as a volunteer on the board of the Friends of the Public Library. I was a volunteer, board of directors of the Friends of the Deputies and Inmates to work to improve the jails. A board member of the Mission Neighborhood Physical Development, which is working with Latino youths. And neighborhood associations. I put together—

Mains: *And you're here reaching out into other communities and other issues.*

[184]

Milk: Right. I put together a merchants' group. I put on a street fair in my area that was so successful that other areas have asked me to help them to put on street fairs. Other areas asked me to help them put together the neighborhood associations.

And it was just committing myself, nine days a week, 25 hours a day. And [with] that kind of commitment, you make friends. And even if they disagree with you on "a" issue, they know who you are. And if you don't do that, you're not going to do it. And that's my whole thing: It's you've got to reach out. You've got to make the friends, 'cause there's more of them than us.

Mains: *Right. Okay, getting back to the Canadian thing. We've got a few minutes to talk about that. What is the purpose of the boycott?*

Milk: Okay. When *The Body Politic* was—when the case was going on, the Toronto police burst into their office and stole their subscription list.

That, in essence, is what our CIA and FBI do, which we find offensive. And that gives them blackmail, so they blackmail, potential[ly], gay people. It also, in essence, is an economic sanction against the paper, and puts the paper out of business, in essence because its subscription list is gone.

And my feeling is that while—like today, I'm speaking out against South Africa—I think we have to speak out wherever we are. And when I see economic sanctions being taken against the gay community, then I can play back [with] economic sanctions.

At the same time, being a little bit of Machiavelli here, knowing that Canada's going through the internal strife of separatism, know that [in] Quebec, even though that there is some oppression on gay people in Quebec [the province] and Quebec city and in Montreal, the Quebec government did pass a pro-gay rights bill.

Okay. By asking and calling on Americans, gay[s] and supporters, to not boycott Canada, but to boycott *English-speaking* Canada and go to *French-speaking* Canada, the entire Canadian government is not suffering. They're [Americans are] still putting the dollar bill into it [Canada]. But what's happened is, if the Quebec government is seeing support from the gay community, maybe they'll become more supportive of gay rights, and say, "Hey, these gay people have

[185]

given us money because we were so much supportive. Let's become more supportive, let's show it back."

At the same time, if the Quebec government is smart, they would say, "Hey, this is great. If we become very open about gay rights, then gay people throughout Canada and Vancouver and so forth, and in Toronto and so forth, would start to say that the Quebec government is good, let us vote for separatism, or let us lean toward separatism."

That, at the same time, tells the local government of Vancouver that if they want to go ahead and get back the gay dollars, and they want the people within Vancouver to support [corrects himself]— not to support separatism, that the Trudeau administration must speak out stronger.

So it works on several levels. It is playing the same game that they played against *The Body Politic*.

In the United States here, we've had in California, especially— and specifically in San Francisco—a very successful boycott against Coors beer. It's taken four years. Last year, Coors lost ten million dollars in sales, plus they're now spending a fortune in advertising—which they never did before—to recoup. We are *economically* hurting their company. And every time a gay person buys a bottle of Coors beer, they are putting money against themselves.

That's a whole other story. We know economic sanctions work. They work. If we can let the Canadian government know that we are going to do that—economic sanctions—then they make [the Canadian government] get the message and not get very harsh at gay people.

Mains: *But why Canada as a whole, why not Ontario?*

Milk: Because what we want to do is, we want the people in Vancouver to go to [Prime Minister Pierre] Trudeau and say, "Hey, wait a minute. You know, we're suffering." We want the people in all English-speaking Canada to go to Trudeau.

Mains: *It really was the Ontario government that brought down that action.*

Milk: Right, but Trudeau supposedly speaks for Canada, and he is remaining silent on this issue. And the only way to get him to

speak out is to get people from within Canada, saying, "Hey, we are suffering. Say something."

It works. And, you know, people are hurt; yes, economically hurt. But you realize how many people will be hurt if nothing is said. And so by the fact that the people in Vancouver keep quiet, that is giving a green light—a sanction—to the government in Toronto to pick on gay people.

Mains: *Yeah, well, certainly most gay groups across Canada are now supporting* The Body Politic *in their fight in the National Gay Rights Coalition. But one of the disturbing things about the thing is the fact that the article, "Men Loving Boys," came to be used by a lot of people in the common attacks against the gay community, saying—you know, promoting this myth that we all know is a myth, about gay people and young boys.*

Milk: Well, it's not really a myth. It does take place.

Mains: *But that is a minority.*

Milk: But what must be pointed out—and this is the way that Trudeau must be able to point it out—is the fact that we do not judge all Italian people by the Mafia. We do not judge all black people by the black criminal. We do not judge all Irish people by the Irish criminal. We do not judge all French people by the French criminal. Why must we judge all gay people by the gay criminal?

We have gay criminals. We have gay people [who are] offensive. We don't judge every single person that drinks by the drunken driver. We don't judge every heterosexual person by the rapist. Why, in this one case? All of a sudden, we're condemning and entire group of people because of the bad apples.

I want to hear Trudeau say that. He knows it. And if he's going to go out and crack down on the gay people because of one article, because of one child molester, then he must do it—

I'm being called to conference.

Mains: *Okay.*

[187]

26.

"A lot of people don't realize the importance of opening dialogues. It's the only way you change people's views."

Nob Hill, Fisherman's Wharf, and the Castro are famous San Francisco neighborhoods. Another legendary neighborhood is Haight-Ashbury, called by locals "the Haight" for short.

Since the 1960s, the Haight has been celebrated as the birthplace of hippies, flower power, the Summer of Love, psychedelic rock music (the Grateful Dead, Jefferson Airplane, Janis Joplin), psychedelic art (Wes Wilson, Victor Moscoso, Alton Kelly, Rick Griffin), and underground comix (Robert Crumb, S. Clay Wilson). As a former hippie now disguised in short hair and a tie, Milk must have been delighted to have the Haight as one of his District 5 neighborhoods. Before the election he had worked in the Haight for years, active on projects to benefit the neighborhood.

Milk's interview for *The Haight Ashbury Newspaper* was unusual in that he was interviewed by a group. The newspaper was run by a collective, so "Four or five of us interviewed Harvey," remembers collective member Calvin Welch. "We all knew Harvey, because we'd worked with him on neighborhood issues for years. To us, he was a neighborhood activist." After the group concluded the interview, Welch edited the discussion into the story "District 5's new supervisor: an interview with Harvey Milk," which appeared in the newspaper's March 1978 issue, its first.

Welch recalls that in the 1977 election for District 5 supervisor, Rick "Stokes was the *gay* candidate. Harvey

THE **HAIGHT ASHBURY NEWSPAPER**

MONTHLY BY AND FOR RESIDENTS OF THE HAIGHT

VOLUME 1 NUMBER 1 MARCH 1978

NAME THE NEWSPAPER CONTEST
$50 Prize SEE BELOW

"A LOT OF PEOPLE DON'T REALIZE THE IMPORTANCE OF OPENING DIALOGUES. IT'S THE ONLY WAY YOU CHANGE PEOPLES VIEWS"

"YOU DON'T CHANGE A PERSON LIKE QUENTIN KOPP OVERNIGHT..."

HARVEY MILK

—INTERVIEW
SEE PAGE 2

The people of San Francisco now have easier access to their government than they did before, we must take advantage.

[189]

was the *neighborhood* candidate. He didn't try to hide that he was gay, but he talked about neighborhood issues and what he had done in the Haight. It was smart positioning."

From his work with Milk, Welch remembers "He was skilled at creating coalitions, and bringing people to a common view. There isn't anyone who can do what he did in San Francisco politics now."

The interview's opening question refers to the fact that when votes from all of District 5 were counted, Milk received 170 percent as many votes as second-place Terence Hallinan and more than twice as many as Rick Stokes, making Milk the clear winner district-wide; however, in the Haight-Ashbury precincts, Milk's opponent Hallinan

received 29 percent of the votes from the Haight's precincts, compared to 28 percent for Milk, fourteen percent for Rick Stokes, and tiny percentages for the fourteen other candidates. In the Haight, Milk came in second.

Q: *How will the fact that you lost in the Haight-Ashbury affect your role on the Board of Supervisors?*

Milk: I don't care who anybody voted for. I feel I represent the district; I feel I represent the city.

As far as issues, right now we're spending a lot of time trying to solve the problems of Muni. That affects not only the people of the Haight, or District 5, but of the city. And I will fight to repeal the RAP [rehabilitation assisstance program] program in the Haight, which I think is offensive and has driven a lot of people out. I will do my best to save the Straight Theatre.

Q: *Is there anything that can be done to save it at this point?*

Milk: I think lobbying. Going to the owner and other people to see if we can do anything with private rather than public funds.

Q: *Do you see a big difference now, with the district election of supervisors, in the ability of communities in San Francisco to better pursue and protect their own interests?*

[190] **Milk:** Yes, definitely. That was what district elections was all about.

Q: *I still run across a lot of apathy and pessimism as to whether people have a voice in government.*

Milk: What you're saying is that after three weeks of government, they expect us to be God. After the end of two years, don't expect any major, significant changes in the sense of new roads being built, but you will see the old roads re-striped. Let's take one or two concrete examples. Let's look at what would never have happened under the old board. We never would have had Centro de Cambio having a drug rehabilitation center where it was located, and we never would have had the Market Street plan pushed through the way it was. We would have had a freeway through upper Market Street.

It's very conceivable that we will get through city funding for a voter registration drive in minority communities. That did not happen in the old board.

I don't know where we will be at the end of the two years, but I think you'll see the whole trend change, and those supervisors who have been unresponsive to the needs of the districts voted out.

Because we have a very conservative Finance Committee and because we have a somewhat conservative president of the Board [Dianne Feinstein], we won't be able to get through all we wanted. On the other hand, if we had Gordon Lau as president of the Board and a more progressive Finance Committee, you would have seen some more drastic changes.

But just because of district elections we won't get everything we wanted, because in some districts they elected some very conservative people.

These people who throw up their hands in apathy now are people who want it all their way today. And that is not what government is about. That's disregarding the other point of view.

Government is about negotiation, and compromise, and bending people. You don't change a person like Quentin Kopp overnight. You may never change him. But it takes a long time, and the Board of Supervisors will not all of a sudden become the district Board that some of us hoped for, because of the Dianne Feinsteins, the Quentin Kopps, the Lee Dolsons. They are not of the same political viewpoint as the Harvey Milks and Carol Silvers. But what you will see on the Board of Supervisors, very strongly, is the dialogue opened, which never existed before. And that itself is a major victory. A lot of people don't realize the importance of opening dialogues. It's the only way you change people's views.

[191]

I'm not pessimistic, but I'm not optimistic, in the sense that all is going to be well by December 31. But we've seen some changes, and I hope we'll see a lot more changes.

Q: *Do you think it's true that communities have a stronger voice on the Board of Supervisors now that they have only one supervisor to lobby, rather than eleven, all living in a few affluent neighborhoods?*

Milk: It wasn't where they lived, it was what they thought.

If the old days, if you had a problem, you didn't know who to call. You'd call up a supervisor and the supervisor may have been responsive or may not have been responsive. A lot of times, they'd say, "Well, you've got to find somebody else to do that. It's not my problem." Or they would say, I'll do that if you find me five other votes."

Like the upper Market Street problem. It was up to me to do the lobbying to put the votes together. I remember the old days, you'd call up and get somebody like John Molinari, and he'd say, "Okay, I'm there. Now you go out and find five other supervisors."

It's hard for a constituent to do lobbying like that. When the upper Market Street thing came through, it was up to Harvey Milk to put together the effort to get it through, and it ended up with nine votes. And that's the difference. Certainly the districts will get more response.

But when you say "the districts," that means everybody in the district. You take a district like District 5, you have everything from Diamond Heights to the Haight and to the Duboce Triangle, and that area just north of Duboce Park, part of the Fillmore neighborhood. There's no way that all the district will agree on any one issue. It's a very diverse district. The people of Diamond Heights have different interests than the people of the Haight.

It's up to me to try to guide and make sure everybody gets what they want as best as they can. But also to explain to people that it's a big district and very diverse. Some people want RAP. Some people don't want RAP. It's up to me, listening to both sides, to do what I think is best. And for me to try to convince those who disagree and to show leadership. In the particular case of RAP, I've been convinced that the RAP program in the upper Haight is awful. There will be a lot of people in the district who say, "Right on"—they agree. But there'll be a lot of people who disagree. And that's the position I'm in.

[192]

Q: *Do you plan to implement some of the policies you've favored in the past, such as opposition to development?*

Milk: Lobbying. Legislation. We'll have the Planning Department's rezoning of the city coming up before the Planning Commission. When that's finished, it comes before the Board.

We tried to stop airport expansion through a technicality, but we lost. We only had three votes. If we had had one more vote we would have won that. Last year, there was only one vote.

I might do something against [the planned] Yerba Buena [convention center]. I don't know yet if it can be done legally or not. But on the old board, there was no opposition to any of that.

I don't think Harvey Milk or Carol Silver will be able to stop Manhattanization by ourselves, but we will certainly be advocates to stop it. And that's more than ever existed before.

Getting through the narrow version of upper Market Street is very significant. It stopped the master plan to make it a freeway and link it up to Interstate 280. We stopped it—cold. And that's one step.

Also, I think we'll be able to stop the Franklin Hospital expansion. If we stop enough little ones, then the word is out.

Q: [Real estate] *Speculation?*

Milk: I'm on the record on this, and we have hearings coming up. I don't expect anything out of the Finance Committee too stringent or too strong. On the floor, it's up to some of us to amend the legislation to make it significantly strong.

I just talked and voted against condominium conversions as just one more avenue adding to speculation. Prior to that, almost nobody on the Board talked about it.

Q: *Do you support the anti-speculation ordinance?*

Milk: Yes.

Q: *Do you see any problems with it?*

Milk: Too many loopholes.

Q: *What kind of loopholes?*

Milk: Well, take, for example, someone who buys a house and then for some reason—say they're transferred or there's an illness or change in the household size due to a death in the family—and they can't afford the house anymore. We have to have loopholes to take care of people in that kind of situation. But when you open up any loopholes, you are opening up possibilities for speculators. We will have a review board on the ordinance soon.

Q: *You've said you favor redistributing the hotel tax to neighbor-hood groups. What kind of groups?*

Milk: First of all, I think the hotel tax under the CAO [chief admin-istrative officer, a senior manager equivalent to a city manager or county executive] is against the Constitution. It's taxation without representation. The CAO is not an elected official, and for him to take tax money and say how it is spent I find offensive. Unless there are some major changes, I'm going to try, either through an ordinance or through a ballot proposition, to remove that from his control. He has ignored community groups. It's supposed to help tourism, and I'd like to see that money go to the neighborhoods to develop the neighborhoods so that the tourists will go to the neigh-borhoods. A lot of tourists go to street fairs. Tourists come to see the gay community. Not just to gawk, but to see that it exists and that there is cooperation, coexistence, and that it is a phenomenon that is unique and, if successful, will be a major breakthrough in life. And yet no money comes from the hotel tax to help improve that quality.

We have to see the hotel tax go to the people of San Francisco and not necessarily to the traditional forums—not to ignore them, but to use the money fairly and equitably.

Q: *You've also come out in favor of placing a greater tax burden on the business property owners—*

Milk: No. I've never said that.

[194]

I'd like to see a re-assessment of business property. I'd like to see them pay their fair share. Let's look at the J.C. Penney building. That's assessed less than some apartment buildings. We're paying the tab for that. We're also encouraging them to keep it vacated.

I find it offensive what the assessor has done to this city. I'd like to see the Downtown Association and the Chamber of Commerce admit that they have ripped off the city. I'd like to see the business community assessed the same as private homes.

Q: *How would you counter their argument that the more taxes they pay, the more consumers are going to pay for their products?*

Milk: That's true of anything. But then it's up to the consumer to decide what to pay and what not to pay. If I don't feel like buying

a pair of shoes at Macy's because the price is too much because of taxes—maybe I'll fix my old shoes. I don't have to buy the shoes, but I do have to pay the goddamn taxes.

Q: *What do you plan to do to implement more effective affirmative action programs?*

Milk: That's a tough one. Right now there's a statewide signature drive to end affirmative action. But I will do whatever I can to increase it.

Q: *Is there anything the Board of Supervisors can do to make Alioto, as president of Pacific Far East Lines, pay his rent to the port?* [Joseph Alioto was the mayor of San Francisco from 1968 to 1969. He owned Pacific Far East Lines, the largest tenant of the Port of San Francisco. As mayor, Alioto appointed the Port commissioners. The Superior Court ruled that this conflict of interest violated city charter protections. Alioto resolved the conflict by "selling" the company to his sons, which the district attorney, who was Alioto's man, accepted as correcting the conflict. Pacific Far East Lines was mismanaged by the sons and went bankrupt. Then it was discovered that the Aliotos' company had not paid the city its rent.]

Milk: We met in caucus on that already. If we had demanded the back rent, we would have forced him into bankruptcy and probably gotten nothing. By having him go into voluntary bankruptcy, we'll get operating costs as we go along. We have to find who is responsible for allowing him to go so long without paying rent, and call them to the carpet. If we force him into bankruptcy he's not bound to his lease, and we may be stuck with the empty facilities with no income. We may insist that those $125,000-a-year salaries be cut so they can pay some rent. In a period of time, I think we can get the back rent out of them.

[195]

If nothing else, it finishes the bright rising star of Bernard Ossi as the next mayor. Shows he can't handle it.

* * *

The interview ended with a discussion of his spending on the campaign. He said he had intended to spend only $6,000 to $8,000 but

was forced by the spending level of his opponents to go into debt and to increase his spending to about $20,000. He pointed out that two of his opponents had spent a great deal more than that. (Hallinan spent about $35,000 and Stokes spent $56,000.)

Besides creating a Board of Supervisors more responsive to community needs, another major goal of the drive for district election of supervisors had been to reduce the amount of money needed to campaign for a seat on the Board so that candidates without access to big money would have a reasonable chance of getting elected. This hope was not fulfilled completely at least for this first district election. According to a Bay Guardian *survey, the six winners in this first district election of supervisors (excepting Kopp, who ran unopposed) spent an average of $6.76 per vote, whereas the six winners in the last city-wide election spent an average of 44 cents per vote. On the other hand, $20,000 is a lot less than the total amounts spent in 1975 by Supervisors [John] Molinari ($66,000), [Robert] Gonzales ($35,000), [Ron] Pelosi ($24,000), and [Quentin] Kopp ($73,000).*

And the fact that one of Milk's opponents outspent him by close to two to one and another opponent outspent him by almost three to one indicates that money may not always be the determining factor in district elections.

The proliferation of candidates in this election was, most probably, the major reason for the continuation of high levels of spending. Since this was the first district election of supervisors in seventy years, there were few precedents or statistics on which to base predictions of the vote, and a lot of candidates were probably attracted to the campaign because of this unpredictability and because of the excitement generated around the election. Fewer candidates in the future would mean lower costs for campaigning. But even if this theory proves to be wrong in the future, there is still the possibility of imposing spending limits through legislation. In any case, the people of San Francisco now have easier access to their government than they did before, but we must keep it in mind that it is up to us to take advantage of that easier access. Someone else will if we don't.

27.

"Keep involved!"

College student Kenneth Cravey wrote to Milk asking for permission to interview him, proposing five questions for their interview:

1. Does Milk view homosexuals as an oppressed minority similar to ethnic and racial minorities?
2. Do people evaluate Milk's performance as an elected official differently because of his sexual orientation?
3. Do the pressures of Milk's public office hamper his effectiveness as an activist?
4. What kind of public services should be made available for gays, and do California communities discriminate in providing services to gays?
5. After Milk's term of office as a Supervisor expires, what are his career plans?

Milk responded by writing the letter below.

City and County of San Francisco
Board of Supervisors
City Hall, San Francisco 94102
Supervisor Harvey Milk

March 17, 1978

Kenneth Cravey
PO Box 93
Deer Park, Ca 94576

Dear Kenneth:

Thanks for your letter and your interest in what I am doing.

 I have looked over your questions and will answer them in written form here. If you have any further questions, please contact me and I will try to be of help.

1. Homosexuals are, by law, the only minority group which it is legal to discriminate against. There is no legal protection for gay people against discrimination and in that regard, we are in a much worse position than most minority groups. I believe that the attitudes of prejudice and oppression against gay people are the same sort of attitudes that have been used against other minorities. But in the case of gays, there is probably even a longer and stronger history of severe oppression.

2. I think some people do scrutinize my performance differently than other elected officials. But there will always be people that do that, and there probably isn't much that I can do for them. My work as an elected official speaks for itself and the great majority of people in my district and the rest of San Francisco support or [do] not support me on the basis of issues, not my sexuality.

3. Having the power of an office has definitely strengthened my position as an advocate for gay rights. Many people will listen now who might not have done so before. I spend most of my time working on the everyday affairs of the City, but I have always been interested in the issues of the community. I don't see that this gets in the way of being a strong voice for equal rights.

4. Gay mental health, alcoholism, recreational and cultural programs are severely underfunded. Government funding of such programs does not reflect at all the amount of tax money and economic importance the gay community contributes. Fortunately, we are making progress in this regard in San Francisco, Los Angeles and other cities. But other areas of the state are sadly lacking in providing services for their gay residents.

5. I have not projected too far into my political future. I've been on the Board of Supervisors only three months and will have to run for re-election again next year. After that, I will have a four-year term and that's as far as I am planning for now. I try to work on the issues facing our city and not worry too much about political plans.

I appreciate your concern. Keep involved!

Warmly,

Harvey Milk

28.

"This country has taken senior citizens and treated them like a can of beer — you drink it and toss it away."

After his narrow defeat in the 1976 Democratic primary for the U.S. Senate, political activist and author Tom Hayden and his wife Jane Fonda founded the Campaign for Economic Democracy (CED), a progressive political organization that successfully influenced the outcomes of several local elections in California in 1977 and 1978.

Hayden visited Milk in his Castro Camera store on March 22. The resulting interview appeared in the April/May issue of the *CED News*. [Bracketed] comments are mine.

EDITOR'S NOTE: *Harvey Milk, elected to the San Francisco Board of Supervisors last November, is the first avowed gay to hold that office. Milk, a long-time activist in progressive movements now raises those issues at City Hall.*

CED Chairperson Tom Hayden interviewed Harvey Milk in his camera store in San Francisco.

Hayden: *In retrospect, how do you appraise the Anita Bryant crusade now?*

Milk: It's probably the best thing for the gay movement. The day after Miami I put a sign in my window that said, "Don't let it happen here — register to vote." Now we always had a voter registration drive here. It was slow but steady; and in the 48 hours after Miami we registered some 700-some people right in front of the store. Right after this a large number of gay people formed a political club [the San Francisco Gay Democratic Club], which is now the most activist club in the city.

Milk's tiny, cluttered office in City Hall displays a toy cow named "Milky," a gift from the supervisor's friend Michael Wong.

[200]

The weeks before and after Miami every newspaper in this country had the word "homosexual" on the front page somewheres or other. More was put in print on homosexuality in that week than in the history of mankind. Every household talked about it—they'd scream at the TV, "You f---ing faggots!" But that's the opening of dialogue. Before, they never would have even said that. She (Bryant) did to the gay community what Richard Nixon did to a lot of people. A lot of people realized what's happening.

1977 saw Miami, saw people talking about gay rights, saw a gay person elected in San Francisco, and saw a convention in Houston which was the convention of conventions so far. And you tell me where the movement from the right is coming from. It's a media hype trying to convince people it's really happening.

Hayden: *How do you view the gay community's relationship to the economic issues?*

Milk: In the gay community we have everything from the ultra-right wing and the ultra-left wing. But I would say my own feeling, based on this city and knowing it as well as I do, that anywhere from 50 to 80 percent of gays will vote as a block on an issue that's explained to them very carefully, no matter what the issue is.

Most gay people are not wealthy. They have been cut out, you understand, and more and more gays are coming to realize that we've been paying our taxes for too long and getting nothing in return. Even gays that are well off and are concerned about conservative politics have come to realize that they have gained nothing in return. So those of us who realize where we should be are trying to head it off by explaining to people, "It's the same people who you are for on these economic issues that also want to put you in jail, so let's be very careful." So we are swinging them from that to people who have economic ideals that a lot of us feel.

Hayden: *That perspective is very progressive. Sometimes when I talk about unemployment, gays say, "Our problem is not unemployment, we have jobs. Our problem is discrimination."*

Milk: No. Unemployment in the gay community is very high. The unemployment factor is perhaps a misguided figure because due to discrimination and other conditions, gay people have jobs, but they are economically miserable jobs.

Discrimination does take place. Two years ago the employment office of PT&T [Pacific Telephone & Telegraph] said on TV that they wouldn't hire any upfront gay people. That's changed now, but that was two years ago. So it takes place and that discourages people from even applying for a job. The fact that you can't get advanced up through the corporate image, that you are sooner or later going to have to show the wife around, discourages people from going into certain fields—that's discrimination, subtle discrimination. Why try to build a career when you know you're only going to become the fifth junior clerk?

Hayden: *What is the gay middle class buying into? Is there enough there to make some independent economic base for politicians?*

[201]

Milk: The same people who discriminate against gays are the people who are for the capitalist free enterprise system. And that sounds good to a gay person who has no children to leave money to and just wants to preserve the income that he or she may have, and therefore politically becomes more conservative.

Actually, thanks to Anita Bryant and Senator Briggs, those people are starting to realize that they're wrong. But I don't think at this stage of the game in 1978 we can appeal to the massive gay community on an economic base.

A political movement can only appeal to them [conservative gays] on who wants to deny you the right to work and who wants to put your ass in jail. At this point that's the only consciousness level. Someday, once you overcome that, then I think you can work on the other.

Sheriff [Richard] Hongisto was real popular in this city among gay people not because of economics or anything else—but just because he related to the gay community and tried to make some improvements.

Hayden: *What is the economic drum you've been beating? You've been talking about speculation?*

Milk: Speculation has many different factors most people don't realize. They say, "I own my house. I have no intention of moving or selling, so it doesn't affect me." What they don't realize is four houses on the street are in the hands of speculators. When the assessor shows up next year, you're going to get it! [A large tax increase.] People don't realize that.

The latest game here is the conversion to condominiums. People don't realize that. They say, "Well, all the people living in this building, they want it." They want it because they see a quick buck in it. They buy it at a cheap price and then sell it at profit in six months. And it's just pushing out the rental units. And when you're pushing out renters, you're pushing out a 60-year-old woman who doesn't want to spend 20 years paying off her mortgage so when she's 80 she can go out and burn her mortgage.

You're pushing out the poor people who can't afford a down payment, pushing out the new family, and you're pushing out people who don't want to own a piece of property.

And we still have a Board of Supervisors here who, for whatever reasons, are tied into the developers—to make the money and are not sensitive to human beings. And so we have rampant speculation.

Hayden: *Do you see a big change in the last two years between racial minorities and gays?*

Milk: Yeah. It's even to the point where there's a conflict and the conflict comes because the gays are no longer sitting back and saying, "We'll just go along."

The gays started demanding their piece of the crumb—by demanding their piece of the pie. And the other minorities see this as a potential immediate threat. But once they get over that fact, then they start to cooperate.

I work very closely with all the minorities—very close. And the rank and file. And I see that within the next five years—you see, right now the city is over fifty percent minority, and that's not counting feminists, not counting gays. We should have control of the city and we don't, because they're not registered [to vote].

So it's my job to put the coalition together as best I can. That's where my energy is going.

At the same time, we're going statewide, putting a gay caucus together so that we will have some impact on statewide elections. I'm doing it on my own and working with the Lt. Governor [Dymally].

Hayden: *What is it like to be on the Board?*

Milk: I was sworn in on January 9 and on January 10 I had a fund-raiser to pay off my campaign debt. It was an excellent dinner, best political dinner I've been to.

A lot of the [real estate] developers showed up—all the people who have an economic interest in this city. These are people who I have never met, probably don't know how to spell my name, or at least didn't want to prior to the election. So there they are sitting down to eat and I'm getting ready to give my speech which was going to be and was about the responsibility of the business community to save the cities.

So prior to that I couldn't resist telling them the old story that Fred Harris told me when he was running for Senator of Oklahoma the first time. He attacked the oil companies, and in Oklahoma

[203]

that's oil companies, Mom, apple pie, God, and the flag. The week before the election a poll in the papers said that he was going to win and the next day he gets a check from and oil company for five hundred dollars and he said, "F--- 'em, send it back," and his treasurer said, "Fred, Fred, we need the money." And he [Fred] said, "F--- 'em, deposit it!"

I told that story to all these people and they looked at me and realized that their checks had been deposited, that they had eaten already, and that I was about to speak. And while I wasn't going to attack the oil companies, there was a chance I was going to attack them. And lo and behold, they were right. Most of them sat on their hands [to withhold applause] through the major part of the address.

I talked about their responsibilities and how this country has taken senior citizens and treated them like a can of beer—you drink it and toss it away. And after your mother and father raise you, we just toss them away. And the corporations that ruin the city move out when they find it economically more feasible. They pick up and leave on the city that nurtured them. And when they move they leave scars, as well as unemployment, and the problems of the city will seep out.

One of the things they must do is realize that the people walking around unemployed are their customers. And they must move back and take care of those people and put those people to work. That's their responsibility. Naturally that means lower profits.

[204]

The most powerful economic and military nation must start to talk about the people.

About five or six years ago we had a childcare initiative on the ballot with the slogan, "Wouldn't it be great if the navy had to do a bake sale every time they wanted a new battleship and the daycare centers got all the money they needed?"

I got them another way, too. Most of them don't live in San Francisco. I told the Chamber of Commerce when I spoke to them, you tell me what's best for the city, but you won't live here. Frankly, I don't want to listen to you until you move back here. I regarded the developers and business people in my talk the same as I do the police department, most of whom live in Novato—as occupying armies.

Mayor Moscone and Supervisor Milk chat
during intermission at the San Francisco Opera.

That's what it's like to be a supervisor. To be able to say these things that have never been said before because people relied on those people for money. To open up the dialogue on issues like drug rehabilitation centers which were never discussed before. IT'S GREAT!

29.

"*I think San Francisco has enough mental complexes without adding physical complexes.*"

Viacom provided cable television for San Francisco. As part of its services, the company produced television series covering San Francisco news, arts, and politics. One was the half-hour interview series *Viewpoint,* for which *San Francisco Chronicle* city editor Jerry Burns interviewed Milk on March 30, 1978. Burns was liked and respected by the staff who worked for him and was respected by the leaders of San Francisco's political establishment as well, including Milk. Dan Nicoletta, Milk's employee at Castro Camera, told me, "One of my responsibilities was to answer the phone. Harvey told me always to put calls from two people through right away: Jerry Burns and Jim Jones."

Jerry Burns: *Welcome to* Viewpoint. *Our guest this evening is Harvey Milk, the supervisor from San Francisco's fifth district, which includes the Castro area, Noe Valley, and the Haight-Ashbury. Mr. Milk is in real life a camera store owner. Supervisor, one of the things you've been associated with lately is you were sponsor of the law which prohibits discrimination against gays in business and housing in San Francisco. Very briefly, can you describe the detail of that law?*

Milk: The law would make it a[n] offense, a crime in essence, a civil crime, if you refused to hire somebody, or if you actually fired somebody who had employment because you found the person was a gay person; or you refused to rent; or you refused to allow public accommodation *solely* on that—those grounds.

Burns: *And this applies to private—*

Milk: Right.

Burns: *—industry, to private housing?*

Milk: Hotels.

Burns: *Everything in San Francisco.*

Milk: What it does in the city of San Francisco in effect brings the discrimination laws that exist in a statewide level against—protection of blacks, minorities, women, physically handicapped, mentally handicapped, religion, national origin—extends those coverages to gay people in the city of San Francisco.

Burns: *What's the significance in a broader scope in terms of—is San Francisco now the first city in the country with such an—with such an ordinance?*

Milk: There are other cities which have some versions of it, but nothing that has—that I know of, at least, or we can find any that has the penalties involved in case you are found guilty of such discrimination. And that puts teeth into the law, and makes it more than a resolution type of thing.

Burns: *Could a law like this have been adopted a year ago, even, in San Francisco?*

Milk: Well—

[207]

Burns: *Or five years ago, say.*

Milk: Less than a year ago, a similar ordinance was submitted to the Board of Supervisors and stayed in committee. So I think the answer is—

Burns: *So this time it passed ten to one. What happened?*

Milk: Well, a couple things. One—

Burns: *Politically, what has changed?*

Milk: Harvey Milk. [He laughs.]

Burns: *Well, that's modest enough.*

March 30, 1978: San Francisco Chronicle
city editor Jerry Burns interviews Milk.

Milk: I mean, you know, it's always hard to say that. But I'm *there*. And you know, like, I'm a *supervisor*. When the mayor was out of the state, I was acting mayor; in essence, I ran the city. You know, for two days. The next day, I could have gone to, [for] example, Macy's; applied for a job, and they could have refused to hire me solely because I was gay. I could have walked into the Saint Francis Hotel. They could have refused to give me a room solely because I'm gay. It doesn't make sense. And so, in essence, Harvey Milk and what Harvey Milk stands for, I think, changed [the Board].

Burns: *Well, there were ten votes this time in favor of the ordinance. Harvey Milk is one vote. What convinced the other nine? Is—is the gay voting strength in this town now that strong that the other nine saw that this is something that enough voters want [so] that they voted for* [it]?

Milk: Not—I don't think it's strictly that. I think that's part of it. There's no question that some people on the Board of Supervisors (and all politicians) do count votes of their constituents. But I think it's a coming of age. It's a significant education process that has been

taken for a long time. It's pressures coming to bear from church leaders, other legislators in different levels, business people saying, you know, "It's time." And I think it was just a maturing of age, as well, and maybe even more so, as the voting bloc pressure.

Burns: *Well, there's some objections. Supervisor Dan White voted against it; and some of the things he said I think ought to be raised and answered. He said, for example, his constituents were concerned, he said, that this would, for example, force private schools and parochial schools in the city to hire gay teachers when they wouldn't want to. Is that accurate? Or was he wrong?*

Milk: It doesn't *force* you to hire. It says that you can't discriminate on those grounds. And all we say, basically, if a person is qualified to teach, that's the only grounds you should hire or refuse to hire. The arguments that Supervisor White brought forth—and his constituents—are the same type of arguments that we heard generations ago about *black* people. Before that, about *Jews*. Before that, about *Irish* and so forth. And history has proven that those arguments are basically the—come out of fear and myths. And once those minorities were accepted into the mainstream, they became assets. I think we can see the same thing. Also, I think Supervisor White did something that many legislators do. And that is, follow the will of the constituents rather than show leadership. And that's where I think some of the other supervisors who *equally* have pressure from constituents not to vote for it, they chose the route of leadership rather than a popular vote.

Burns: *Supervisor Feinstein, who did vote for it, along with all the other supervisors, apart from Supervisor White, said at the time that she felt convinced it was the right thing to do. But she expressed great concern— I don't know exactly how to put this—maybe you don't either* [Milk chuckles]*—that—that gays should exhibit some sort of self-control—*

Milk: Gays. Right.

Burns: *—and standards. And I noticed some letters in the newspapers with—from gays, saying "You're absolutely right," and others saying, "Wait a minute. Nobody else in this town has to toe the line." What she was talking about, I assume, was outrageous behavior in public.*

Milk: Right.

Burns: *Did—*

Milk: You know, I found that—

Burns: *And you smile, but didn't she have a—*

Milk: She's offensive! She's offensive. Let me just say that.

Burns: She's *offensive? Or the behavior in public is offensive?*

Milk: That statement. Both are. That statement is offensive? Richard Nixon sets the standards. The legislators who are on the take. The Watergate. The mediagate. The crip—

Burns: *Well, Harvey, that's apples and oranges.*

Milk: The—no, no! Let me get down to it! The mafia. Every single element—blacks, Jews, *every group*—has criminals and myths. We *do not judge* those groups by the criminal element. We judge them by their leaders. But with the gay people, she's saying, "You have to clean up the act for those." We have criminals. We have people who are offensive. There's myths. We should not judge just gay people by that. If we are, let's judge *all Italians* by the mafia. Let's judge *all* blacks and Asians and Spanish by the stereotypes and the myths. Let's judge *all* politicians by Richard Nixon. Let's judge *all* people who drink by the drunken driver. Let's judge all husbands by the fifty percent of husbands who beat their wives. You know, it's a *double standard.* And to just apply that standard to one group is *offensive.* And she was *offensive* on those remarks.

Burns: *But you just said you think some of the behavior is offensive, too.*

Milk: Right. But you don't judge a *whole community* by that. You show me *one group* of people who have a *hundred percent* great standards among their people. I mean, do we judge—did she say the same thing about the *Asians* because of the—the—the gang wars among the teenagers taking place? Is she judging the entire Asian community by that? No! Is she judging *any group* by the criminal element or the offensive element within the group? We have gay people who are offensive. We have gay people who are criminals. But you don't judge a

Milk appears pensive during his televised interview with Burns.

group by the bottom of the barrel. You judge it by the leaders. And for her to do that I found was *completely* off base—was just *grandstanding.*

Burns: *Does it concern you at all that there is any kind of outrageous public behavior in the gay community?*

Milk: It concerns me that there's outrageous public behavior in *every* community. But I understand some of that behavior, too. You know, and I'm not excusing it.

[211]

Burns: *But you know where—you know what her background—I—I hesitate to use the popular expression, "where she's coming from?"*

Milk: Right, that's the trouble!

Burns: *You know, there are a lot of people out there who, you know, drive or walk through Castro or Polk and say, "Oh, my God! At least if they're—if these people are gonna—*

Milk: Okay.

Burns: *—have homosexual relationships, let them do it do it in private, not in public."*

Milk: ~~I agree. Don't scare the horses!~~

Burns: [laughs]

Milk: Okay. Let's get down to the—let's get down to that aspect, but first let me touch on one thing. Dianne [Feinstein] seems to have trouble with anything that's not in its proper little neat place. And look into her whole record on pornography. And she, she once made a statement that the crime wave in the city is because of the dirty bookstores, and when I asked her, "How many of the thousands of automobiles stolen each year are [a] result of the dirty bookstore?" because, you know, people stealing the car to get down there fast, she couldn't answer. She's great at statements, but without any facts.

Let's take a look at the Castro area, which seems to be the example we were talking about. Gay people historically and even today, really, are thrown out of their homes. Most families don't accept their child when they're gay. The church throws them out. The Most Holy Redeemer [Catholic church] a block and a half away from Castro will not accept them in. The Lions Club, the social clubs don't accept 'em. The unions, basically, most of 'em don't accept 'em. There's no place to go. The *gay bar* becomes the family, the church, the social club. It becomes a meeting-gathering place because there's nothing else. So naturally they come meet there. And so you've thrown them *out* of anyplace else, and so you push them into the street and into the bar syndrome. And then you object to that. So I say the answer is for Dianne not to object to that, but for Dianne Feinstein to go to the archbishop and say, "Open the doors of the church." And to go to the rabbis: "Open the doors of the synagogue. To go to the—the social clubs, the yacht clubs and everything else, the Bohemian Club: "Open the door to gay people." You see, you can't *exclude* them from everyplace and then say, "You can't do that."

Burns: *Do you feel—you obviously feel that Harvey Milk in public office makes a difference. And you give credibility to the whole gay movement—*

Milk: No.

Burns: *—the whole gay political movement. Wait, you just said a gay ordinance is the result of you being in office. I wonder whether you feel*

any responsibility. Do you feel constrained in your own personal life-style because of the—the responsibility heaped on your shoulders now?

Milk: Okay. Let's say—first, let me correct you. I'm not responsible for everything or a spokesperson for the whole movement. I represent a lotta people, a lotta people views. A lot of gay people didn't vote for me, and a lot won't next time.

There's no way that anybody could represent a whole movement. I stand for Harvey Milk and what he symbolizes. There's a big difference. I just happen to be the person. I do accept a lot of responsibility, to a point where I don't go over fifty-five. I don't even want a traffic ticket. I'm super-careful.

And I know that a lot of people, both bigots and gay young people, are looking at me for two different reasons: the young gay people for hope, that I do a good job; and the bigots hope that I fowl up, so they can jump on me. So I'm quite careful. I'm not perfect; I'm gonna make a lot of mistakes, and I know it's gonna happen sooner or later. But I do accept the responsibility. I'm knew it ahead of time, I knew what it was going to be like.

When you get a letter from a person in Southwest Africa asking for hope, when you get a phone call from a seventeen-year-old child in a small town in Minnesota who is *handicapped* and whose parents found out that he is gay and want to *commit* him to an *asylum* and you become his lifeline, then you know you're gonna do a good job. But that's not so awesome as it sounds. It's just something I knew would happen.

[213]

Burns: *Well, let's bust out into another direction.* [Milk chuckles.] *Now there is also Harvey Milk, the soon-to-be-sponsor of the anti—of an anti-speculators tax. Tell me the detail—you intend to introduce next week—*

Milk: Monday.

Burns: *—on Monday an anti-speculators tax. Tell me the details. What will it be? Eighty percent on the profit on the first year, sixty percent on the second year?*

Milk: Right.

Burns: *And then decreasing over how many years?*

Milk listens to Burns.

Milk: Five.

Burns: *Till five years.*

Milk: Let me just say, the reason that we need it is more important than the specifics of the legislation. The fact is that there is no new housing—really, no new housing—being built in the city. That the speculation and the second wave of speculation effects and the third wave are hitting the city now. And unless we do something now to prevent it from getting out of hand, we will drive out more poor people, more young people, people who are *just starting out* to make it economically, and certainly the senior citizens, who are on fixed incomes, will be driven out as less and less places become available for renting, or the rents go too high. So there's a need for it desperately.

Burns: *Will it discourage, though, people from improving their property?*

Milk: No! Because in it is built in that if you buy a house for a hundred thousand dollars and you show ten thousand dollars worth of improvement, and you sell it for a hundred twenty thousand, the profit is not twenty thousand, it's the difference. There's a lot of

[214]

loopholes. Till now. It is mainly to discourage as much as possible something—you see, the speculation of housing is not just a San Francisco problem. The higher you paid for your rent or your property taxes or your mortgage payments, the less disposable income you have. The less you have for ties (he holds up his necktie), the less you have for vacations, eating out. San Francisco is a city that *thrives* on disposable income. It's a tourist city. And if people are spending—all over the country—too much money for housing, they're not gonna be spending it for jackets, ties, glasses of water. And cities like San Francisco will be hit.

Burns: *But isn't the price of housing really a mix of the* demand *and the* supply? *San Francisco has a very limited—you said yourself—a limited supply. No new housing is coming into the market.*

Milk: That's the answer.

Burns: *What's the answer?*

Milk: The answer: We *must* encourage housing to be built in those areas of the city that are devastated now. The Western Addition and South of Market area. Not just complexes but—but *neighborhoods* must be created that people move into it. And if we *must* give tax incentives, then so be it. We've *got* to do something to build new housing. Until you build new housing, this ordinance and anything else you may talk about is meaningless. It's not gonna solve the problem, as you so well stated. You've got to have more supply.

[215]

Burns: *But you're not afraid this ordinance, if and when it passes, will have the same chilling effect on property in San Francisco that some say rent control has on property in New York? Removing the incentive of a landlord, a property owner, to do anything to upgrade his property.*

Milk: No. This has nothing to do with the person who wants to build—build for an investment's sake or build for their own use. It's strictly those person—people—who are turning it over fast. This is almost the same type of legislation—the degree is different, naturally—but it's the same theory as was put on the stock market when they increased the margin requirements years ago. It took the speculative *out of it.* Cause the market *crashed* and killed the economy

because of the speculators, and we had to go in and stop the capitalist system. We had to put a control on it. The most capitalist aspect of the capitalist system was the stock market, and we put margin controls on it to do that.

This is somewhat the same type of situation, of putting a control on the speculative part of housing. And it's vital.

Burns: *Well, I don't know that it puts controls, it obviously puts penalties. Some say—*

Milk: That's a control.

Burns: *Some say that landlords, property owners, speculators would simply increase their prices even more, assuming they could get them, to absorb the cost to them of the fact that eighty percent or sixty percent is gonna be taxed, eighty or sixty percent of their profits.*

Milk: I doubt very much that they'd be able to sell it at those prices. People are not gonna be able to do—you know, there is a *limit* of supply and demand where you're just not gonna *pay* for it.

Burns: *To what extent in your mind have speculators—and there ought to be a different word, it has such an awful connotation. But anyway, in response—*

Milk: There's one under your bed. There's a speculator under your bed! [laughs]

[216]

Burns: *Oh, my God! Hit him with a shovel! Have speculators really contributed at all to the city in terms of upgrading, say, the Castro area, the Haight area, the lower Pacific Heights area?*

Milk: Not the speculator. The person who renovates a building, the person who—

Burns: *How do you distinguish?*

Milk: How soon, and how fast do you turn it over? The person who buys a building and within one year, with no intent to live in it, not even fix it up—maybe a coat of paint—and turns it over. Or the building is turned over two or three times in two years. Or there's paper transactions were not even cashed. That's speculating. I'm

not talking about somebody who goes in and takes a building and fixes it up, puts improvements into it, and then sells it. There's a lotta difference. We're talking about somebody who just churns it over. And that's why we—at least, in the ordinance we're going to introduce, there's a review panel. To allow those people to go in and do a rehabilitation of buildings.

Burns: *There was a property—an anti-speculation ordinance—that the Board was considering just this week. It didn't even advance out of the finance committee.*

Milk: It didn't even—it didn't even *exist.*

Burns: *Why—*

Milk: It was a *skeleton.*

Burns: *Why is your proposal—does your proposal have a chance politically?*

Milk: Pragmatically? [He laughs.]

Burns: *What does that mean?*

Milk: I don't know. You mean, do I have six votes?

Burns: *That's what I mean?*

Milk: [laughs] Right now, I doubt it.

Burns: *Would you consider putting it on a ballot in November? It's too late for June, but*

Milk: [nods yes] It's too late for June.

Burns: *Is it something that the voters should have a chance to—*

Milk: No. Yes and no. I'm tired—one of the reasons I ran for office is I was tired of seeing the voters have to make all the major decisions. That's what you're supposed to elect people for. They don't make the right decisions, you throw us out.

Burns: *Well, you put—you voted to put several charter amendments on the June ballot.*

[217]

Milk: Well, I'm voting also—no, through the works. But I wanted to have charter modernization so we don't have to go through that. I think the supervisors should make the decisions—more decisions. I think we should have a stronger Board of Supervisors and a stronger mayor. Not weaker. Every time you go to the voters, you're saying—well, that's why we got into trouble with the poor, they got into trouble with education. It's getting rid of power. It's piecemealing it, so nobody could be responsible for the major decisions. And I am frankly tired of the old Board and some of the philosophies of not making decisions. Let the voter make the decision and wash my hands. We have talking about the salaries of the city and everybody gets up there and harangues about it. Well, the supervisors didn't pass the salaries. But they passed on the *responsibility* to other people. And I think I'm tired of that. I think the supervisors should stand up and be counted and not turn everything over to the voters.

Burns: *You'd like to see a charter that would be very spare and not go into every detail, but leave it to the elected officials?*

Milk: Right.

Burns: *But don't we have a charter that's filled with detail because the elected officials were giving away the kitchen sink and the bath?* [Milk chuckles.] *Why should we trust you any more than the past?*

[218]

Milk: Well, the last—this current Board of Supervisors—the outgoing one—they put on several years ago Proposition M, which gave huge pensions to the fire and police. And then after they said [it] was wrong, and they redid that. And then two years ago they put on Proposition D, which set salary standards. Now they say it's wrong, you know. Charter amendment is hard to change once you get one on. It's costly and everything else. I'm not saying that we're any better or any worse. But it'd be a lot easier to make the changes [to a law passed by the Board as an ordinance] if we do make a mistake. And we will.

Burns: *In connection with the anti-speculation ordinance, I wanted to ask you: Where do you stand on proposed rent control?*

Milk: Any form I've heard of it, I'm against.

Burns: *Why?*

Milk: I think it's wrong. First of all, rent control is the wrong battle. It pits landlord versus tenant. And that's the wrong battle. Again, as we talked about anti-speculation, the answer to rent control is more housing. If you had—for argument's sake, let's say we need rent control [unintelligible]. We can get into that. It has to allow the landlord an incentive to build. If you can put your money in a bank and get, say eight per cent, and go off to Tahiti—you're smiling. [chuckles]

Burns: *It sounds good!*

Milk: I'll go with you! No headaches, and you get eight per cent. Then if you're gonna put that same amount of money into housing, and have the headaches of a landlord, and insurance and leaky faucets and everything else, you've gotta do better than eight per cent. So you've got to build in the incentive for—for capitalism.

And I have yet to see a rent control bill that does that. And that's—that's a major thing. But if we don't do something about the housing problem, what is going to happen is that the rents keep going up, and—and—and the elderly keep getting driven out—the alternative, I'm talking about—the poor people being driven out. What are we going to do with the senior citizens? And usually say to someone who says, "Are you for rent control?" I usually say, "Are you for the alternative? Are you for driving out those people who can't afford the high rents? And I don't think I'm for rent control, and I don't think you're for driving out the senior citizens, so we must look at the alternative of building housing. And we've *got* to do that, we've got to address that problem. I don't see the real estate industry, the real estate board who is so concerned about real estate, addressing that—that question. And I think they should be.

Burns: *Well—*

Milk: I don't see the *unions* addressing it, and they must. And I don't see the people at City Hall who have the *power* to address it, or the Chamber of Commerce, to address those issues.

Burns: *There isn't a lot of empty land, of course, in the little-known—*

Milk: It's true.

[219]

Burns: —confines of the city. Do you think they should build housing, for example, out at the Playland at the Beach site?

Milk: No. [smiles]

Burns: Well, you just said we should build more housing.

Milk: Okay, well, there is plenty of land south of Market. And there is plenty along Third Street.

Burns: Let me ask you about that. You think housing should be build where Yerba Buena [convention center] is supposed to go?

Milk: In that area, yeah. It's be nice.

Burns: Not—not on the Yerba Buena site.

Milk: Well, I don't know if Yerba Buena should be built there. They're talking about, in order to build it, now we have to increase the hotel tax from six to eight per cent. If we build the convention center on the piers [which are owned by the city]; see, 'cause we're saying that the waterfront can't be saved—everybody's telling me— and if it's not going to be saved, it's going to be *used*. And if we build a convention center on the pier, it might be much cheaper—least, I know it's going to be cheaper—and we may not have to increase the hotel tax. Again, if Jarvis-Gann [Proposition 13 property tax reduction] passes, we may need that hotel tax money for other things. There won't be any money for Yerba Buena Center. So I don't know if that's the right site. The only reason that I hear it's the right site: it's closer to the hotels. And I don't think the distance between there and the hotels—or *those* hotels—and the distance between those hotels and the waterfront is that far. In fact, it would encourage people to see San Francisco.

[220]

Burns: Let me drag you back to the ocean for a minute. What do you think should be done with the Playland site then?

Milk: Ah! [chuckles] I have a vision. [spreads his hands wide apart to indicate size] Actually, it should be a park. There's so precious few ocean spots that come up. When one does come up, I think—you know, we have to decide what—what's more important: standard of living or quality of life. And to me the quality of life is very

Supervisor Milk laughs.

important. An open space park. There's only one exception what I would like to see there—

Burns: *What kind of park? You mean a Golden Gate Park park?*

Milk: Right. For people to enjoy. I would also wouldn't mind putting in there—at least talk about—in fact we are—putting the—right now, the de Young Museum is overcrowded. And the de Young cannot show everything that it has. And they are looking for new space to add—the de Young. And I've thrown out the idea, and I'd like to get [a] reaction to it, of putting on that park where Playland used to be, a[n] Asian Museum. Since it looks out to Asia. It's on the Pacific coast. House the Asian collection there, in the—in the park in a new building, and that would give the de Young room for the rest of its collection without expanding there. So I've thrown that out, and I'm waiting to get the feedback on that.

Burns: *You mentioned the possibility of more housing south of Market. You don't mean—or you do mean the sort of high-rise senior citizen housing that we're seeing, some of which is being built there now? Or what?*

Milk: The complex types?

Burns: *Yeah.*

Milk: I think San Francisco has enough complexes—mental complexes—without adding physical complexes.

Burns: *I walked right into that.*

Milk: I know you did. I couldn't resist. I'm sorry.

Burns: *What kind of housing did you have in mind? You mean in all where those—where those two, three-story industrial buildings, many of them empty, stand now?*

Milk: Right. Right. I would like to see like almost like neighborhood-types built, with shops and everything else, so that it's more than just a place to build houses, it's a place to *live.* And with those industrial sites, if we can bring in some light industry, then people could walk to work. You see, Levi Strauss did something interesting. They're moving out of their high rise, and they're building a new complex on the other end of the waterfront. It's low, a low-rise. You know. And I think they understood what the trend [will be], that building up is not always the answer.

Burns: *How would your anti-speculation tax affect someone who is building new housing? Would that person be able to build a house and then keep his profits after—I mean, you build a new house to sell it, you don't build a house to live in it.*

[222]

Milk: Okay, you see, but that's not—

Burns: *How would that be affected by your anti-speculation tax?*

Milk: [It] has no affect at all. Speculation is somebody who *owns* something already and selling it within a timeframe. To build it and sell it: [he shakes his head "no"]

Burns: *It wouldn't apply to new construction.*

Milk: No. You can't do that. I mean, in fact, I'd do the *opposite.* Do everything I can to encourage new construction, in new areas rather than to rebuild the old areas. See, right now most of the condo conversions and most of the new building is to rip down what

we have and make something new there. We have all this other opportunity, and I think we should use it. Of course, I have a couple [of] dreams of what else I'd like to see there. I wouldn't mind seeing that South of Market area also ban the automobile.

Burns: *Well, that's the New Yorker in you talking, I guess.*

Milk: No, that's the Disneyland in me talking. You see, we have to go to Disneyland or Disney World or amusement parks to have a pleasant place to walk and stroll and transportation. No pollution. Not going to be hit by cars. People could ride bicycles, strollers with babies, everything else. I mean, it's *great* just to—to move around in those amusement parks. We have to go to [an] amusement park for good transportation systems.

Burns: *Let me drag you back to reality for just a second.*

Milk: No, Disneyland *is* reality! [laughs]

Burns: *Well, I know you only go to reality as a tourist. What—are you satisfied with the way the city administration has been handling the—the parking meter scandal so far?*

Milk: According to the [San Francisco] charter, I can't interfere with any other department, but as you know—[laughs]

Burns: *But in your opinion?*

Milk: The answer is "no," Jerry.

Burns: *Why is that?*

[223]

Milk: I think—first of all, let me just preface this by saying I think the administration of the city by charter is fouled up. We have a mayor, we have a chief administrative officer who is like a city manager. We have a—a two-headed executive branch, and the chief executive officer, there's no accountability to the voters or the taxpayers. He's appointed for ten years, and that's it. So I think that there's a problem there [in] that there's no responsibility for certain departments.

In this particular case [the parking meter scandal], we've run into that—that Catch 22. We have some people on the streets who are accused—the lower jobs are accused of taking some money. Then we have a bunch of lieutenants and colonels and captains. So

we finally have a *general*. The general being the CAO. The way I look at it, I don't know all the facts, because I'm sitting on the other side of the hall. You don't accuse a lieutenant or a colonel. If—if the privates are on the take, you wait and see if they are guilty. But if you are gonna go ahead and crack down because you are afraid there's been mismanagement, the general's at fault. In a—in a—in a war zone, when you have a battle, you lose a battle; and because the troops didn't fight properly, or whatever it is. You could blame the troops. You don't blame the lieutenants and colonels, you blame the general. You get rid of the general. And I don't have all the facts, so I may be wrong, but to get rid of or suspend Ted Brown, the tax collector, is like getting rid of the colonel. I think that if anybody should have been—and I don't know if anybody should have been— it would have to be the top man who has the ultimate responsibility.

Harry Truman, the reason I loved him so much, is he said, "The buck stops here." Or "The nickel stops here." [Both men chuckle.]

Burns: *A buck then is worth a nickel today.*

Milk: A nickel today.

Burns: *You think that Roger Boas, the chief administrative officer, whoever it is, bears responsibility for* [unintelligible]?

Milk: Naturally. He may have facts I don't know about. If he does, that'll come out. If he doesn't, then I think he took the wrong step.

[224]

Burns: *We have about half a minute. Do you—do you support getting rid of the chief administrative officer's job? I don't mean Roger Boas.*

Milk: Oh, yes. I strongly—I think we need charter modernization, as you hinted on earlier. That means to get rid of it, put *more* responsibility on the mayor. This is a *big* city. It's not just 670,000, it's over a million people living and working here. We need a *powerful*, powerful executive officer to make those hard decisions, and the responsibility and the removal of that person if their decisions are wrong.

Burns: *Very good. Thank you.*

Milk: Thank you, Jerry.

30.

"When you get into a philosophical change in government, then it takes time."

In 1978, probably in early April, Joshua Weiss called Harvey Milk at City Hall and scheduled an interview. Josh was 14 or 15 years old. The interview was likely arranged by his father, Mike Weiss, a San Francisco reporter—although neither Weiss remembers for certain.

The younger Weiss planned to write a story for the *Everett Echo,* the school newspaper of Everett Middle School. He brought along his classmate Aaron Berg to take photos of Milk to go with his article.

"I shouldn't have gone," Josh Weiss recalls today. "I was unbelievably sick, and barfed in the bathroom. I never even met him."

Aaron Berg photographed Milk and conducted the interview himself. He later gave his thirty-minute recorded interview to the elder Weiss, who used it when researching his book *Double Play: The Hidden Passions Behind the Double Assassination of George Moscone and Harvey Milk.*

Aaron Berg: *What—what happened with your camera store exactly?*

Harvey Milk: Oh. Well, that—we found a new location, on our camera store, the—because of the speculation [that] takes place in the city, my landlord got greedy, too, and he raised the rent from 350 to twelve hundred dollars. Which economically makes it very difficult for a service-type store to maintain business there.

Berg: *Yeah.*

Milk: So I found a smaller location, but for a very reasonable rent on Market Street near Castro. So after five years, I've moved from Castro to Market.

Berg: *Why do you think the rents went up so much?*

Milk: Well, it's greed. Strictly greed. The whole speculation market is—the whole real estate market is a market of greed. You'll find in the real estate market today speculation. People who ten, fifteen, twenty years ago were the type of people who were in the stock market—when it was an easy way to make a quick buck. And they got in there. And what happened was that they, because of—you found doctors and lawyers throwing money into the stock market ten, fifteen years ago. I was *there*. I was watching. And it got inflated. And the bubble busted. And everybody got hurt, especially the people who were really investing, the people who were using investments for—for retirements and so forth. They got hurt because the speculators came in. So the stock market became a dead thing. And now all of a sudden you find in the last five or six years or so the *same type* of people, you know, doctors and lawyers and dentists and so forth throwing money into the housing market.

Berg: *And real estate.*

Milk: And real estate. And they're pushing that way out of line. And again, the people getting hurt are those on the fixed incomes, the people who only own homes and [are] getting hurt. And there's three levels that the speculation hurts. One is the actual speculation of a particular building where it changes hands two or three times over the course of a couple [of] years. That you know is speculation. Then there's like my landlord, who's held his building for six or seven years, but as the speculation on the street goes up, and rents go up, he keeps jacking his rent up.

Berg: *Right, because he can, he knows he can.*

Milk: Right, [unintelligible] man. And then finally, you have the person who owns a home, who lives in the home, has no desire to sell it, no desire to rent it out or high rents—wants to live there. But because of the speculation up and down the street, the assessor comes by and jacks up the assessments on everybody—

Berg: *Right.*

Milk: —and that person's tax bill goes up, and maybe it goes up to a point where they have to sell because they can't afford their home any more. And even though they made money on the selling, they didn't *want* to. They're being forced to do it. So the speculators are a very greedy group of people, very short-sighted, very narrow-minded, very offensive.

Berg: *Yeah. Okay. Well, that* [unintelligible]

Milk: [laughs]

Berg: *What are you going to do about that? Are you going to do anything about the rent increase?*

Milk: Actually, there's nothing you can do about rent increases outside of rent control, and rent control laws are usually the wrong kind of laws. Basically, a rent control law usually pitches a tenant versus a landlord.

Berg: *Yeah, right.*

Milk: And that's the wrong battle. The only *real* thing that can be done, we're going to try and get some anti-speculation laws through. [Of] course I don't think we'll have the votes to get it through this Board, 'cause the Board is still conservative. The only real solution is building more housing—housing stock. And you can build that and you have Western Addition and you have all of South of Market—Third Street, Yerba Buena, China Basin, India Basin, all the way out there—where you can build housing. And *not* complexes. The city already has enough complexes. If you pardon my pun. But to create new neighborhoods, so that it's not just housing out there but shops, parks, schools, whatever—services, so that people would *want* to live there, and that eases the pressure. And unless we build housing, we're not gonna be able to solve the problem.

[227]

Berg: *Well, how can you make it appeal to the people that, you know, are like in that I—is it the—um, that hotel?*

Milk: International Hotel?

Berg: *Yeah, International Hotel. Like, they didn't want to move, you know. They wanted to stay in the neighborhood.*

Milk: You have to go—you see, we're getting into a philosophical thing here, which—let me just tell you where I'm coming from philosophically. And when you get into a philosophical change in government, then it takes time. And it has to be, unfortunately, because the nature of human beings of not wanting to change and wanting to resist change, the dialogue has to take place over a long period of time.

Berg: *Right.*

Milk: So philosophically, the United States of America has proven over the years it can be the military giant of the world. Okay. I'm sure if need be we can go ahead and become the military giant again, mass produce for war. We have also in the past proved we can be the economic powerhouse of the world. We are in trouble economically right now. We've been for a few years. The dollar is very weak, the balance of payments is wrong. *But* if need be—the government knows it—they could put on controls and whatnot, and we could once again we could become a very powerful economic nation.

And what's happening is that once we've proven that, the only aspect of—of life that we haven't proved is that people are more important than buildings. And what I see taking place in this nation, ever since incidents like the Watts riots to the International Hotel, is the struggle is going on between do we put the government services and money to use for people or for buildings? And we have some people do want us to have the B-1 bomber, keep the Panama Canal, that's the military people. Then there are people who want more highrises, more highways—those are the people who want economic power.

On the other side of the coin, you have people like the minorities in many cases, the I-Hotel people, people like myself who are saying, "We now, now must direct our energy to the human being: child care centers, healthcare, senior citizen care." These are the kind of issues that are starting to come up. And what this country is going through to me is a turmoil battle between the materialistic needs and the humanitarian needs that, that—are so desperate. And I think that's what's happening in the country. And the speculation battle in the city, and in other cities, is that battle.

Berg: *Right. And I see. So what you want to do is you want to build houses that are going to be fixed rent houses?*

[228]

Milk: Not necessarily fixed rents. But if you build *enough* housing, then supply and demand takes care of itself and keeps the rent down. When you have only two or three percent vacancies in the city, and they're not choice vacancies, then the landlord can raise the rent. It's the same thing that if you want to buy a new camera. And nothing wrong with your Pentax, but if you want to buy a new camera, and I want to buy a new camera and there's only one camera around, we're gonna bid for it. But if there were *three* cameras around, we don't have to bid very high. And the same thing with housing. If there's not enough housing, then the landlords just raise the rents. But if we were to build overnight, say—you know, say do I be God, and tomorrow morning there's fifteen thousand more housing units in the city—

Berg: *Right, then—*

Milk: Right? Then the price of the housing—then I'm not going to have to pay my high rent. I'll go someplace else.

Berg: *Okay, the city will build the houses, right?*

Milk: Well, the city itself can't, but what we can do is encourage private industry to do it by giving them tax incentives. Say, don't charge you property tax for five or ten years.

Berg: *Oh, I see.*

Milk: To give them the incentives to build. We have to, in other words—it's expensive to build. But we have to make it worthwhile for them to build, and so we have to give them some kind of incentives.

[229]

Berg: *Right. Okay. Do you know—so the landlord's position in your, in that situation, is that he was forced to, right?*

Milk: No. Not forced to. He didn't have to. Just that he saw a chance to make [a] quick buck. Greed.

Berg: *Is he selling—is someone willing to buy it* [unintelligible]?

Milk: I'm sure he will find somebody sooner or later to pay the high rent. And that's called greed. And he's just taken advantage—he's not a speculator, but he's taken advantage of the speculation that's taking place all around. And so while he himself is not a speculator, he sees the, what's happening and his greed—

Berg: ~~Catches on?~~

Milk: Catches on.

Berg: *Yeah. See, he wouldn't let us interview him. 'Cause he would, but then he called us up at eight o'clock in the morning, got all nervous and said he wouldn't. So. Do you—let's see—in the gay rights law that just went through, people are going to be fined it said two hundred to four hundred dollars?*

Milk: Well, actually, you could be fined *more*. See, if, if, if I denied you a *job* because you were strictly—I mean, you were *competent* doing your job but you were a gay person—and denied you a right to a job, and you took me to court, and let's say it becomes a battle, and because of timeframe and whatnot, it's six months before the court comes to a settlement in your case, and they say, "Okay, you were right." And you could have been working for those six months, let's say, three hundred dollars a week for argument's sake.

Berg: *And you can sue them for that.*

Milk: You can sue them for that much. *Plus* attorney fees. Plus court costs. So—it's very stringent. It's probably the most stringent— it *is* the most stringent law in regard to that issue in the nation.

Berg: *Is it just gay people, or is it lesbian people, too?*

Milk: This one is just gay people. The reason why is that there are state laws that cover discrimination against race, religion, sex, physical handicap, mental handicap, national origin. That's all covered. Every group is covered under state law. Except for gay people. And the state hasn't passed anything, so the city of San Francisco, which has had a similar type law in existence for companies doing business with the city, this now extends out to the private industry. And in essence, what this—the gay rights bill does is to give to the gay people in San Francisco the same rights that every other minority has. But instead of doing it through the state level, it does it through the city level.

Berg: *Okay. Have you—has your being gay helped or hurt your political career, do you think?*

Milk: I would say both. There are some people who vote—gay people who vote for me strictly because I'm gay, and there's a lot of

people who will *not* vote for me because I'm gay, and I don't know what the balance is. There's no way of ever knowing. I would say that in hindsight and retrospect, I think it's probably more of a handicap.

Berg: *Well, but—but in the, in the supervisors, with the supervisors when you're trying to pass something through, does it help or hurt is what I'm saying?*

Milk: I don't think there's any effect. For the gay rights bill, it helps. Because I can be able to speak as a person and—you know, and some of them have to relate to me, you know. As far as all the other legislation goes, I don't think it has any effect one way or another. The, the fact that I happen to be a very progressive person on issues, a lot of gay people aren't. I'm very progressive. I believe in, in, in a very *activist* approach, a very *fair-minded* approach. Those are my *political* positions. That shows where I am, and that affects my legislation and my record and so forth. I just—while you were waiting and while Josh [Weiss] was getting sick, I was meeting with five members from the Chinese community who are very active politically. They—they—they feel much the same way I do on issues. And what many of us are doing—not only in the city but in the state—is trying to get all the minorities together, the traditional minorities—black and Spanish and Asian—Filipino—and add to that coalition, getting the gay population and the feminist movement. And if we can put that together and, and bury the differences we have and work on the issues that we have in common, we would have a very effective force.

[231]

Berg: *You'd have a lot more power.*

Milk: [laughs] Incredible amount of power. Now, the lieutenant governor, Merv Dymally, is trying to do that on the state level, and I'm helping him on that. And some of us are trying to do that on the city level. So that we *do* have more power, so that many of the, the injustices of the past don't happen anymore.

Berg: *Yeah, okay. When you said that [Gov. Jerry] Brown fired Mondero because she was lesbian, what kind of facts did you have on that?*

Milk: Well, there was no justification for her firing. First of all, he claimed this letter with some offensive words in it. It was a personal letter. And somebody had to go through her files, looking for

something to hang on her. And it wasn't where this was—and this was an *old* letter. It wasn't even a recent letter. And they had to dig it up. Brown is very paranoid. Brown's running for reelection this year. He's single. A lot of people will question whether *he's* gay or not. And he's trying to cover up any, any implications that he is. And, so he's trying to be pure, whatever it may be. And so he's very paranoid. And the fact that she was an up-front gay woman, I guess had him nervous. So he went looking for a reason to get rid of her. He came up with the thing, "offensive language." I don't who in your, who's in your class, but I doubt if there's a person in your class who has not used quote offensive language, whatever that may be. I don't even know what that means.

Berg: *Yeah.*

Milk: I'm sure that your parents have used language. I'm sure the governor has. We know that the ex-president of the United States, Richard Nixon, used *highly* offensive language. We know that President Eisenhower used *highly* offensive language. So, to fire somebody just because they used an offensive word—which I don't know if it's offensive, because those words appear in newspapers *every day*.

Berg: *What words* [unintelligible]?

Milk: I think she used the word "asshole" and "bastard" or something like that. And we see words like the word "dogshit." "Shit" appears in newspapers.

Berg: *Yeah.*

Milk: You know. So who—in fact, what makes the words offensive is not using them. I don't know if you know much about Lenny Bruce. You should read about Lenny Bruce. Lenny Bruce summed up what an offensive word is by using a little analogy. He used many things. He was trial—put on trial for using offensive words in a *nightclub*, where you had to pay to go hear it, you know. But he used the analogy, the fact that if—he used—he got into the black situation. And he said—this is in the early sixties, mind you—he said that if the president of the United States was to get up at a press conference and said "Now I'd like to introduce the nigger in my cabinet." And if he said, "Oh, there's a nigger there" and

used the word "nigger, nigger, nigger" as common everyday language instead of any other word, you know, that eventually the word would lose its nastiness. It would lose its derogatory tone. And eventually, no young black child would ever be upset or cry or frustrated or mad because somebody called that child a nigger because the word would have no meaning anymore—offensiveness. And what made the word offensive—the word "nigger"—was the very seldom use of it except only in a derogatory term. The same word—the same thing with the word "asshole" or "cocksucker." If it was common language every day, it would not be offensive.

Berg: *Right. Okay, but you think that the only reason that he would have* [unintelligible] *because he was just trying to pin something on her?*

Milk: Well, he was trying to pin something on her. Nothing else came out as far as her competence goes. And the fact that the review board reinstated her, gave her a clean bill of health, showed that he was *wrong*.

Berg: *Right.*

Milk: And so, why *did* he try to get rid of her? Because she was, certainly, she's *highly* competent. The language *really* was not offensive. I mean, it was printed in newspapers. So why *did* he try to get rid of her? And you'll have to answer that question yourself.

Berg: [unintelligible]

Milk: I think just about everybody who's watched the case and listened to it carefully has to sit there and laugh at him, that he made a fool of himself. It was strictly [unintelligible] it was strictly because she was gay. Instead what he should have probably done is just never even mentioned it. And, you know, and why bring it up? In fact, maybe he should appoint more gay people. That would be the answer.

Berg: *In the* Chronicle, *it had a thing on you after you won, and it said that you wanted to be supervisor because you were fed up with taxes?*

Milk: Fed up with—fed up with *not* taxes: fed up with the system. See, we need taxes. We need money to run government. It's the *way*—it's who's paying the taxes and what's used for the tax money that

[233]

bothers me. ~~What bothers me is the~~—allowing all the tax loopholes, so that the large corporations and the wealthy people don't pay their fair share. And I can give you example after example after example.

Berg: *Yeah. But what I'm saying—what have you done to help that situation?*

Milk: Okay. One, to talk about it. You have to open up a dialog before you can change something. Going back to my original premise. Before you can change the whole tax structure you have to talk about it. But just last week I asked the President Feinstein to introduce, or to set up a select committee of supervisors to, to review the entire tax structure of the city. But if we can start to make effective change here, then we can make maybe some effective change in Sacramento. I think if the Board of Supervisors takes a strong stand that we have to change the tax structure that can have some impact on Sacramento because then maybe San Jose or Santa Clara or Stockton will also—their Board of Supervisors will follow suit, and finally pressure will come on Sacramento. Unfortunately, the legislators of Sacramento are basically under the controls of the large lobbyist[s]. I even know—they're not supposed to be, but they are. And they have no indication [he meant "inclination"] to change tax laws. The reason Jarvis-Gann that you hear so much about is where it is is the fact that Sacramento has done nothing.

Berg: *Well, would you* [unintelligible] *tax things? Like if you set up a new tax code, would the public vote it?*

[234]

Milk: Oh, I would certainly bring it to the public to vote on it. What I would personally like to see—my own personally—is to do away with every single tax we have today. Everything we have. Wipe them off the board. And have one tax and that's an income tax on individuals and businesses based on a progressive tax. The more you make, the higher the percent. Based on a person's ability to earn money.

Berg: *Okay, what happens if someone inherits a lot of money and has a lot of property and so they don't need to have that much—they don't get that much income, they don't need it, but then how would they be taxed?*

Milk: Well, strictly the income. Strictly the person's ability or corporation's ability to earn money. To me—I'm not saying I'm right,

or wrong—to me, the only fair way is if you have the ability to earn money, your corporation's ability to earn money, that's where the tax is. The reason why is right now we have a lot of people, you pay taxes. You pay sales tax. You pay property tax. You pay [unintelligible] tax, this tax, that tax, and the individual [unintelligible] a limited income, be they a senior citizen retired, be they a handicapped person who [is] living on a fixed income they are paying property taxes go up and these other taxes go up. They pay more, more of their fixed income. They're paying a high percentage, and they can't afford it. Whereas the large businesses that are making all this money are getting away scot free.

Let me give you one tiny example to, to pinpoint what I'm saying. Downtown on Market Street is the empty J.C. Penney building—a huge building. That is assessed less than half the apartment buildings in the city. So as land speculation goes up, the owner of that building, he pays property taxes on it, but he writes it off against his other incomes from other buildings. So he writes it off. In the meantime, as the value of the land goes up from speculation, someday he's gonna sell it and make a big killing and you and I are not going to share in that killing. But you and I, because he paid so little income tax—I mean, property tax—compared to what it should be, you and I are subsidizing that building because your home and my home have to pay higher taxes to make up for the lack of income coming in from that building. So the property taxes are very unfair, and on top of that, that adds to a blight in that area, which depresses the area so *all* the business taxes [unintelligible]. So that's there. So it is an unfair situation. Some of the large hotels and downtown office buildings pay less now in property taxes than they did five, ten years ago. And where your home goes up. So the homeowners pay the larger burden, and alotta the homeowners are retired people on fixed incomes, and they can't *afford* it anymore. Whereas if we have an income tax based on the ability to pay, right? Then if you retired, you don't have to pay any taxes. You don't have to get caught in that bind. And the corporation that is making all this money downtown has to pay. So I think—personally—and I'm not saying I'm right or wrong—personally, I feel that the only fair tax is an income tax. With *no* loopholes whatsoever.

[235]

Berg: *None?*

Milk: ~~None. And I'd like to put that to the voters.~~

Berg: *Well, in a corporation, like a large corporation, how would you, would you tax them on the bulk amount* [unintelligible]?

Milk: Profit.

Berg: *Just on the profit?*

Milk: Profit. Like, see right now a corporation, you know, they write off the business lunches. You know, you and I have to go out and pay for our lunch. If we were a big corporation we could write off our business lunch. You know, that's not fair.

Berg: *Yeah.*

Milk: Business trips, all that stuff. You know, first class, the three-martini lunch. Why should I—why should you or your business be allowed to deduct [unintelligible] lunch three martinis?

Berg: *Yeah, I agree with you totally on that. But has Dianne Feinstein done anything about it?*

Milk: No.

Berg: *Or has she picked anybody?*

Milk: [unintelligible] Not yet, she hasn't picked yet. I don't know if she will. She may decide not to. It's her right. We'll go before the Rules Committee sometime in the month of April. And she may decide to, and she may decide to fight it. We'll find out.

Berg: *Okay, let's see. When I was—a couple—a while back, I saw one of your campaign pamphlets, and it said some things about Muni. About students should go free, or something like that. That Muni—the ones that have to take the buses because there isn't enough school buses.*

Milk: Well, my—lemme tell you what my theory, my theory on the Muni is. Right now, Muni runs at a deficit. Every time a person gets on and puts a quarter in that box, it costs, I guess, about 35, 40 cents actually for that ride. And the commuter who comes in from town and parks the car or whatever it is and then gets on the Muni [and] rides. You and I, as citizens and taxpayers of the city, are *supporting* that commuter. And so not only is it costing you fifteen, twenty

cents extra every time *I* ride it, it costing you fifteen, twenty cents every time a *commuter* rides it. So the commuter's getting away free. On top of that, I think we have a long-range energy problem and a transportation problem [in this] city. I'm very staunch on transit first. I'd like to personally get rid of the automobile in downtown area. Just nothing but Muni. A better Muni, faster Muni—when I say "faster," I mean more frequent. Don't have to drive faster. Better service. And more cross-town service. Eventually the automobile as we know it will not exist in the downtown area. So I'd like to get there now.

In order to encourage people to ride Muni, to discourage them from riding their car, and also to make sure everybody pay[s] a fair share, I'd like to have—make Muni *free*. [unintelligible] for every-body. Take out the coin box.

Tell you what that does: A), we save some cost of Muni because we don't have to have—to pay anybody to count the coins or do any of that or repair the coin boxes. So we even save a little money. But if it's free, and you're gonna ride it, now, how do we pay for it? Since we already pay through taxes, most of it, or a large percent of it, I would then tax everybody who works in the city. Income tax. Since we're paying for it anyhow. And that way you could also tax the commuter. So if there's a commuter who doesn't live in the city but works here, makes a salary and rides the Muni and we have to subsidize him has to pay his or her fair share. So you can go after the commuter who's getting a free ride now. And we're carrying it. And once everybody realizes they could have to pay for Muni through their taxes and doesn't cost you anything to get on it, it's costing you taxes, it's gonna say "Well, gee, since I'm paying for it, I might as well ride it." The same time, you take the parking garages downtown and raise their rates very high. So that if you want to use the automobile, it's going to cost you a lot. So the Muni you can pay for whether you use it or not. The automobile's going to be very expensive. Then it's going to encourage you to ride Muni.

[237]

Berg: *But you're still going to run—you would run an even larger deficit?*

Milk: Right. But everybody's going to pay for it.

Berg: *Okay, but, then what does that do about the commuters?*

Milk: Make them pay. You can tax *them.*

Berg: *But how can you tax them on another district?*

Milk: Well—right now, several cities have income tax. Several *states* have income tax. We have a California income tax. You can live in Nevada and work in California, but you are taxed in California. Not at the same *rate.* But you're taxed where you work, where you make your income.

Berg: *And that's what you could do with the commuters?*

Milk: Sure. Right. And New York City works that way.

Berg: *So that's a pretty radical change, then. In the way that—*

Milk: Well, radical times call for radical changes. No, see, it's not really a *change.* It's just extending from what's taking place from state level to the city level. I mean, it's done from states. If you work in Nevada rather than San Francisco—you work in Tahoe, in Reno, your, your income's coming from Nevada. They should have the right to tax you, and vice versa.

Berg: *Okay. You suggested that a bike lane be put on Market Street?*

Milk: It will be.

Berg: *It will be? It's going to? Great. Have you taken any steps to slow down crime rate in your district, District 5?*

[238]

Milk: How do you slow down the crime rate? If I were able to do that, I'd be elected president of God. The only thing I've done about crime so far, in essence, basically, is—

Berg: *Do you mind if I use a flash?*

Milk: Not at all.

Berg: *Thank you.*

Milk: What kind of film are you using?

Berg: *Tri-Ex.*

Milk: You probably don't need flash [inaudible].

Berg: *Yeah, I'm just going to try it out.*

Milk: Okay. [unintelligible] Okay. The, the difference between the crime situation—first of all, you have to understand I haven't been on this Board for ninety days yet, you know. [chuckles] So you know—

Berg: *You can't get a whole bunch of things yet.*

Milk: But already we are talking about the root causes of crime. You can't stop crime by putting a police officer on every, on every corner. For too long, some of the older supervisors are talking about, you know, "More police, more police, more police." And since I've been elected, some of us are now talking about why people are in crime. And that's a big change, that we're starting to discuss that, reasons why people do crime. That's the solution. Until this election, you never heard that discussion on this Board. And so there's been a change in thinking.

The same time, what I've done in my district is to encourage more and more people to carry police whistles. We have a good whistle patrol.

Berg: *Do they help?*

Milk: Oh yeah. Not to use except you see somebody being victimized or *you* are victimized, to blow it and in the Eureka Valley area, when you hear a police whistle, you know somebody's being attacked or, and to come running. And that has helped a little bit. We also [are] asking people more and more to report the crime to the police and then if the person is apprehended, to prosecute. And even though I *don't* like to see anybody go away, to get put away into the criminal justice system, it seems that that's the *only* way we're going to be able to stop it, is to let them know that we *will* prosecute and put people away.

[239]

Berg: *Does it, it—like a lot of time, someone will* learn *things in, in—*

Milk: Jail.

Berg: *In jail. It's like a person will be—*

Milk: Minor offender will end up a major criminal.

Berg: *Just because he goes to jail—and—[unintelligible]?*

Milk: Okay. You're, you're the Catch 22. You can't just work on one aspect [unintelligible] aspect. In fact we were down in the prison system just the other day.

[A telephone rings. Milk speaks into phone.] Yes? Five more minutes. *Five* more minutes. [Hangs up.]

You have to—I work in the prison system to, to get better rehab, rehabilitation down there. But if you don't put the person in jail, then the person's gonna commit the crimes. [unintelligible] them a green light to go out and commit crime. So you have to do peer pressure, you have to threaten to put him away, and if you do put him away, you have to provide rehabilitation. So it's a—but more important, you have to find out why the person's committed the crime [and] try to prevent it. Most crimes, or a lot of crimes, are committed because of social and economic conditions. And so we have to try to change that. We have to try to bring jobs back to the city. If we can do that, then I think we can make an effective change in the crime rate. I mean, to the crime out of my district would be to push it into another district.

Berg: *So you just try to do it city-wide, then.*

Milk: So you *have* to do it city-wide. Because if—put it this way: If you are black, and you are denied a job, and you have a child who is starving, milk costs fifty cents a quart, you're gonna go out to steal to get that milk to supply that child. So the answer is not to put a policeman out there but to give you a job. And when you tell the black population, the black male youths, that there's probably a forty percent chance that they will never have a job, you tell them to go get into crime.

Berg: *Well, that's what they're going to do if they tell them that.*

Milk: Well, so I'm not—you're telling them.

Berg: *Yeah.*

Milk: So what we have to do is give [them] jobs. Give people jobs. Meaningful jobs. And that's the *only* effective way to end crime. Anything else is, is misleading. Crime's been around since as long as recorded history.

[240]

31.

Supes refuse street closing for parade

At the Board of Supervisors meeting on Monday, March 13, Milk drove his fellow supervisor Dan White into a rage.

In contrast to Milk's blizzard of legislative ideas, his fellow supervisor Dan White promoted just one major item: stopping nuns in his district from selling their school for wayward girls to be turned into a Youth Campus for possibly violent disturbed adolescents. White had met with Milk three days before to assure that Milk would vote "no" against the Youth Campus. Milk prevaricated; he led White to believe that he would vote "no," when in fact Milk planned to vote "yes."

On the day of the Board vote, Dan White expected to triumph. He invited dozens of his supporters to witness his victory, but Milk surprised him and voted to approve the Youth Campus. In front of his supporters, White lost, six votes to five. White was so angry he refused to speak with Milk for weeks. Before this incident, White had supported Milk in several ways. Now he felt betrayed, and he reacted by opposing several of Milk's initiatives. (These events are described in *Double Play* on pages 144–146.)

To close city streets for the Gay Freedom Day Parade and Fair, permission was needed from the Board of Supervisors' Fire, Safety and Police Committee. White was the committee's chairman and he refused permission. Milk worked around him. This article about the conflict appeared in the June 16 issue of the *San Francisco Sentinel*. It is one of the few times Milk was quoted in print about Dan White, his future assassin.

A REQUEST TO close a number of streets surrounding Civic Center Plaza for the Gay Freedom Day Parade and Fair on June 25 ran into a snag at the Fire, Safety and Police Committee of the Board of Supervisors last week when Supervisors Dan White and Ella Hill Hutch refused to pass the request out of committee and onto the full board.

White, who chairs the committee, and Hutch voted to "file" the request for the street closure, which means that the measure cannot go before the full Board of Supervisors unless it is called out of committee by another supervisor, which Harvey Milk promptly proceeded to do at Monday's full board meeting.

The proposal will be considered by the full board June 19.

Milk, angered at the Fire, Police and Safety Committee's action, later asked rhetorically, "What do they expect people to do? There are going to be somewhere around 300,000 people there. It's simply a matter of public safety to close those streets."

"The purpose of that committee," Milk continued, "is not whether they agree with the purpose of Gay Freedom Day or the civil rights of people, but whether they are concerned about the public safety."

"As a former police officer," Milk said of White, "he ought to know that if you have 300,000 people there, you've got to do something to insure their safety, whether he likes them or he doesn't like them."

[242]

White opposed closing the streets around Civic Center for the celebration because "many people in San Francisco do not approve of public demonstrations of sexuality."

However, Milk predicted that the street closure proposal would pass the full board on June 19. The Police Department and the Municipal Railway, which will have to reroute several Muni bus lines, have already approved the closure request.

PART SIX

1978,
Milk vs. Briggs

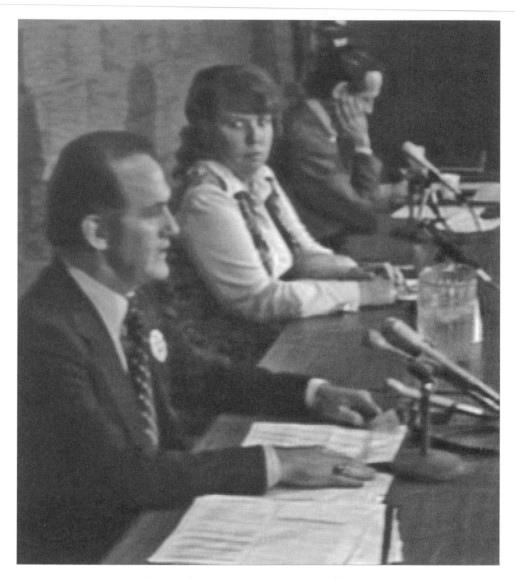

November 1, 1978: State Senator John Briggs, moderator, and Supervisor Milk at the debate in Brigg's home district in Garden Grove, Orange County.

32.

" . . . *the* whole concept *behind democracy and the Constitution is to protect the rights of the minority, not the majority.* "

On June 14, 1977, exactly one week after Anita Bryant's repeal of Dade County, Florida's anti-discrimination law, a California state senator named John V. Briggs announced a petition drive to place an initiative before voters to remove all gay teachers from California schools.

Briggs' proposed law would not only remove teachers and other school employees who were gay, but also employees merely *accused* of being gay (for instance, by a student angry about receiving a poor grade), and those who were not gay but supported equal rights for homosexuals.

On May 1, 1978, Briggs turned in enough signed petitions to the California secretary of state to qualify his initiative to be placed on the ballot for the November 7 election. Proposition 6 was formally named the School Employees Homosexual Initiative, but was quickly nicknamed "the Briggs Initiative."

Even before Briggs filed his petitions, Harvey Milk (who had been a teacher) and other concerned people began plans to defeat the initiative. After the filing, their efforts intensified. One of Milk's most important efforts launched in June, 1978, when he and San Francisco State University professor Sally Miller Gearhart formed the United Fund to Defeat the Briggs Initiative, creating a central organization to raise funds and distribute them across the state. They selected Cleve Jones to head the Fund.

In addition, Milk continued his work as a supervisor. On Monday, August 28, after the Board of Supervisors

meeting adjourned at 6:55 p.m., Milk attended an evening committee meeting. He arrived home about 9 p.m. at the apartment he shared with Jack Lira to find his lover hanging on a rope, a suicide.

Soon afterwards, Milk debated John Briggs in an unusual setting: the New San Remo Restaurant (now Fior d'Italia), one of San Francisco's finest Italian restaurants. Their debate was first scheduled for Tuesday, August 29. Due to Lira's suicide the night before their encounter was pushed back to Wednesday, September 6, at 2:00 p.m., according to Milk's 1978 appointment calendar. The debate was moderated by KPIX TV reporter Richard Hart, and was filmed by producer Bob Klein. An edited half-hour version was shown on the KPIX program *People's 5* on September 22. That program has been lost, but excerpts survive.

Debates between Milk and Briggs are not exactly interviews, but they are more interactive than strictly prepared speeches, so they are included in this book. The New San Remo debate was one of the first between Milk and Briggs, and is one of the liveliest.

In this transcript and throughout Part Six, my comments are in [square brackets]. A division between two filmed shots is indicated by three asterisks in square brackets [* * *].

Briggs: *Let me tell you what* [Proposition] *6 does not do. It does not deny you the right to be a supervisor. It does not deny anybody in this room to have a job. It does not deny—*

Milk: Yes, it does. It denies people the right to *teach!*

Briggs: *Hold on a minute. There's no teachers in this room.*

Milk: But we don't know.

Briggs: *It does not deny anybody the right to a job. It does not deny anybody the right to rent or buy a house. All it does is say that*

parents—parents—*have the ultimate right as to who is going to teach their children.*

Milk: Okay. You see, based on that—now, based—wait—on that ultimate—on that ultimate right, at one time, parents didn't want *blacks* to teach. At one time, they didn't want *women* to teach. You know, the old Bible says women shouldn't be teachers, in the Old Testament. At one time, par—because parents are locked in. They're afraid of new—of something different, they're afraid of change, because of fears and myths put into their heads.

[* * *]

Milk: ... mistake in some quarters, that you don't *choose* homosexuality. Like you don't choose *blue* eyes.

[* * *]

Milk: We are saying that a gay person should have the right to say "I am [a] gay that is a part of society" *period.* No more.

Briggs: *In the classroom? In the classroom?*

Milk: In the classroom, out of the classroom, because it is a part of society.

Briggs: *But not in the classroom or—*

Milk: Why?

[247]

Briggs: *Because we don't allow prostitutes to do that in the classroom, we don't allow dope addicts, we don't allow thieves, and we don't allow alcoholics. Why? Because that's considered to be immoral.* [Sarcastically] *What's wrong with a man being an alcoholic?*

Milk: Wait, but, but talk about *morals*, and you're lumping together different groups of people. Are you talking about what Christ said is moral?

Briggs: *No. I'm talking about what the standards of this society is. We do—*

Milk: Who sets the standards?

Briggs: *People.*

Milk: The people? Okay. The Constitution set by the majority or the minority?

Briggs: [nodding] *By the majority.*

Milk: No, it's by minority. That's why it takes two-thirds. You see, the Constitution and censorship are to protect the rights of the minority. The majority *do not need* a constitution. This gets into allowing the Constitution to be governed by the majority, and there-fore in certain places you can disallow whites or blacks or Jews or anybody else from teaching if you allow the majority to rule. And the *whole concept* behind democracy and the Constitution is to pro-tect the rights of the minority, not the majority.

Briggs: *Morality is that which is the prevailing customs of the people. In some societies, homosexuality is okay. But in this society, homosexuality is* frowned *upon.*

Milk: Why?

Briggs: *Why?*

Milk: Yeah, I wanna know. Where are you coming from? See, because all the myths have been shattered, all the fears, all the—

Briggs: *Not in my mind, they haven't.*

[248] **Milk:** That's it. In your mind they haven't. I'm wondering why. What is the real reason behind it? All the psychiatrists say you're wrong, the doctors say—

Briggs: *Not all the psychiatrists.*

Milk: But the ones who have studied the situation.

Briggs: *The ones you read.*

Milk: No, the American Psychiatric Association.

Briggs: *They just took a new poll.*

Milk: They didn't take a poll, they took a—

Briggs: *They said people like you are sick.*

Milk: That's where you're wrong. There are *some* who do. But the *myths* have been shattered. Child molestation, which you're worried about, is 95 percent a heterosexual problem—usually the parent. Child abusement is a heterosexual problem. *Rape* is a heterosexual problem. Role model we know doesn't work, because if there's role modeling there'd be a lotta *nuns* running around out there in schools. So we know all your arguments are based on fallacies. I wanna know what the real reason behind it is.

Briggs: *You know, Mister—Doctor* [William H.] *Masters of Masters and Johnson said every person is born with a sex organ, and what they do with it, they learn what to do with it. So you've learned what you're doing, Harvey. You're not—*

Milk: By the age of six! By the age of six.

Briggs: *You can't say "every psychiatrist" and "by the age of six." You couldn't prove that if your life depended on it.*

Milk: The American Psychiatri[c] Association—

Briggs: *The American Psychiatric Society just took a whole new poll in June and said that people like you are ill and you're not to be trusted with children.*

Milk: No! It's not! They—

Briggs: [unintelligible] *in the car and I'd like to go get it.*

Milk: Right. Is that the *Time* magazine article?

[249]

Briggs: *Yes. I'll be very happy to show—*

Milk: You believe everything you read in *Time* magazine?

Briggs: *Of course! I read* [inaudible].

Milk: You believe it?

Briggs: *Of course!*

Milk: [unintelligible]

Briggs: *It's printed! Newspapers don't lie, do they?*

Milk: Richard Nixon never lied, either.

Briggs: *Of course not.*

Milk: I believe Richard Nixon lied quite heavily.

Briggs: *People do lie, right? You could be lying.*

Milk: Look at you.

Briggs: *That's right.*

Milk: We know that you've been distorting the truths—the myths and everything else. And I wanna know: Do you have a book coming out on this?

Briggs: *Yeah.*

Milk: How much money you gonna make on that?

Briggs: *Lots of it, I hope.*

Milk: Right.

[* * *]

Milk: Not too long ago, an Asian couldn't own property in San Francisco. Not too long ago, we put Japanese-Americans in jails. We had laws against Jews, against Irish, against many, many groups of people. And when we changed those laws, and judged people by their leaders instead of myths, we found out that they were *assets* to society instead of detriments. And *that's* what's happening in homosexuality. You'll find that the laws are being wiped away from the books because they were *unjust* laws based on myths that have been destroyed.

Hart: *Yeah, but the Proposition 13 analogy here, aren't you using that same list of people who were against Proposition 6 that you just mentioned the same people who opposed 13 and lost?*

Milk: No.

Hart: *The same people who supported 13.*

Milk: [California State Attorney General and Republican candidate for governor] Evelle Younger was for 13. [Republican candidate for lieutenant governor] Mike Curb was for 13. The *L.A. Times* had no position.

Briggs: *Oh, Harvey!*

Milk: The *L.A. Times* were?

Briggs: *They were absolutely opposed to it! And Evelle Younger had no position on it.*

Milk: So Evelle Younger had—?

Briggs: *Who cares what Michael Curb—er, Mike Curb thought anyways?*

Milk: You don't care what Michael Curb thinks? Your own candidate for lieutenant governor?

Briggs: *I do now, but I didn't then.*

Milk: Right now he thinks this is *wrong.*

Briggs: [holding up thumb and index finger about an inch apart] *Yeah, I think about that much about what he thinks.*

Milk: But Senator, he's your candidate.

Briggs: *No, he's not my candidate.*

Hart: *Would you like to see him elected?*

Briggs: *Sure!*

Milk: But he's—he's dead-set against it. Wilson Riles, the superintendent of schools—

Briggs: [unintelligible]

Milk: Wilson Riles and every other—

Briggs: *Younger wasn't my candidate. I was my own candidate.* [Briggs refers to his failed campaign for governor.]

Milk: Right.

Briggs: *And then I chose* [to endorse Los Angeles police] *Chief* [Ed] *Davis* [for governor].

Milk: Chief Davis was says this is not needed!

[251]

Briggs: No, *Chief Davis did not say—*

Milk: Yes, he has. You prove that to me in writing.

Hart: *Where did Chief Davis say anything about Proposition 6?*

Milk: During the gubernatorial race—

Briggs: *Oh, yes.*

Milk: —Chief Davis said—

Briggs: *Yes.*

Milk: —that this was not needed.

Briggs: *That true.*

Milk: Okay, so Chief Davis—

Briggs: *But he does think it is needed today.*

Milk: Oh, he changes his mind like the wind.

Briggs: *Of course he does, I was his opponent.*

Milk: That's what I go back to it, because it's *cheap politics.* You're playing on the political fears of people. It's political opportunism. One day you're *for* it, one day is *against* it. How can you view on something so fundamental on that, whether you, just because you're a candidate or not a candidate?

[252] [* * *]

Milk: Now they say they aren't. So they've *changed* as they've become enlightened about the subject.

[* * *]

Briggs: *I care about this country. And I care about the family. And I really, sincerely, honestly, and truly believe from the bottom of my heart that homosexuality is a real threat to the survival of this country. If we continue to tolerate it and approve it and let it be raised to an equal level and standard of heterosexuality. That's what I truly believe.*

[* * *]

Milk: ... the *oldest* game in the world. That's why I keep saying to you, study. I wouldn't be surprised what your next step is, because you ...

[* * *]

Milk: ... *always*. It is not ever done because of experience.

Hart: *Purely determined before school age?*

Milk: Determined before school age, that is every scientific study, and I say ...

[* * *]

Milk: It is not a *choice*. It is *not* a choice. That's the most fundamental mistake in Senator Briggs' ar[gument] ...

[* * *]

Briggs: *Children learn by example. Children emulate. People need heroes.*

Milk: Okay, okay.

Briggs: *I said if—the reason you wanted to be elected to high office is so you can recruit and convert every young adolescent—*

Milk: [laughs]

Briggs: *Those were your own words! I read it in the* Chronicle.

Hart: *Did you say that?*

Milk: No, no.

Briggs: *What did you say?*

Milk: I said that one of the reasons [for] being elected is that I'm a role model to young gay people.

Briggs: *Right.*

Milk: To young gay people. You see, you mis—turn things around, like you turn everything around.

Briggs: *What about a teacher who's a role model?*

[253]

Milk: To—a teacher should be a, a—to a, to a sexual orientation.

Briggs: *Yeah?*

Milk: You see, Senator, you turned it around.

Briggs: *No, I haven't turned it around!*

Milk: My statement was—my statement was, I'm a role model to the young gay people, people who are already established themselves as gay. *Period!* I didn't say—*you're* the one who keeps bringing up this *phony* recruitment. You know you're lying. You know you're changing the statements around. And you're doing that all the way around, just like you, you shifted the money around in your campaigns. And you talk about *morality.* And I question; what is your *real* motive behind it? What is your *real* ambitions behind this? What are you *really* using this for? And stop this phony issue that you know is a phony issue.

Hart: *Okay.*

33.

"*Just because something has been a law for a long time doesn't make it* right."

On September 15, Milk met Briggs in a debate sponsored by the Walnut Creek Democratic Club. It was held in the Northgate High School gymnasium, was moderated by Ed Skoog, the president of the club, and was attended by a large crowd.

The only known surviving recording of the debate was made by Tim Lewis, seated in the middle of the noisy crowd in the echoey gym with an inexpensive cassette recorder. Sound quality is poor, and the cassette ran out before the debate concluded. Transcription of recorded speech is often a blend of science and art. That is especially true in the case of this transcript. To aid in reconstructing difficult sections, I consulted contemporary newspaper articles and Milk's debate notes. Still, interpretation of hard-to-hear words are sometimes aided by the art of guessing what feels right. Some words, therefore, may not be exact.

Even with many gaps due to the unintelligibilities in the source tape, this transcript is still valuable because it is the most complete known text of any of the famous Milk-Briggs debates.

Skoog: *Senator Briggs.*

Briggs: *I'd like to thank you very much, Mr. President. It's a pleasure and an honor to be here in Walnut Creek at the invitation of the Walnut Creek Democratic Club.* [inaudible] *I know* [inaudible] *forward.* [Briggs pauses for the sound system volume to be turned up.] *Can you hear that?* [applause] *Thank you.*

I'm very pleased to be here in Walnut Creek. I'm here at the request of the Democratic Club. As a staunch Republican [unintelligible], *I never thought I'd be invited to fill a hall for a Democratic club. But in the interest of bringing you an important message, I guess I'll be forgiven. And I'm encouraged by the turnout that we see here, because that means you really want to hear about this issue. The other day I read in the paper that Evelle Younger had a meeting, he only had forty people. So I guess perhaps issues are still* [unintelligible] *of those in California politics who are concerned about the future of this state and the future of this country* [unintelligible] *those who hold elective office.*

I'd like to talk with you briefly about Proposition 6, what it is, and how it got here; why I feel strongly about it. And basically [unintelligible]. *It is an issue that goes to the moral question, the fundamental moral question, that will be placed in front of the people of California on Election Day as to require the highest standard of conduct by those who have such a heavy influence on our young children in California, kindergartens through high schools. And the question is whether the teachers are ready to abide by an act that was enacted in 1975 by the California legislature by a vote in each house, by a majority vote in each house* [unintelligible], *and signed into law, into law by Governor* [Jerry] *Brown. In effect, these people determined for 23 million Californians that homosexuality would no longer be a crime in California, and therefore it would no longer be a crime to be a homosexual schoolteacher, and* removed *from the law books of California statutes a law that had been there for 100 years giving school boards the authority to use as automatic grounds for dismissal, or automatic grounds for refusal to hire, a teacher who was homosexual.*

[256]

Now, this is not a civil rights issue. It is not a human rights question. It is simply a question of morality— [audience boos and hisses]. *It is simply a question of morality, in more ways than one. The first moral question is whether or not parents have the right to determine who shall teach their children. And frankly, ladies and gentlemen,* [unintelligible] *would remove from your authority, whether you favor it or whether you oppose it. When the California legislature made that decision for you three years ago, this initiative put on the ballot, signed by five hundred thousand people, is going to give the* people

of California the right to determine who will be teaching the children in California. Now, that is one moral question that we need to have answered.

And the other question is: Should we continue, as we did for over one hundred years—to hold our teachers to a higher standard of confidence—much higher than what we hold to the average person who [unintelligible] *leadership in California, in all walks of life. Frankly, I believe, and the people that support me,* [unintelligible] *who feel that our children are a very precious resource, and those whom we entrust with their daily care, who we entrust our children to for the role models, for those teachers that we entrust our little children to emulate, to look up to, should not be those who lead a homosexual life, or those who advocate homosexuality, or promote homosexuality, or solicit homosexuality, or impose homosexuality on young little children.*

Now, the initiative does not say [unintelligible]*, and I encourage all of you to read it. It does not say you cannot be a homosexual teacher. What it does say is you cannot be a* publicly *homosexual teacher.* [audience laughter] *To the point—to the point that if your activity is in private, which is your own business—frankly, I don't think there's* [unintelligible] *or anybody* [unintelligible] *what you do in the privacy of your room, or your bedroom, or your friend's bedroom, or anybody's bedroom, or anybody's house, or anywhere. But the Supreme Court of the United States of America has ruled many times that a public right that is a private right ends—a private right ends where public decency begins. And my organization, called California Defend Our Children, has taken the position very firmly that your right to privacy to engage in a sexual practice that has been* [unintelligible] *a law, a crime against nature for over 2,000 years or longer, is a right that ends when it becomes publicly known by the* [unintelligible] *public* [unintelligible]*.*

Now, what has this law produced? It has produced [unintelligible] *a climate that was fostered throughout this country that* [unintelligible] *toward the homosexual* [unintelligible] *country* [unintelligible]*.* [sustained cheers and applause]

Well, [unintelligible]*. It has produced—It has produced massive evidence to me that* [unintelligible] *the floor of the California legislature that when this law was passed in 18—in 1975, known as*

[257]

AB 489, which decriminalized homosexuality, in spite of the fact that thirty-one of the states still consider it to be a crime, that we would soon find the day that homosexuals would be declaring publicly and proudly [unintelligible] the fact that they were homosexuals [unintelligible]. [applause] [unintelligible], according to Tom Ammiano of the Gay Teachers Alliance [the Gay Teachers and School Workers Coalition] has proudly proclaimed that over one-third of the teachers here are homosexual in orientation. Los Angeles. The [unintelligible] there [unintelligible], they said that between ten and twenty percent of the teachers there are homosexual. Well, that's all right, because most of them are still in the closet, and frankly I think that's where they should remain. [applause]

Why? I'll tell you why. They should remain there for one reason; because I don't really care if you're homosexual or heterosexual or bisexual or asexual or what they are. But I [unintelligible] in front of any classroom, and teach reading, and writing, and arithmetic, and geography, and leave their values in the back room and the closet, that's what I want to see. [applause] I [unintelligible], and we're not interested in your sexuality, and we're not interested in giving you a platform to demonstrate to young children that gay is okay, and that gay is even better than the normal family's heterosexual lifestyle that this country was built. [unintelligible] the world.

Now, I would think that if Proposition 6 should be defeated, according to what my homosexual friends [unintelligible]. [laughter, cheers, and applause] In any event, [unintelligible]. In any event, it seems to me that whatever the historical [unintelligible] you that if we do not return to the local school boards the final determination as to whether or not a public homosexual who conducts himself or herself either by activity or conduct should be removed from the [unintelligible] public school children for homosexuality, then I feel the next step that we will take here in California, is to take them out of the public schools, and into [unintelligible] private schools, that Christian, Jewish, and nondenominational schools—that's the next step—for the people of California. [unintelligible] a very big question [unintelligible]—

[Someone shouts something unintelligible and is gaveled down by the moderator.]

Briggs: [unintelligible] *in conclusion, as* [unintelligible] *we will probably then* [unintelligible]*, Jean O'Leary, who is the lesbian co-chair, a National Gay Task Force leader, is that they have the right to have their homosexual demands. They'd like to fill every high school, and every elementary classroom in California and throughout the country,* [with] *homosexual student clubs, homosexual counselors to help the students adjust to homosexuality, and* [unintelligible]. [applause] *And in effect—and in effect, if achieved, that goal is to* [unintelligible] *militant organizations throughout this country that would like to raise homosexuality to equal status to that of heterosexual families in this country.* [applause]

Skoog: *Now Supervisor Milk has five minutes for rebuttal. I would appreciate very much if we wouldn't have the catcalls. We have a tradition in the Walnut Creek Democratic Club that we treat all ideas and all people with respect. And I would appreciate if you would just save your catcalls, please. Supervisor Milk.* [applause]

Milk: I would also appreciate it if you would keep the catcalls [unintelligible]. There's five minutes' rebuttal; before I do that I would like [unintelligible] to also thank the Walnut Creek Democratic Club. It's very interesting that when this battle first started, people were wondering if where the really great debate would take place; would it be L.A., Sacramento, San Francisco? It took place in Walnut Creek. [applause] I think that's—I think that's what America is about. That this debate takes place where you didn't expect it, in Walnut Creek, which means that *everybody* has the opportunity. And that's what America's about, and I think that this issue is about: who has opportunity and who doesn't? And so congratulations to the Walnut Creek Democratic Club. [applause]

I'd like to respond to some of the senator's comments before I read a text or notes. The senator talks about *education*. Some of us feel that the only qualification is *competence*; a good teacher. Apparently, the senator has a little problem with mathematics, and had some *incompetent* mathematics teachers. He said *three people* decided to overturn the sex laws, the Willie Brown law. He named those three people. The *vote* was 44 votes in the assembly, 21 votes in the senate, and the governor's signature; and that's *sixty-three*

people—none of whom are gay. Sixty-three people voted for the state to make a determination that the laws of the State of California, like in many other states, were archaic.

He had a little trouble with math later on, when he referred to San Francisco as "homosexual Mecca." According to the statistics available, the most, based on any percentages, is some sixty to ninety thousand gay people in the city of San Francisco. Based on a much *smaller* percent, if you took four percent of the population of New York, you would find there are something like three hundred thousand gay people in New York. So if you called sixty to ninety thousand "the Mecca," what do you call three to four hundred thousand? His numbers are wrong. If the facts are wrong for those simple mathematical things, then when we get into arguments, we'll see how wrong they are.

The senator talked about moral questions, and the highest standards of conduct for people who have a heavy impact on the children, that we should be careful who teaches our children, because of the *impact* upon them. According to government figures last year, there were one hundred thousand cases of child abuses by heterosexual parents. There are possibly—by the FBI figures—six million rapists, ninety-eight percent heterosexual. That in the state of California, thirty percent of all marriages have domestic violence. That in the state of California, one of every three women who will be murdered this year will be murdered by their *husbands*, and in the state of California, ninety-five percent of the child molestation is heterosexual. He's worried about who's gonna teach your children, and *this means* the highest standards of conduct. [applause]

If, indeed—if, indeed, the highest standard of conduct, *why* is he not concerned about the *heterosexuals*, who are so violent? So—so given the crimes against young people, what is he going to do about that? Based on the statistics, it might be a lot *safer* for our children if they *were* taught by gay people. [applause]

The senator—the senator talked about a law that existed one hundred years that was repealed and he wants to turn it back, bring it back. But sometimes laws weren't just. For *over* a hundred years, we treated blacks as property, and we threw those laws out. They weren't just. For *over* a hundred years, women didn't have the right to vote. We thought those laws were wrong, and we overturned

them. Just because something has been a law for a long time does not make it *right*. In fact, that's why we keep amending the constitution, that's why many of us are trying to ratify the ERA; because *that's* wrong, too. [applause]

The senator talked about morality. And we get into something very interesting about morality, but I only have a minute for this rebuttal, and the parent's right. Who says "morality"? The senator says it. The senator says to decide: Who should teach? "The parents." The parents don't have the right to determine whether the teacher of their child is male or female. The parent doesn't have the right to decide what color the skin is of the teacher. The parent doesn't have the right to decide the *age*, or the sex, or *anything* else about a teacher. Under the State of California, the Board of Educations and the State decide there is only one qualification for teaching, and that is competence. And that is the *only* qualification. A parent doesn't even have the right to decide what subject. The Board of Education does. A parent doesn't even have the right to decide what *school* you go to. The Board of Education. And what the senator wants to do is overturn everything that's on the books. And if you start with one, what's next?

I think my time for rebuttal is up, and so [unintelligible] back. [sustained applause]

Skoog: *Supervisor Milk will now have ten minutes for a presentation.*

Milk: [unintelligible]. On one hand, there is freedom of speech, human rights, and the right to privacy. On the other hand is Proposition 6.

There are already laws on the books to protect our children. Everybody from Superintendent of Schools Wilson Riles to [Governor] Jerry Brown to newspaper editors across the state agree that indeed we have the laws to protect our children. This law, Proposition 6, is misguided, confused, dangerous, deceitful, frightening, and un-American. It is based on the same type of attacks on basic human rights that gave us witch hunts, Nazism, and McCarthyism. It comes from the same pattern that Richard Nixon used to parley himself into the U.S. Senate, when he wanted to find Communists under every bed, and rode that to the senate. We now

have a person who's trying to shove the gay back into the closet for political power.

If this is allowed to pass, it could become part of an epidemic which will spread to other individuals who are minorities by virtue of their race, religion, sex, political beliefs, or national origin. The Constitution of the United States is meant to protect the minorities, not the majority. And that's why it's been changed from time to time to protect groups which were not included—such as blacks, and now women. The senator has come up with his usual arguments referring to Dade County tonight. In each case, as we repudiate argument after argument that use the same McCarthyian tactics: Throw down the lie, over and over again, hoping that you believe it, trying to get through to you.

And each time, they have to shift the argument. They originally started with child molestation, until we showed the figures that child molestation is indeed a heterosexual problem, and usually the parents. And now they don't talk about it, but they still throw the lie out—and this out, and they say, "Would you want your child—your son—to go to camp with this man as a teacher?" And that's to, to bring up the image of child molestation, even though the figures show that they're wrong.

And the senator tells us—and this line is key—so they don't use "child molestation," but they use the buzzwords.

They used to start talking about the Bible, until they found out that in the gospels—in the gospels—the teachings of Christ, and the life of Christ, it's never mentioned—it's never mentioned once—homosexuality. And if they start going back to the Old Testament, of what's morality, they'll find out that people who eat shrimp, lobster, men who cut their beards, and on and on, are immoral. And so they don't use the Bible. They now decide that *they* are going to say what's moral, and you are immoral if you are gay. And if they think—Senator Briggs thinks *he* is better than Christ, that *he* decides who's moral—better than Christ— then maybe you should elect *him* pope. [laughter, applause]

And the next—the next argument no longer holds up. In fact, Anita Bryant thumps the King James version of the Bible—it was [unintelligible] by a gay person. *They*—they decide what is moral. And so that argument is dead.

And then they use the argument of role models.

I was born to heterosexual parents. I was taught by heterosexual teachers, in a fiercely heterosexual society with television ads and newspaper ads—*fiercely* heterosexual—a society that *puts down* homosexuality. Then why am I a homosexual if I am *affected* by role models? I should have been a heterosexual. And no offense meant, but if *teachers* are going to affect you as role models, there'd be a lot of nuns running around the streets today. [audience laughter]

We know—we *know*—that a *teacher* does not—and stop and think how *weak* this argument is to heterosexuality and the family— if the senator thinks that *one gay teacher* can *change* all society. So much of society is heterosexual. The child wants desperately to be like his or her own peers. And the senator thinks that one child being taught by a gay teacher will go ahead and become gay. That's almost like saying how *fragile*—how fragile—his own opinion of his own [unintelligible] is, that you can convert people that easy.

So role models don't hold up.

And there were—the other argument the senator uses is that the parents have a right to decide. One time, in this nation, the parents decided blacks shouldn't teach. One time, in this nation, the parents decided *married women* should not teach. And if you go back to the Old Testament, the parents wrote that so that women totally should not teach. And sometimes parents, being restricted under the same kind of narrow-mindedness, and afraid of the unknown, will impose. The parents of Germany under Hitler agreed with Hitler that Jews should not be allowed to teach. And we know that Hitler started by not allowing the Jews to teach. And we know where he went with that. And it's interesting that Hitler did it in the name of the law.

And so as we knock down every argument—and there are many more that we can knock down—[unintelligible], we come to: *What* is really behind this? What is the senator's real reason? He *knows*, logically and intelligently, that he's wrong on this issue. And so I have to come to the question of: What is behind him? Is he, indeed, a person who is a tyrant? Does he want to become a Hitler? That would be frightening, and I don't think so. Is he in [it] for the money? Last week, he admitted he had a book coming out, and he would make a ton of money. We know he admitted that he [unintelligible] campaign taken money that was given to him for the

governor's race and put it into the Initiative drive. So we know he manipulates money. But is he in it for the money? I don't think so.

So what else? Maybe he did it to rise to political power, to run for the U.S. Senate, much like Nixon did by saying there were Communists under the bed. And we know what Nixon turned out to be. The moral is—[applause] The moral is, [unintelligible]. And we found out how he was going to *save* America; *save* the family. And we found out what *he* was like. Hiding behind [unintelligible] everybody else is immoral [unintelligible]. And so I wonder what's the real reason behind the senator, because he has never given an argument that can be held up. Religious leaders across the state say he is wrong. Oh, the Bible thumpers say he's right. But Bishop [C. Kilmer] Myers, the head of the Episcopal church for the entire state, says he's wrong. Newspapers after newspapers have checked with religious leaders, and they say he's wrong. And yet he keeps talking about morality. We don't know what's really the reason. And so we come down to the final conclusion, that I think: He's using it for his own personal gains, whatever they may be.

And I want to remind the taxpayers of this state what the initiative says; that the cost factor of this is unknown but potentially so great. And so I will tell the senator, the taxpayers of this state, what's gonna happen if this passes. According to the way it's written, you don't have to be gay. You don't have to be gay to be removed. You can *advocate* homosexuality. Every legal organization says, that means a straight person who says "It's okay"—or even if you belong to an organization that says "It's okay"—it's grounds for dismissal. It doesn't mean you're gonna be, it's grounds. So if this passes, I am going back to the teachers' union, both teachers' unions who said this is wrong, and ask them if it's still wrong. And if those teachers' unions say, "You [Briggs] are wrong," then I'm gonna make sure every one of the three hundred thousand teachers in this state who belong to those unions, are challenged. At a cost to taxpayers of two to three thousand dollars per case, this initiative will be substantial—in the neighborhood of eight hundred million dollars to taxpayers [drowned out by applause].

And if—and if the taxpayers in this state want to shell out eight hundred million dollars to finance his campaign for higher office,

[264]

[unintelligible] gay people, that would be their [unintelligible]. But they must know what's gonna happen if it passes. Every teacher who belongs to those unions, if those unions stay on course, will be challenged. And we'll see if the taxpayers want to shell out.

But we haven't got into the heavy part. Because time's running out, that the constitutionality of this: what the Constitution of this country was meant to be, when it was founded, what this country was all about, and how this initiative, based on every single lawyer, based on the lists of analysts, says it's so vague, that it flies in the face of the basic values of this country. And not just the Constitution, but what this country started out to be.

Thank you very much. [sustained applause]

Skoog: *Senator Briggs, now you have five minutes for rebuttal.*

Briggs: *Thank you very much. Really, I always thought that Disneyland and all the Fantasyland entertainment was in Anaheim, California. It's really eye-opening to me to come to Walnut Creek and hear the new Fantasyland [unintelligible] and hear all these wild accusations, which probably have little or no truth in them. But I really don't want to speak of myself. I want to take a few moments to focus on people I think you may know, and hopefully have some respect for. Let me tell you what George F. Will, who's an editorial columnist for* Newsweek *magazine the other day, said. He said, "Surely homosexuality is an injury to healthy functions, a distortion of* [unintelligible] *to the extent that homosexuality is, in some cases—*

[265]

[Gap in recording caused by switching sides of tape cassette.]

Briggs: *—[unintelligible] government to do about this issue?* [unintelligible] *the issue is: homosexual teachers or no homosexual teachers. He said: "For us to engage in homosexual activity, for us to steal, for us to* lie, *all these are a sin."*

Doctor [unintelligible] *of New York Medical Center: "Parents are absolutely correct to be fearful of the effects all of this is having on their kids."*

Doctor Charles Socarides, who is professor of psychiatry, psychiatry at State University in New York, he said, quote: "There is no doubt in my *mind that if homosexuality is further normalized, and*

raised to the level of a [unintelligible] *social disability there will be a tremendous rise in the incidence of homosexuality."*

[California State] *Attorney General Evelle Younger: "Society tolerates but should not encourage homosexual activities. Nor should society tolerate conduct by adult homosexuals exercising any control or supervision over children which promotes homosexuality or attempts to portray it as a legitimate alternative lifestyle."*

And in conclusion, I think U.S. Senator S. I. Hayakawa. [Mumbles and boos from crowd are gaveled to order.] *He said, "Homosexuality is a failure of emotional development. It is a failure of maturation. I believe they need medical support or psychological help, although I guess that they are entitled—although I guess that they are entitled to remain as sick as they like, as long as they like."*

That happens to be my position. I really don't care what your sexuality is. I feel that the people of California were shortchanged in 1975, when three people who provided the majority of the [unintelligible] *that it took to pass these bills sponsored by the homosexual community of the city of San Francisco, which has become the* [unintelligible] *capital of the world, that* [unintelligible] *people of California to have said your sole conduct as moral. Those of you who are homosexual or who engage in that kind of activity, or those who promote it, or who advocate it, or would like to encourage it on the rest of the state of California: I disagree with that. I* [unintelligible]

[266]

to disagree with you. I'm glad you disagree with me. I'm proud of the fact that you're here. [unintelligible] *That's* [unintelligible] *though. Why, you folks are here because you care, because you agree with me. I'm sure that* [unintelligible] *difference of opinion* [unintelligible] *agree with you.* [audience chuckles and applauds]

At the conclusion of this meeting, I hope you will respect my First Amendment rights. I have the right to disagree with you. You have the right to disagree with me. And basically, by all the charges, [unintelligible]. *Because, I believe I'm right. And, as Edmund Burke* [unintelligible] *said, "When good men do nothing, then evil will triumph."* [unintelligible] *good part of California, that respectfully agrees to disagree with homosexuals teaching children in California. You can be police. You can be doctors, lawyers, politicians, whatever*

the adult world will allow you to be, [unintelligible] *to protect our children from you* [unintelligible]. [applause]

Skoog: *We're going to have questions coming on in this, after the opening phase, and I wonder if those—if those who are interested in asking your question, you could put up your hands, and Bob Goldman will go around and select the questions and pull five at random at a time. And then we will* [unintelligible] *of the audience for the questions from the audience. We're now going to a thirty-minute open phase. We're just going to let Senator Briggs and Supervisor Milk take the initiative from there.*

All right. Supervisor Milk?

Milk: The senator—you quote psychiatrists, and I can quote an equal amount of [unintelligible] from the other side. In fact, over ten thousand psychiatrists of the AMA, they voted—and it's kinda strange to me [unintelligible] *Time* magazine [unintelligible] a poll of twenty-five hundred *possible* psychiatrists, and [unintelligible] were [unintelligible] most of those [unintelligible]. Doctor Jack Weinberg, the head of the AMA—APA [American Psychiatric Association], he issued a strong statement that the questionnaire was loaded; there were loaded questions, and most of the people who answered weren't psychiatrists. Just about every one of the *leading* psychiatrists say that those figures are wrong and [unintelligible].

But you can always find somebody. We can still find today psychiatrists or people who find blacks inferior. And we know how ludicrous that is. We have found for years people saying *Jews* are inferior. [unintelligible] It's always easy to reach into the back and find somebody with a title who doesn't like somebody else [unintelligible]. So just by polling the quote "experts" is wrong, because the psychiatrists themselves don't even always [unintelligible], and they split on that. But the ten thousand members of the APA—the ten thousand members of the APA say that those figures are wrong, that indeed homosexuality is *not* an illness, just as many other things have changed as we've learned about them and become educated. And part of the problem, Senator, is the statement you made in your opening statement, that you [unintelligible] wanted young students to have gay counselors. [unintelligible] gay. And the thing is, you say you don't. So my question is: Do you want a young gay person—a

[267]

young person at school who is gay—to go without help? To go unadjusted? Not to have the best that the medical profession has to help ease that person to accept his own life? Well, we've got to help that person be a success without any help.

Briggs: *Well, Mr. Milk, I'll tell you where I'd like that young person to go to. I'd like him to go to a pastor, or to a priest, or to a psychiatrist who would help lead him* out *of that depression rather than push him further into it. Frankly, I—*

Milk: How would—how would you expect to do that?

Briggs: *Well, I think that* [unintelligible] *people who* [unintelligible] *homosexuality who* [unintelligible]. *As a matter of fact,* [unintelligible] *approximately two-thirds of* [unintelligible] *of shedding that lifestyle, which is a* chosen *lifestyle, a* learned *lifestyle; one which you can un-learn or choose to get out of if you choose to do so. These young—or even old—homosexuals and lesbians were led* out *of that. I mean, you talk about the AMA* [unintelligible]. *According to the* Time *magazine on February twentieth, 1978, they had a article called "Sick Again? Psychiatrists Vote on Gays." Now this is* [unintelligible]

Milk: [unintelligible] twenty-five [unintelligible].

Briggs: *This was the American Psychiatric Association, which polled ten thousand members—*

Milk: But—you just—I said Doctor—Doctor Jack Weinberg, the *president* of the APA, *repudiated* that questionnaire, and said *most* of the people polled probably weren't even legitimate psychiatrists.

Briggs: *Well, that's not* [unintelligible] [audience laughter] *Anyway,* Time *magazine* [unintelligible]. [audience laughter] *And the chairman—the chairman of the* Medical Aspects of Human Sexuality Journal, *same questions, ten thousand members of the ACA, and* [unintelligible] *the first twenty-five hundred, and sixty-nine percent said they believe homosexuality is usually a pathological adaptation. Even the American Psychiatric Society today* [unintelligible] *deal with that question. They did say, sometime ago, about four years ago I believe, that homosexuality was* not *a pathological*

adaptation, but was a sexual disorientation. So I ask you, you normal people who have children, who think [unintelligible]: *Do you want a sexually disoriented person teaching your child? I would urge you to vote "No" on my initiative if you want a sexually disorientated person.*

Milk: Senator, one of the statements you first started talking about, people who found their way out of being homosexuals [unintelligible] the Bible; you know, I want to give you an analogy.

When I was young, at that time there were blacks who didn't have rights. In fact, many of them were lynched. Blacks couldn't vote. They couldn't get decent jobs. And there was an expression called "pinky." And that was where a black with a very light skin, and they were able to pass [as white]. And sometimes you didn't blame them for trying to pass, so they could get a decent job, and not be beaten up, and not be lynched. And sometimes it would lead them to turn against their own [unintelligible] came out. In Nazi Germany, there were reported cases of Jews denying their Judaism, turning other Jews in to protect themselves.

In the society that you [unintelligible], where a gay person can't get a decent job and is called "sick," it is no wonder that the pressure's on some of them to want to change, and to look for *any way possible* to change. Instead of trying to foster into that, if you would accept them, as Christ would accept everybody, to *love*, not hatred—[applause]. If you would accept them, they wouldn't try to seek a way out. And Senator, as a *Christian*, it is interesting that you don't seem to understand what Christ was about. He was about accepting people and giving love, not carrying the Bible in one hand and hatred in the other. [sustained applause and cheering]

[269]

Briggs: [unintelligible] *question the Bill of Rights. I never met a homosexual who was forced to ride in the back of the bus. And I can never, ever recall any homosexual being denied service at Howard Johnson. You know, blacks worked during the 1960s to achieve the Bill of Rights, and I'm proud of that. And I've got* [unintelligible]. *They worked very hard for it. But this is not a civil rights issue.*

The Supreme Court of the State of California, the Supreme Court of the United States of America, have said over and over again they do not hold that homosexuals are entitled to teach in

public schools. That's very clear. As a matter of fact, the State of California goes on to say, for some strange reason, that homosexuals can be denied a license to be married *in California. So you can't get* married *if you're a homosexual. I don't know* any *religious denomination, other than the Metropolitan gay church, that started out as a proper church, that will* [unintelligible]. *So you can't get married, you can't preach. But somehow or other, the State of California says, "They can teach our children." Now that—that I don't understand.*

Now, Harvey, I don't hate anybody, you know. I mean, I will defend your right to be elected every single day [unintelligible]. [unintelligible] *people who have elected, or the franchise to vote, and they're elected. That's their choice. And I have nothing against homosexual doctors or lawyers or politicians or newspaper people or presidents of Democratic Clubs, or anybody* [inaudible due to laughter]. *But, the majority of us, probably ninety percent of us—*

Milk: Senator, Senator—

Briggs: *—who take to time to* [unintelligible] *our lives; who take the time to try to* [unintelligible] *with our children* [unintelligible] *teach to give them a* fighting *chance* [unintelligible] *pornography on the movies* [unintelligible]—

Milk: Senator, now—

[unintelligible because both men talk at once]

Milk: Before you go on preaching your sermon, [unintelligible] does not make sense. [applause] [unintelligible] over and over again, and [unintelligible]. Let's go back to the civil rights thing. At one time, people segregated them out, and said, "Blacks have no civil rights." And what happened?

Briggs: No—

Milk: We *changed* that!

Briggs: No—

Milk: At one time, women had no civil rights. We've *changed* that.

Briggs: [unintelligible]

Milk: At one time, *in this state,* we built concentration camps to put Japanese-Americans in. [unintelligible] [applause] Now each time—each time—

Briggs: [unintelligible]

Milk: [unintelligible] fight for the old ways. And the Constitution was changed. And maybe once again, the same mentality, the same Hitler-like mentality of trying to suppress a minority doesn't change; this, too, is just the latest change. And you have to be enlightened. You have to be educated. You have to be led [unintelligible] to understand that human beings are human beings. Franklin Roosevelt said it very well, when he said "The four freedoms of [unintelligible]: freedom of speech; freedom of religion; freedom from want; and freedom from fear." And you take away the freedom from fear. Where does this lead to next, Senator? Because already in the streets of San Francisco, [unintelligible] here today, and there are quite a few of them. And Senator, you [unintelligible] that all you want is a camera in people's bedrooms. And we must [unintelligible]. You are opening up the floodgate to a situation that *is* like the Holocaust. Because Adolf Hitler *did* first eradicate gay people before he got to the Jews.

Briggs: [unintelligible]

Milk: [unintelligible] everything—

[Both men talk at the same time and are unintelligible.]

[271]

Milk: —and inside—inside [unintelligible] look at. You just look at the outside [unintelligible] and that's why everything that [unintelligible].

Briggs: *Okay,* [unintelligible] *straight down?*

Milk: Straight down? [cheers and applause]

Briggs: *You see, Harvey,* [unintelligible] *where they fall apart. Because people know that the State of California never voted to put the Japanese into internment camps.*

Milk: But they—

Briggs: *That was—that was President Franklin Delano Roosevelt,*

the one—the man you just got done quoting a moment ago. He's the man *who put the Japanese into concentration camps.*

[Both men shout at the same time; unintelligible.]

Milk: But, Senator, don't you understand? [unintelligible] people like you who made decisions that were wrong! Decisions that [unintelligible].

Briggs: *Harvey—Harvey, I trust and respect you and request that, I do not interrupt you,* period. *And I would just like a chance to finish now. It was the* government *that made decisions for the people, and in particular, it was* your own *Democratic governor and president that did that.*

Milk: Okay.

Briggs: *It was* the government *down in those Southern States that made decisions that black people could not vote. It was not the people who* voted *to take away the rights of the* [unintelligible]. Now you go back to the [unintelligible] *and you will find out, the elected representatives of the* government *did that. The difference between that and this is Mister Hitler, the first few Jews, it was the government, it wasn't the people. The people never had the right to vote!*

Milk: Senator—

Briggs: *Let me continue* [unintelligible]

[272] **Milk:** [unintelligible]

Briggs: *In this issue, in California, we are* [unintelligible] *Democrats. I may be wrong, but at least I'm right in my commitment to putting this to a vote of the people of California: Do you or do you not want to give homosexuals* [unintelligible] *access to your children? If they do,* [unintelligible].

Milk: [unintelligible] eighteen lies, eighteen, over and over again. First of all, the government and Hitler: Hitler won from a democratic election. He went to the *people.* The senator was wrong. He won through a democratic election. So don't say that [unintelligible] people. The people in the South who—and not just the South, but throughout this country—who had laws against blacks, were elected

by the *people*. And you [unintelligible] leader. At one time [unintelligible] said [unintelligible] morality [unintelligible]. And out of that same morality came the greatest crime in this *nation*—the most horrendous murders in this nation came [unintelligible]. So sometimes, people don't always know right but the leaders are wrong.

But let's go back to one thing you keep saying over and over again, about homosexuals teaching. First of all, in no way is anybody saying they are teaching homosexuality. Let's clear that up. That isn't covered in this issue. It never was. What is covered in this issue of who they are. The subject matter is determined by the rules of engagement, and you know that. And yet you keep throwing that out. You keep throwing that old recruitment [myth] out. All the [unintelligible] repudiate. Do you want this person to teach? Do you want to teach, the child molester who is heterosexual? The rapist who is heterosexual? Most murderers are heterosexual. Do you want those people to teach our children? [unintelligible]

One more lie that you keep bringing out, this "chosen lifestyle." Let me go back once again to that. People are born—most people— to heterosexual parents. They're raised with heterosexual teachers; in a heterosexual society. Children want nothing more than to be equal to their peers. People like you who degrade homosexuality tell the child not to be a homosexual. What child, faced with that, is gonna come home one day and say, "Gee, Mom, I wanna be gay"? It's not *chosen*. That is where you are fundamentally wrong on a very basic point and need to be educated. Nobody chooses homosexuality. *Every* psychiatrist; every educator; everybody who has studied it, researched it, has determined that homosexuality is caused by one of two reasons: either through birth, or through the environment [unintelligible] from the first months up to the age of six. By the time of age of six, a child's sexual orientation is embedded, and nothing any one teacher can do that will change that. And *that* has been stated over and over again. You can reach back into the files, and find what somebody once said a long time ago, just as I can reach back into the files, and find that [unintelligible]. But the current—the current thinking of that you cannot change a child's sexual orientation by the age of six, and *you know it*.

Briggs: *Harvey, I will give you one thousand dollars as—bring*

[273]

home if you bring me proof of that, because you can't do that any more than I can do that.

Milk: [unintelligible]

Briggs: *You know for a fact that there is* no *way of proving that. But I can tell you this:* [unintelligible] *in terms of our environment. I'm certain the air I breathe and the roads I drive on and people I live around* [unintelligible] *to create a very healthy, moral environment in the classroom, and that's why, in Tacoma, Washington, in Gaylord vs. Tacoma, the Supreme Court on that date* upheld *the right, just two years ago, of the school board to* remove *a teacher, solely based on the fact that teacher was an admitted homosexual. And that right was upheld by the U.S. Supreme Court when they refused to* review *that law case, and in effect said they* do *have the right to determine the moral fitness of a teacher.*

Now I want to read you about ten lines why they did that. First of all, the Supreme Court said if they did not *remove that teacher— the school board—then students would* "treat the retention of a high school teacher by the school board as indicating adult *approval of his homosexuality, and it would be* unreasonable *to assume as a matter of* law"*—not opinion, but* law*—"a teacher's ability to perform as a teacher required these principles of* morality *is not impaired and creates no danger of encouraging expression of approval and of"—"and of imitation.* Likewise *to say that school directors must wait for* prior *specific overt expression of homosexual conduct before they act to prevent* harm *from one who chooses to remain erotically attracted to a notable degree towards persons of his own sex and psych—and is psychologically, if not sexually disposed to engage in sexual activity prompted by this attraction is to ask the school directors to take an unacceptable risk in discharging their fiduciary responsibility of managing the affairs of the school district."*

And they conclude in asking, "It is not fair to the school, it is not *fair to the parents, it is not* fair *to the child to put a* known *homosexual in the* classroom *and expect that teacher to teach morality and ethics* [unintelligible] *immoral* [unintelligible]."

Milk: [unintelligible]

Briggs: [unintelligible]

[274]

Milk: Senator; you *quoted* from the Supreme Court ruling. There are Supreme Court rulings in this country that said that blacks should be treated like property. There are Supreme Court rulings in this country that said that women could not vote. You can always go back in history and find rulings of people who maybe meant well but didn't have the awareness. You can find a nation that said Jews should be put into concentration camps and murdered. You can always find something to quote from against a minority. It is so easy, and you're basing your whole argument on the same argument that Adolph Hitler used: that these people are immoral, should not teach. He used that against the Jews.

Everything you said just now, if you strike away the word "homosexual" out and put the word "Jew" in, would've come out of the mouth of Adolph Hitler. I don't equate you with *that*, but that's the same *tactics* you're using, that's the same *logic* you're using, and for *God's sake*, person, can't you understand where that will lead to?

Briggs: *Mister Milk, I'm only quoting*—[Drowned out by applause for Milk.]

Milk: I can quote *anything* from *anybody!*

Briggs: *I'm only quoting President Carter, Evelle Younger,* [unintelligible], *Senator Hayakawa, the Supreme Court*—

Milk: [unintelligible] the other side: Benjamin Spock and Jerry Brown and Mike Curb and—

[275]

[Both men talk at once.]

Briggs: *—homosexual, immoral—*

[Both men talk at once.]

Milk: I mean, are you gonna line up a popularity contest to see who's the most? Because the most people at one time *killed* every other species. Catholics killed Jews. Jews killed others. Catholics and Christians have fought. You can always line up a list of great names to justify murder. You can always find people who will do that. It's so easy to find people who hate. *Can't you* give me a list of people who *love?*

Briggs: *Yeah, John Briggs, his wife, his children, you.* [audience laughter]

Milk: How about Jesus Christ? How about Jesus Christ?

Briggs: *Jesus Christ. You know, Harvey, when you first ran for office, you said when you were interviewed on television and radio, that you wanted to be elected as supervisor because you wanted to provide a role model for young adolescent teenagers—*

Milk: No! [unintelligible] Richard Nixon lives. You got that straight out of him. I said that one of the things as an elected official I would be is a role model for young *gay* children; *gay.* Not "adolescent." Drop that whole word out. It's so easy for you to do that.

And that's the whole strain of your arguments, over and over again: manipulating the words, dropping words out. What is the real reason that you [unintelligible] out?

Briggs: [unintelligible] *today,* [unintelligible] *statewide* [unintelligible] *that he wanted to have teachers who could provide role models for young, adolescent students to come out of the closet. You made that statement* [unintelligible].

Milk: But Senator, you also said that day that when you took money from Arco—when you took money from Arco, and you took it from your government [unintelligible], Arco knew about it. And it's on tape. I've checked with Arco. They deny it. Either *you* or the leadership of Arco is lying. Your own statement a little while ago that the government—the president of the United States—that lying is immoral. Either *you* are lying, or the head of Arco is lying. One of you is immoral.

[276]

Briggs: *I tell you, it wasn't me, because I never* [unintelligible] *a lie.* [Audience laughs and boos; Skoog raps gavel to restore order.] [unintelligible] *name-calling* [unintelligible].

Milk: You call me immoral, you call gay people immoral. He says, "I'd like to get away from name-calling." Yet *you* name-call. You know, the same thing this morning I heard in the press, or on the radio.

[Both men talk at once.]

Milk: You know; in this game, we all [unintelligible]. I could bring in a bushel basket of letters. But you're threatening hundreds of people all over the state, thousands of people with their careers, their livelihoods. And *you* complain about a threat. It's so easy to take that Victorian attitude. [applause] [unintelligible] call me immoral, and nobody can say, [unintelligible]. And it's not name-calling; it's calling it like it is.

Briggs: *You know, I can—I can agree with—. If I had a choice, after being in office for twelve years, people would just be critical, calling me "immoral." They call me that once, I can be so happy. I can get rid of all the other forty-five thousand things which I have been called for a period of years. And—so if we want to at this point, let's just call me immoral* [unintelligible]. *But I want to talk about* [unintelligible] *thousands and millions of people—* [audience laughter]

Skoog: [Raps gavel three times.] [unintelligible]

Briggs: *Millions and millions of people that were led to their death and they couldn't—no one could understand how that can happen. How could a nation, and the community of nations not do anything? How can these people just let themselves be led with no activity, no action, no* [unintelligible] *I—*

[End of tape.]

34.

“*If more people got involved on every level—both sides, all sides—this nation would be a lot better off.*”

After a year as an intern at KCBS radio, Juana Samayoa was producing, writing, and directing three-minute segments on special topics. She leveraged her work to get hired by Field Communications to produce and host *El Amanecer*, a weekly news program for Latino audiences on KBHK-TV, channel 44 in San Francisco. About two months after she started, the host of KBHK's daily program *News Talk* went on vacation, and Samayoa was told to fill in for her. "They really wanted to get rid of her," Samayoa explains, "so they used her vacation to audition replacements. When she came back from vacation, they fired her." At the age of 29, Samayoa had beaten her goal of hosting a San Francisco television program by the time she was thirty. She was the on-air host of not one program, but two: *El Amanecer* and *News Talk*. In addition, she was the station's public affairs administrator, and was raising two young daughters, Sara and Marie.

News Talk consisted of three segments. The first was traditional television news reporting, and the second two segments were interviews. "On one of my first shows, I interviewed Ali Marrero of the Daughters of Bilitis," recalls Samayoa. Her managers were not pleased that Juana had invited a lesbian to appear on their television station. "I got called into the office and told they didn't want shows like that on the air."

In September 1978, Samayoa ran a week of interviews focusing on controversial ballot propositions, including Proposition 6. She had interviewed a woman who

supported Proposition 6, but unexpectedly had trouble finding someone to speak against it. She contacted BACABI, the Bay Area Coalition Against the Briggs Initiative, which had a list of approved speakers. "I had scheduled BACABI twice, and twice they did not show up," explains Samayoa. "Harvey was the only one who I knew to call. We may have booked him that morning or the morning before. He came on as a favor at the last minute."

KBHK-TV's managers "were very unhappy that I was doing the show on homosexuality and having Harvey as a guest. They brought me into their office and told me to warn Harvey we were on live TV, so he can't use any swear words or mention anything sexually explicit. I didn't say anything about that to Harvey. I felt that would be disrespectful."

In spite of these tensions, the result is an enjoyable and warm conversation. Of her encounter with Milk, Samayoa says, "Anyone who stands up for the rights of a particular group always stands out. He was a hero in my eyes. He was taking the heat for standing up for these rights, and I admire and respect that."

The interview below was broadcast live at 11:00 a.m. on Tuesday, September 26, 1978 on *News Talk* on KBHK-TV. Unfortunately, the technician responsible for recording the live event forgot to start the recorder until seven minutes into the segment, so the interview's first seven minutes have been lost and this transcript starts with Milk in mid-sentence.

[279]

Milk: —people shouldn't teach.

Samayoa: *Okay.*

Milk: People who can't physically have a child shouldn't teach. Okay. We all—we know that's—okay?

Samayoa: *Okay. All right. What about it* [homosexuality] *being sinful?*

Milk: Sinful—it's sinful. *Read* the gospels. You know, everybody *thumps* the Bible. *Read* the gospels: the teachings of Christ, the life of Christ—books of the gospel.

Samayoa: *Mm hmm.*

Milk: And it's never mentioned once. In fact, Christ talks about *love*. It's very interesting. They carry this Bible in one hand and *hatred* in the other hand, and said, "It's sinful." Christ himself said nothing about it.

Samayoa: *I don't know the Bible that well, but I'm sure—*

Milk: Aha!

Samayoa: *—but I'm sure there must be some reference in the Bible to—*

Milk: No! In—in—in the teachings of *Paul*, whose own *life* was questionable, there's reference to it. But the *gospels*, which is Christianity, you know—Jesus—

Samayoa: *Mm hmm.*

Milk: —his life and his teaching, it is never, ever even *hinted* at, suggested, or even in—in any kind of context can you find anything like that. Just the opposite.

Samayoa: *Okay.*

Milk: Christ says, "*Love* thy neighbor."

[280]

Samayoa: *Okay.*

Milk: "Do unto the neighbor as you'd want the neighbor to do unto you."

Samayoa: *Okay.*

Milk: So these people who thump the Bible have *never* really read the Bible, the gospels.

Samayoa: *Well, I'm not a Bible-thumper, but—*

Milk: Aha. [Juana laughs] [Milk addresses the camera] To the Bible-thumpers, to those who are out there, re-read the gospels, and *live* the life of the gospels, and you would do what Christ says, [Milk

turns to Juana] is to accept everyone. It is so *ironic* that these people carry the Bible in one hand and anti-Christ attitudes in the other.

Samayoa: *Okay. Harvey, we have to take a break.*

Milk: [laughs] Get your Bible!

Samayoa: *We'll be back in just a moment.* [Both chuckle.]

[After break]

Samayoa: *Welcome back. We're discussing Proposition 6 this morning with Supervisor—from San Francisco—Harvey Milk, and Harvey, just before our break, you asked our viewers to go get the Bible.* [They both laugh.] *I'm not sure how many of those did that. But really, you know, what I think we're dealing with here is a right-wing conservative backlash, or a movement. And the polls show that the Briggs initiative, the anti-gay initiative, is winning in the polls by a 63 percent margin. Do you think that speaks of Northern California, or Southern California, which is more conservative?*

Milk: There are all kind of polls, and the final poll will be on November seventh.

Samayoa: *Sure.*

Milk: And if we can shatter the myths enough, I think the polls are going to change. But you brought up something very interesting, and I think you have been victimized, like so many of us, about this right-wing movement. I think that there is no right-wing movement.

[281]

Samayoa: *There is not?*

Milk: There is not. Let me explain. I think that the right wing has *talked* about it, and *packaged* it, and put it on a shelf like a box of cereal, and people are *buying* it. And the legislators are buying it, and so the legislators are acting that way. And the liberal-progressive people even are buying it, and starting to act that way. But let's look at the *facts*. We've seen four states—cities—throw out gay rights bills. So now 38 cities have 'em. Five years ago, none. We talked about ERA [Equal Rights Amendment] being stopped and its cold and have to have an extension. Seven years ago, *not one state* had ratified

ERA; *sixty* percent of the nation has. We talk about marijuana. The state of Mississippi—*Mississippi*—has almost decriminalized marijuana. We talk about—

Samayoa: *And it may be coming here in California.*

Milk: Right. [Republican candidate for governor] Evelle Younger himself says he'd sign the bill.

Samayoa: *Right.*

Milk: We talk about the convention of conventions in Houston last year, the women's convention—

Samayoa: *Right.*

Milk: —which was the most exciting thing ever came out of there. And finally, I guess, if you want to sum it up—and this is going to come out a little wrong, but: Richard Nixon is in exile, and Harvey Milk is in City Hall. [They both laugh.] What I'm saying is, the right movement has *talked* about it so much that people are buying it. When in essence what has happened is that we have gone—the progressive-liberal movement of this nation, the human rights movement—has gone six steps forward, and one step backwards.

Samayoa: *But this is so much different from all the other—the, the Dade County initiative, which was a repeal of a—*

[282]

Milk: Right, a repeal. This is actually denying peoples' rights.

Samayoa: *This is not a repeal, this is actually a—*

Milk: This is the *first time* in *this nation* we've gone after a group who already had rights—

Samayoa: *Right. And it comes right after Proposition 13.*

Milk: You can't compare the two. Proposition 13 was an economic issue that cuts across all lines.

Samayoa: *But people are fed up. They want order to their society.*

Milk: No they don't. People are not fed up. There are certain people who are bigots, who are racists, who are fed up. [If you] don't think that Proposition 13 was the most racist bill we voted on—the

September 26, 1978: Juana Samayoa interviews Supervisor Milk

people who got affected most are the minorities. We have the Republican Party in this state saying now, "No income tax." As long as—this was last week, in San Di—in L.A. As long as the income tax went for highway expansions, airport, golf courses, and so forth, it was good. Now that income tax is going for senior citizens, abortions, and so forth, all of a sudden income tax is no good.

Samayoa: *Okay, I guess—I guess what I want to get is a feel for what is happening. Why a Briggs initiative? Why an anti-gay initiative? And, also—I mean, it seems very interesting to me that Briggs had another initiative on the ballot, too, and that is the death penalty.*

Milk: You have—I think Senator Briggs could care less one way or another about the gay issue. Senator Briggs is—because of his demagoguery, because none of his arguments hold up under *any* kind of scrutiny; I think he's using this to get name identification to run for U.S. Senate like Richard Nixon did: "I'm going to sweep the Communists from out under this table." Richard Nixon became *famous* for sweeping Communists that did not exist out under your bed, and ran for power. I think John Briggs is using the same type of thing.

It's very interesting to see who's on both sides of the issue. Against John Briggs is [Republican candidate George] Deukmejian—the most conservative person running, he's running for attorney general. You have Mike Curb, the lieutenant governor, Republican candidate. Ronald Reagan has come out against it. Group after group, every—Wilson Riles, superintendent of schools—

Samayoa: *Right.*

Milk: [Episcopal] Bishop [C. Kilmer] Myers—

Samayoa: *What groups are for it?*

Milk: Well, I understand the—I'm saying this, I have to smile, laugh, but I understand that the California Nazi Party came out for it, the ultra-conservative wing of the Republican Party's come out for it, and I think the L.A. Sheriff's group has come out for it. And that's the *only groups* whose come out for it. And every—every *teachers'* union, every *union*, every *minister* of a large denomination except for the Bible-thumpers, *name* after *name*—boards of *education, newspapers.* You know, anybody who *understands* it has come out against it.

Samayoa: *You know, I guess—*

Milk: So he's playing on—I really think his real thing is to build up that mailing list.

[284]

Samayoa: *You think that this is just a political—a ploy—*

Milk: He's honest.

Samayoa: *—to further his ambitions?*

Milk: He has even—he's admitted on television that he's writing a book and is going to make money on the book coming out. He's admitted that he gets huge amounts of money in from the mailing lists he has and things.

Samayoa: *Yeah, now that we're talking about politics, I have to ask you this. And this is somewhat personal.*

Milk: [chuckles] Politics?

Samayoa: *Yes. I had scheduled another person to be here, and there was a last-minute cancellation, and you were kind enough to be here on a last-minute notice.*

Milk: Right.

Samayoa: *And I got a comment from someone in the committee* [referring to BACABI, the Bay Area Coalition Against the Briggs Initiative], *saying that "You shouldn't have Harvey Milk on. He's just using it to further his political career. He's really not a spokesperson for the Bay Area [Coalition] Against the Briggs Initiative."*

Milk: I'm not. I am not a spokesperson. I was called because you had nobody else.

Samayoa: *Right.*

Milk: My own political career—if I was going to be using something [for] my political career, I'd be out there shaking hands in my district and spending more time putting stop signs up and filling potholes than I would be spending time traveling up and down the state fighting Briggs.

Samayoa: *I—okay, I guess the reason I asked that is because, you know, you were leveling, you know, criticism against Briggs, as this just being something to further his political career, and someone in your position, you know—*

Milk: I'm running for reelection next time, not for any higher office like Senator Briggs is.

[285]

Samayoa: *But what would you say about that criticism? I mean, what does that say about the Coalition's forces?*

Milk: Every group has the same problems, that rather than go out and do something positive, there are people within every group who look at those who have accomplished something and sit there and criticize. The lieutenant—the governor of—of New Mexico, [Jerry] Apodaca who's Spanish-American, his biggest—*biggest*—opposition comes from the Spanish community. Because of other Spanish-Americans who are jealous, and rather than doing something *positive*, it's easy to pick. It's always easy.

Samayoa: *There's always a—*

Milk: You get so used to it that you know that's unfortunately that it's so easy to sit back and criticize rather than go out and do something positive, and I just usually pay very little attention to the critics. I would like to see them go out and walk the streets, knock on doors like I've been doing.

Samayoa: *Okay then, so how close are you then, to the gay community, do you feel?*

Milk: Well, no one person is a spokesperson for the gay community. BACABI is one group. In fact, there are three campaigns, major campaigns—

Samayoa: *I wondered about that.*

Milk: There's a statewide campaign, which is the No on 6, which is the media campaign.

Samayoa: *Are they all coordinated?*

Milk: Oh, yes. BACABI does speakouts and endorsements. And then there is San Franciscans Against Prop 6, which is going to do the door-to-door voter registration and get out the vote. Three distinct levels—

Samayoa: *Levels, right. Okay.*

[286]

Milk: How close am I to the gay community? Nobody can be close to the entire gay community, because we go from the extreme left to the extreme right. And I am good, old-fashioned Harry Truman-Adlai Stevenson Democrat. I sit in the middle. Those on the extreme left think I'm too conservative. Those on extreme right think I'm too liberal.

Samayoa: [laughs] *Can't please all of the people—*

Milk: There's no way.

Samayoa: *—all of the time. Right.*

Milk: And I have no intention to try to. I just put my views out and just keep going forward. I think that if more people got *involved* on *every* level—both sides, all sides—this nation would be a lot better off.

35.

"Who are we to say that another person must be put to death? I cannot make that decision over another's life."

Noe Valley is a charming residential neighborhood in San Francisco. It was part of Milk's supervisorial district. The neighborhood's monthly newspaper, the *Noe Valley Voice,* featured an "Election poll" article in its November, 1978 issue. It asked several people about Proposition 6 and other initiatives on that month's ballot. Here are Supervisor Milk's opinions.

T o focus attention *on several key city and state issues on the Nov. 7 ballot, the* Noe Valley Voice *conducted its own informal primary with city and neighborhood luminaries. Here is a sampling of the responses.*

Prop. 5: *Smoking shall be banned in most work areas, cafeterias, clinics and other health facilities, half of space in company lounges, most public arenas, museums, galleries, public restrooms. It would be allowed at roller derbies, rock concerts, semi-private hospital rooms where both patients smoke, segregated restaurant areas, hotel and motel rooms, and private offices. $50 fine/violation.*

Milk: No.

Comment: I do not smoke, but this prop. discriminates against small businesses and is not equally applied in all cases.

Prop. 6: *Provides for filing charges against school teachers, teachers' aides, school administrators or counselors for advocating, soliciting, imposing, encouraging or promoting private or public sexual acts . . .*

between persons of the same sex in a manner likely to come to the attention of other employees or students.

Milk: No.

Comment: It would legalize discrimination and is a deceitful attack on basic human rights.

Prop. 7: *Enlarges the list of crimes calling for death penalty to include murder based on racial prejudice; murder of a peace officer, fireman, witness or elected official; murder for financial gain; murder with use of bombs.*

Milk: No.

Comment: Who are we to say that another person must be put to death? I cannot make that decision over another's life.

Prop. U: *Shall there be a one-month rent stabilization for December, 1978 (calculated on basis of June 6, 1978 rent) and a rental reduction for calendar year 1979 (calculated on June 6, 1978 rent minus the property tax saving on the rental unit)?*

Milk: Yes.

Comment: The alternative—driving out seniors and those on fixed incomes—is unacceptable. Greed by some has brought this forward.

Prop. W: *Declaration of Policy: We, the people of San Francisco, demand that the District Attorney, along with the Chief of Police, cease the arrest and prosecution of individuals involved in the cultivation, transfer or possession of marijuana.*

[288]

Milk: Yes.

Comment: It'll be legal soon anyway, so why waste money trying to enforce unjust laws?

36.

"*John Briggs, how many careers ruined, how many lives destroyed, before you are satisfied in your thirst for power?***"**

On November first, the day after Halloween, Milk and Briggs debated on Brigg's home turf, at Pacifica High School in the Orange County city of Garden Grove. The debate was sponsored by the Pro-Family Coalition, a group allied with Briggs. In Walnut Creek, a substantial portion of the audience was on Milk's side, but in this Orange County debate the majority applauded Briggs.

KOCE-TV videotaped excerpts, but never aired them. I found the roll of unviewed videotape in a not-yet-cataloged box in the GLBT Historical Society archives in San Francisco.

Square brackets containing three asterisks [* * *] indicate gaps in the recording due to breaks between camera shots.

[289]

Moderator: *So first we'll hear from Senator John Briggs.*

Briggs: *Thank you very much. I'm delighted to be here with you in Orange County after returning from Bay Area. You know, Proposition 6 has been a very interesting dialogue across this great state of California.*

[* * *]

Briggs: *They had a grievance. They had a teacher there that they felt was abusing his position as a teacher, which would have an adverse effect on their children in regards to homosexuality. The school board told them, "Well, I'm terribly sorry, but you need a new law."*

[* * *]

Briggs: . . . didn't decriminalize dope addition. Did decriminalize homosexuality. And it raised to a level of heterosexuality, homosexuals—of which my opponent [he gestures towards Milk] is one of the leading opponents of. [audience laughter] Now, it appears to me, the question becomes—the question becomes: Why homosexuality? Why was it decriminalized?

[* * *]

Briggs: And the California legislature, when they passed what we call AB 489, the Homosexual Bill of Rights, giving homosexuals the right to teach our California schoolchildren, to use their California classroom to publicly advocate and flaunt homosexuality, to the point that when the school boards . . .

[* * *]

Briggs: . . . to determine who will teach their children. Not some— [applause]. But the California legislature disagreed back in 1975, and without a vote of the people, without asking anybody's opinion, they just passed a law by the barest minimum vote—one in each house—matter of fact, we had to fly the lieutenant governor [Mervyn Dymally] up there to break the tie vote—and then Governor [Jerry] Brown signed into law a bill that took the right away from parents, teachers and who the role models will be for their children. Now why—why should we have this right? It seems to me that in a heterosexual society when we want to enfranchise people—give them a license to teach our children—that they give up certain rights. In other words, everybody has the liberty to do what they want. What people do in private is their own business. But what they do in our classrooms is our business. What they do in—[applause]. What they do in private and then wanna brag about on Monday is the public's business. We don't allow people to fall down in the gutter drunk every Saturday evening and continue to teach our children.

We—we have the responsibility, we have the right as parents, we have the right as citizens, to exercise our free speech. And our free speech, and our right to petition our government, is [unintelligible] Proposition 6. And the question is for California voters as we head to

Election Day is this question: Is gay okay? And if it is, is it okay in the *classroom? And I—I hope, and I'm counting on, and I'm doing a little* *praying, that the people of California will* realize *that what they're* *about to do on November the seventh next Tuesday is to affect the* *life—lives of every child, and every person, and* not just *in California,* *but throughout the* entire country, *on this very profound social issue* *of whether or not gay is okay in the classroom.*

A "yes" vote means, "Gay is okay, but not in the classroom." *And a "no" vote means, "We're out, and we're out of the classroom."* [applause]

Milk: I'm glad that Senator Briggs has finally accepted my challenge and has invited me down here to debate him in his home territory, because I think it's very interesting to see what he had to say in front of his own territory and his own people. On one hand, there's freedom of speech, human rights, and the right of privacy.

On the other hand, there's Proposition 6, which is a misguided, confused, dangerous, deceitful, frightening, and un-American attack on the basic rights. [audience shouts of disagreement mixed with applause]

Please—let 'em yell. Hold off. I'm talking to those people. [He gestures toward a section of the audience.] Let 'em yell. Let 'em yell.

The same kind [of] attack, based on lies, myths, and most important, *fear*—uninformed people, that at one time spawned witch hunts in this nation, McCarthyism, and Nazism. And as educator after educator, religious leader after religious leader, and psychiatrist after psychiatrist—and especially if you've read today's *Los Angeles Times*—every one [has] repudiated the myths and fears except those people who want to keep themselves shrouded behind myths and fears. And that is why—that is why these people have come out strongly against this proposition. Because there *are* laws on the books already, and *enforceable* laws, that do protect our children.

This initiative comes from the same tactics that Richard Nixon used to reach the U.S. Senate: a self-serving, political, ambitious person, dreaming up a moral crusade to rise to power. To satisfy his crusade and attempt to run for higher office, he had to find a scapegoat. If this is allowed to pass, it could become part of an epidemic,

[291]

State Senator John Briggs debates Milk in Garden Grove.

which will spread as it did in Nazi Germany to other individuals who are minorities, by virtue of their race, religion, sex, political beliefs, or natural origin. John Briggs, if you've been reading his statements and listening to him, changes his tune from day to day, contradicts himself from time to time. Each time we debate, he comes up with a new reason why Prop 6 is on the ballot. Last night, as I debated [the] professor of law that supported him and signed his ballot argument, they had a new reason. And the professor of law, who signed this ballot argument, said last night on television, "It doesn't make a difference what Prop 6 says. That's not the real issue."

And I wanna know what the real issue is, because it changes. I think the real issue is: John Briggs' thirst for power. [mixed boos and applause] The reason why I say that—the reason why I say that is, *every argument*, every single argument he has brought forth, and one time or another during this campaign has been thoroughly repudiated. Yet he continues his moral crusade, and he contradicts himself, sometimes during the course of the same debate. He has no hesitation of being a contradiction person to fit his audience. He is willing to teach our children—*your* children—that hatred of some people is more important than the love of Christ. [mixed boos and cheers]

And I have to—I have—I have to ask—I have to ask the rhetorical question: John Briggs, how many careers ruined, how many lives destroyed, before you are satisfied in your thirst for power? It's very interesting. Other people have asked the same questions.

And John Briggs talks about the political *clout* of the gay community. I want to know what political clout got the archbishop of San Francisco, the Catholic [Arch]bishop [John R.] Quinn, head of the archdiocese; Bishop [C. Kilmer] Myers, the head of the Episcopal Church in this state; the Methodist ministers—how do they buckle under to political clout? I want to know how the gay community made the *Teamsters* buckle under to political clout. [audience laughter] I wanna—I want to know how—how the political clout of the gay community affected Senator Hayakawa; Ronald Reagan; Gerald Ford. And it's interesting, because *that* is only *part* of the multitude of people and groups who are supporting the anti-Briggs Initiative, the "No on 6" position. And if you think that politics can influence the church, if you think that the gay community can influence all the unions, then you are really in for a shock.

But at the same time—at the same time, there is some groups supporting him. And you must understand that the Nazi Party in this state, and the Ku Klux Klan have come out on his side. [applause] [inaudible]. I think tonight, before it's over, you will hear John Briggs contradict himself more than once. So listen carefully to what he has to tell you. [applause]

[293]

Briggs: *Abraham Lincoln one time said, "If you can't answer another man with logic, you can always resort to calling him names."* [applause] *Unfortunately, this campaign, like all campaigns, as it winds down seems to get into the* [unintelligible]. It's unfortunate, but it does.

[* * *]

Briggs: . . . *as to whether or not we are gonna have our children exposed to the homosexual lifestyle, gay identity, as good and nice and natural. And I think it is a matter of contention as we move into the final campaign as to who and who is not supporting this initiative. It is true that the state Young Republicans and the Los Angeles Young Republicans are supporting me. California Farm Bureau, some school*

boards, some teachers, some priests—Catholic priests—, Baptists, Protestants—[recording glich] who would rather be president than be right. Now, you have to remember that when you put 240,000 people on the streets of San Francisco, and you can deliver up money and you can deliver up votes, that is a whole new bloc of votes that a lot of vote-hungry politicians are looking for, and they've made a decision in my opinion that they can ignore—they can ignore—the Bible-believing, God-fearing, family-oriented person and go for the new bloc vote out there. Well, I think they're going to be surprised on Election Day. I think— [drowned out by cheers and applause].

You have to remember the educational establishment by—headed up by Wilson Riles and other [unintelligible] —they're opposed to this initiative. They have good reason to be opposed to it. Do you know, that under California law, school boards are the only governing board that has no authority to fire the people they hire? They have to turn it over to a commission. And in this one area of morality—who's gonna be teaching our children—school boards will recapture the ability to fire the teachers they hire.

In California, eighteen teachers a year are fired for all kinds of reasons: incompetency, unprofessional conduct, immorality, and so forth. Eighteen a year, out of 200,000. The politicians are scared to death, including some school boards. They may get the responsibility put back in their lap to fire teachers. And this could lead to a whole series of problems for the Teamsters and other organizations that are labor-oriented. And that is, the local people could come in once again and take control of their schools. We have—we have lost control of our schools. We have lost control of our educational system. We had to pass a law this year that says, "If you can't read or write by 1980, well, you can't graduate."

But we don't need new laws, we need new teachers. And we're going to begin on this one area. First, in the area of morality. Then we'll get in the area of incompetency. We have a million teachers in California. 200,000 of these teachers—out of those, maybe eighteen of these teachers will lose their jobs. The most protected species in the entire world. And that's why the educational establishment is in such opposition to this bill. They are afraid of local control. This is a local control bill. But [unintelligible] in San Francisco, where they are now teaching homosexuality as an alternative lifestyle,

Milk debates Briggs before a hostile audience in Garden Grove.

we don't want *in Garden Grove. We don't* want *in* [unintelligible]. We— [applause].

Milk: [unintelligible] "We don't want to teach homosexuality in Orange County." That "we don't want 'Gay is okay' in school." "We don't want it in the classroom." He said that tonight.

I will quote from his statement in the *Bay Guardian* a couple of weeks ago. The question was, "Do you think sex, including homosexuality, should be taught in schools?" John Briggs' answer: [Milk reads aloud from a newspaper] "*Yes!* I'm on a committee in Orange County that was very controversial a few years back. I said we should *have* sex education classes. I think homosexuality should be talked about. A school board could lay down the guidelines for that. We can't ignore it." [applause]

And every—and every one of his promises and every one of his campaign slogans, he does that: different things at different times to different audiences. The senator himself can't keep consistent. That's why he himself is confused about the whole subject of homosexuality, and that's why he plays on people's fears.

He also talked about role models. You know, in today's *Los Angeles Times*, it talks about role models. [Milk reads aloud from

[295]

newspaper:] "Does role modeling ever create homosexuality? The scientific answer is unequivocally *no*." And it goes on and so on. Those people who believe in role models had better read this and see what the psychiatrists are saying. They all say that by the age of *six*, the sexual orientation is established. It's in your own papers, your own psychiatrists in Southern California. Read it. The *mother* and the *father* and the *family* determine the sexual orientation. But because some people cannot *face* that, they have to find a scapegoat. And who's the scapegoat? [inaudible due to applause]

Just stop and think—think of the indictment he is doing to the heterosexual family. He says that for five or six years, or seven years, the mother and father have this child. And this child goes to school in a very *fiercely* heterosexual community. Television heterosexual, everything heterosexual. Most of the teachers are heterosexual. *One* teacher, for one hour a day, is going to [snaps his fingers] convert that child. What a weak indictment of heterosexuality that is! And if—if—if—if role models were by the teacher, I was born to heterosexual parents. I was raised in a heterosexual community. My teachers were heterosexual.

[End of video]

On November 7, California went to the polls to vote on Proposition 6 and other initiatives. It was the first time an entire state had voted on gay rights. The results were clear: 58.4% of voters voted "no" and only 41.6% voted "yes." The Briggs Initiative was crushed by a margin of more than one million votes.

Milk was not alone in contributing to the victory; thousands of men and women across the state worked together to make voters understand the consequences of the Briggs Initiative. But Milk's extensive efforts, from setting strategy to organizing behind the scenes to acting as the initiative's most visible opponent, gave him prominence across the state. He had always been a ham—he loved being the center of attention—and now his star shone brighter than ever.

1978,
The City Weeps

The City weeps

San Francisco Examiner

★ ★ ★
Streets edition
Closing stocks

114th Year No. 148 Thursday, November 30, 1978 20¢ S

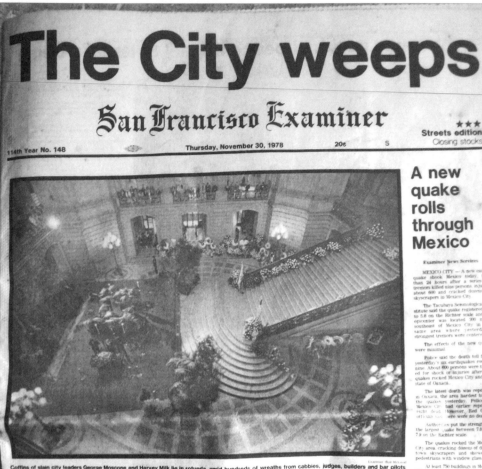

Coffins of slain city leaders George Moscone and Harvey Milk lie in rotunda amid hundreds of wreaths from cabbies, judges, builders and bar pilots

A new quake rolls through Mexico

Examiner News Services

MEXICO CITY — A new earthquake shook Mexico today, less than 24 hours after a series of tremors killed nine persons, injured about 600 and cracked dozens of skyscrapers in Mexico City.

The Tacubaya Seismological Institute said the quake registered 5.5 to 5.8 on the Richter scale and its epicenter was located 200 miles southeast of Mexico City in the same area where yesterday's strongest tremors were centered.

The effects of the new quake were minimal.

Police said the death toll from yesterday's six earthquakes rose to nine. About 600 persons were treated for shock or injuries after the quakes rocked Mexico City and the state of Oaxaca.

The latest death was reported in Oaxaca, the area hardest hit by the quakes yesterday. Police in Mexico City had earlier reported eight dead. However, Red Cross officials say there were no deaths.

Authorities put the strength of the largest quake between 7.8 and 7.9 on the Richter scale.

The quakes rocked the Mexico City area, cracking dozens of downtown skyscrapers and showering pedestrians with window glass.

At least 750 buildings in Mexico City were damaged and two older structures collapsed, forcing the evacuation of thousands of office workers and residents.

One nine-story building split open at the top, the two halves separated by about six feet. Another building tilted to one side, sinking about two feet, said firemen who helped evacuate the area.

Two high-rise buildings in the capital's Polanco neighborhood swayed so much that they collided. Many windows shattered under the stress and fell into the streets below, sending residents and tourists scrambling for cover.

Police spokesman Jose Madrid said that of the eight killed, two died of heart attacks, two when a lamp pole fell on them, one from a collapsed wall. Two construction workers were killed while working on Mexico City's Rochasoria Sur prison.

Another victim jumped to his death from a third-story window, apparently fearing the building was about to collapse, Madrid said.

The first shock yesterday afternoon lasted 20 seconds. Five more tremors were felt in Mexico City before 6 a.m. The aftershocks in Oaxaca lasted until 10 p.m.

It was a strong earthquake, said Alan Alanis, 22, a visiting Houston businessman. I was sitting on the 21st floor of the Fiesta Palace Hotel and suddenly the hotel began to sway, covering...

Last farewell to Moscone

☐ Photos / Pages 4 and 24

The bells of St. Mary's Cathedral began tolling slowly shortly after 10 a.m. today as 6,000 people gathered inside and outside the cathedral for a Mass of Christian Burial for slain San Francisco Mayor George Moscone.

Although one woman collapsed in the central aisle of the cathedral and had to be carried outside before the Mass began, and thousands of others spilled into Geary Boulevard, the general temperament as the service began under leaden skies was one of solemnity and restraint.

Hundreds of dignitaries from around the country came to pay their last respects, including mayors, U.S. representatives and senators, and a large contingent of legislators from Sacramento, where Moscone served 10 years.

Gov. Brown was among the last to arrive, being ushered to his seat as the cathedral choir began its chorus of Alleluia. He was seated next to The City's Chief Administrative Officer Roger Boas, Police Chief Charles Gain and acting Mayor Dianne Feinstein.

Others in the cathedral, where 2,300 were seated and another 2,000 stood in back, were Lt. Gov. Mervyn Dymally, Chief Justice Rose Bird and other members of the state Supreme Court, former Mayor Joseph Alioto and his wife, Kathleen, former Mayor George Christopher and such other notables as Sally Stanford.

Gina Moscone, wife of the mayor, and her four...

The front page of the November 30, 1978 San Francisco Examiner shows Milk and Moscone's caskets lying in state beneath the dome of City Hall and a headline that sums up San Franciscans' sorrow.

37.

"Rights are not won on paper. They are won only by those who make their voices heard."

On Friday, November 10, Dan White gave Mayor George Moscone a letter stating that White was resigning from the Board of Supervisors. The following Tuesday, White changed his mind and retrieved the letter from Moscone. Unfortunately for White, his letter no longer mattered. On Monday the Board of Supervisors had accepted White's resignation. It was now up to the mayor to appoint someone to the vacant seat that had once belonged to Dan White.

At first Moscone said he would reappoint White. Then he took a more pragmatic view; White had consistently opposed Moscone's legislation, often casting the deciding vote to sink a Moscone initiative. Milk reminded Moscone of White's opposition, and worked behind the scenes to have Moscone appoint a more liberal person instead of White.

White tried to persuade Moscone to reappoint him. On Saturday, November 18, Moscone met White and told him that Moscone needed two things:

1. Evidence that District 8 voters still supported White;
2. White's promise to support Moscone in the future when voting on measures before the Board.

Over the next few days, White focused on providing Moscone with evidence that some District 8 voters still supported him. However, he ignored Moscone's second condition, so Moscone decided to appoint someone else.

White became aware that Moscone had changed his mind and was going to appoint someone else, and that

Milk sits on the edge of the reflecting pool across the street from City Hall.

Milk was working against him. He felt humiliated and instead of taking responsibility for his own actions, blamed Moscone and Milk for his feelings.

On Monday, November 27, former policeman White cleaned his police revolver and loaded it. He strapped on a holster that concealed his gun under his suit coat. He wrapped ten extra bullets in a handkerchief that he stuffed into his pants pocket. He phoned his City Hall aide Denise Apcar and asked her to pick him up at home and drive him to City Hall. He told Apcar three times that he wanted to see both Moscone and Milk. She dropped him off at City Hall, where he avoided metal detectors by climbing through a window.

White met Mayor Moscone, and in the mayor's private study, shot him twice in the body and twice at point-blank range at the base of his skull, execution-style. This left White with one bullet in his five-shot revolver. He left the mayor's office through the back door. Six witnesses saw him run a full city block to the supervisors' offices on the far side of City Hall. He went to his now-empty former office and, he later confessed, reloaded his gun there. He called Milk in and shot Milk in the body three times and twice at point-blank range at the base of Milk's skull.

White fled City Hall but turned himself in to police half an hour later and confessed to the double murder.

The city was in shock. That night, in a spontaneous demonstration of grief, 25,000 silent mourners carried lit candles along the same route that Milk had taken marchers, from Castro Street down Market Street to City Hall,

for a candlelit memorial. Among the speakers remembering Moscone and Milk was Harry Britt, who said, "Harvey was a prophet. Like Dr. [Martin Luther] King, he lived by a vision. As I look out over this crowd, I think this city has bought this vision. Something very special is going to happen in this city, and it will have Harvey's name on it."

* * *

Many people agreed: They had felt something special about George Moscone and Harvey Milk. The *San Francisco Examiner* headline three days after the double murder read: "The City weeps."

Earlier in 1978, Pamela Brunger, features editor for the *San Francisco Examiner*, had had the idea for a series of stories about life for gays in San Francisco. She hired free-lance reporter Lenny Giteck, who wrote a thirteen-week series of articles called "Gays in the City." It was one of the first detailed looks at gay life ever published by a major American newspaper. On November 29, two days after Milk's assassination, the *Examiner* published this "Interview with Harvey Milk" as part of its series.

H ARVEY MILK was one of the new breed—an up-front, openly gay politician. His death sends shock waves of grief and anger to every corner of San Francisco, especially to our city's large gay community.

I liked Harvey Milk. I found him friendly and funny and interested in my job as editor of the Scene section of this newspaper. He thought it was about time women were winning the war of acceptance, too. He cared about all minorities, not only his gay friends. He frequently scribbled little notes on bright orange paper, story ideas or comments when he found something of interest in the paper, and sent them to me.

In order to share our insight into this rare man, we are printing an extensive interview conducted with Milk, by Lenny Giteck, shortly before last month's elections. The interview was scheduled

[301]

for publication next Monday as part of our continuing series on The City's gays. It is more appropriate today.

Milk, of course, did not speak for all of San Francisco's gays. He was, however, a symbol of the determination of gays to take an active role in all areas of The City's life.

In his tiny office at City Hall, Milk discussed his hopes and dreams for all of San Francisco and his special concerns for his followers—all of whom he urged over and over again to say "I'm gay."

Pamela Brunger
Scene Editor

Giteck: *People have often contended that the gay rights movement seems to grant homosexuals a special, privileged status in society, and that to support gay rights is to condone homosexuality. How do you answer that?*

Milk: That's wrong. That's their lack of reading below the headlines. All gays want is what everybody else has. No more, but no less. We don't want any favors, and we don't want any more than anyone else is getting as far as protection under the law and our right to participate in all aspects of society. We just want equal protection. People are equating gay rights and affirmative action programs. Nobody that I know of is asking for affirmative action for homosexuals. I think that's how people misconstrue what the gay rights movement is all about. What we do want is equality.

Supporting gay rights does not mean supporting homosexuality, just as supporting black civil rights does not mean you have to like or love black people. But you respect their right under our democratic system and under the Constitution to have equality. You don't even have to accept the idea of homosexuality; what you are accepting is the right of all people to exist. You are just reaffirming what the Constitution says, and what is chiseled into the Statue of Liberty.

Giteck: *Some gays here think the gay community in San Francisco is so well-accepted that an Anita Bryant-style campaign couldn't succeed. Are they right?*

Milk: Unfortunately, I think they're wrong. It's true that we've done our homework, but we've taken the "getting to know you, getting to know all about you" approach. That's vital and important, but we never really addressed the myths that Anita Bryant used in her campaign. The Anita Bryants will talk about child molestation and role models, and unless we address that we're in trouble.

The survey in Miami after the vote said that most people voting against us thought we were child molesters. In California 95 percent of child molestation is heterosexual. Unless we talk about that we'll be labeled child molesters. The same thing about the Bible—unless we address the issues that are brought up about the Bible, we're in trouble. We must address the real issues that will be thrown at us—the smear campaigns, the myths, the lies, the distortions—and expose them.

Giteck: *What do you say to gays who feel too much money, time and energy are being devoted to the political process, rather than educating the public about homosexuality?*

Milk: You don't educate people overnight. You've had centuries of discrimination against blacks, and there's still rampant prejudice against them. Against gays it's gone back thousands of years, and you can't eradicate that in one generation.

We wouldn't have to be fighting Briggs so hard and spending all this money to educate when for a much smaller amount of money we could probably have elected some gay people to Sacramento. They would have been working and showing what gays are like, just as I'm showing people here that we're involved with taxes and dogs—and Muni and everything else. So that people say, "Hey, you know it doesn't matter if a person is green with six heads. That person is good—good on human issues, good on taxes, good on environment."

Every poll says that people who are on the gay side are people who know a gay person well. How do you get to know a gay person well? They have to be out of the closet. And who is more out of the closet and more exposed than a gay official?

The reason so much has been accomplished in the black movement in a short period of time is that blacks have gotten into elected offices and many have shown great leadership qualities. That has done more to educate people than education has. My involvement

with issues in this city—and I'm not saying if you agree or disagree with my stand—has done more to educate the public about gays than standing outside with pamphlets, writing literature and making TV ads. And why should there only be one elected gay official in this city? So many of these people who are against putting money into politics feel there can only be one gay leader, and if it can't be them they're against politics. I think history will show that's the wrong approach.

Giteck: *How would you like to see gay people address those issues?*

Milk: What they have to do is to come out to their friends, their neighbors, their relatives, the people where they work, and dispel that myth. So you're telling the gay people what they must do, and you're educating everybody about what the real facts are. Unless you're willing to get down to that nitty-gritty and talk about those issues, then the Anita Bryant campaign will work.

Giteck: *There seem to be a great number of factions in the gay community, and often they appear to be fighting among themselves more than working toward a common goal.*

Milk: That's true in any community. You name me the black leader who controls the black community in this city. There isn't one. There are 40 or 50 black leaders. The same is true of the Chicano community. There's not one group that's ever had it all together, and gays are even more divided because we cover all economic strata and racial and ethnic groups. Blacks are all black. But gays are black, Asian, Chicano, white, men, women, wealthy, poor and so forth. And to expect a very wealthy, white well-educated gay man to relate completely to a very poor, black lesbian—as an example—is ludicrous. A lot of us are doing our best to bring them together. But it's difficult when you have gays who are staunch socialists and gays who are reactionaries. To sit there and expect that we will all unite under one common banner is crazy.

Giteck: *One of the divisions in the gay movement is between lesbians and gay men. Do you see the two groups working together toward common goals?*

Milk: It's happening right now. I'm working with a group called A

United Fund to Defeat the Briggs Initiative. Most of the lesbians in the group are strong separatists, yet we are working together. The group has been in existence for just a short while and it seems to be working. What's important is what happens to the coalition after the election in November. I think many lesbian separatists and gay male separatists will be very surprised. If you look at the letterhead of the group, it says in a bold headline, "A United Fund," and underneath in smaller print it says, "To Defeat the Briggs Initiative." You can be sure if we defeat the Briggs initiative, the big headline will remain "A United Fund," but the smaller line may change to "To Support the ERA" or "Bring Back Abortion." We have structured it so that the concept of working together will continue to other issues.

Giteck: *Many gay people think it's a mistake to link the gay movement with other questions, such as the Bakke decision or abortion, for example. Where do you stand?*

Milk: I don't think it's wise to tie other issues into the Briggs initiative by itself. But I think it's imperative that those people who have been disenfranchised work together on all issues. We must work together on Bakke, abortion, the ERA, the American Indian issue, Latino issues, etc. So the blacks, for example, must come to the aid of the gays on the Briggs initiative—as anti-gay as some black people are. They must come together with us on this issue, just as we must come together with them on their issues. That doesn't necessarily mean linking the campaign literature, because that's not the way it works politically. But we must join forces.

If you look at who's against gays, who's against blacks, who's against women, and on and on, you find that it's the same people— the Richard Nixons of this country. And if the blacks and browns and Asians and women and gays are all going to fight each other for the same crumb, they're all going to be disenfranchised.

I think the gay community has to stop voting its pocketbook. There were gays who voted for Jarvis-Gann. They voted for their economic interest, despite what a racist bill it was. I think it's time to educate the gay community that it's no good having a lot of money if you're in jail because you're gay. So what some of us are trying to do is to put together a coalition of all the traditional

[305]

minorities—people who have gotten nothing over the years—so we can stop fighting among ourselves and work together.

Giteck: *Graffiti urging "Gay Riots Now" have been appearing on some walls in The City. Do you think gays would—or should—turn to violence to protect what they see as their basic human rights?*

Milk: I don't think anybody should turn to violence. I am non-violent. I believe in non-violence. But I think I would be remiss in my duties as public leader not to discuss the definite possibility for violence, given the fact that a certain percentage of the population is violent by nature. Let's say for argument's sake that one percent of all people are violent by nature. Then you're talking about 100,000 to 150,000 gay people nationwide who are violent people. If they watch their rights being chipped away, that is justification for them to come out with their violence. In the city of San Francisco, you're talking about 500 to 1,000 gay people who are violent by nature, and will react in the same way.

Gay people are angry ever since Dade County and they're getting more and more angry. After the vote in Eugene, Oregon, there were a thousand people marching in the streets of San Francisco, and when they walked past City Hall most of them were shouting, "Civil rights or civil war!"

On the other side of the coin, there is violence being committed against gay people every day. If Briggs wins, there will be a green light for more violence against gay people. Look what happened in New York City recently, when young gangs took baseball bats and went through the city and Central Park beating up gay people or anyone they thought was gay.

Do you think gay people are going to go with their heads bowed into the gas chambers? I mean, I'll go kicking and screaming before I go with my head bowed. I've read history; 300,000 gays went into the gas chambers in Germany, and then six million Jews. I don't think the Jews are going to go quietly the next time, so why should gay people?

Giteck: *Even if it doesn't reach a point where gays turn to violence, some have argued that civil disobedience should become a tactic of the gay movement.*

[306]

Milk: Rights are not won on paper. They are won only by those who make their voices heard. They are won by activists and militants. Silence never won rights. They are not handed down from above. Rather, they are forced by pressures from below.

Civil disobedience won blacks the attention, and black violence frightened a lot of people. There are gay people studying history, and they are learning that lesson. They're realizing that Jimmy Carter is more concerned with the human rights of people in Russia than he is about gay people in the United States. A lot of them are apparently deciding that civil disobedience is the route. History is going to show that gay people are eventually going to win their rights, no matter what. So I would tell Jimmy Carter that he has the chance to turn the pages of history faster and prevent violence and civil disobedience from happening.

Giteck: *Gays in San Francisco are covered by a number of city antidiscrimination ordinances. How well do you think these ordinances are actually being enforced? Are gays really protected against discrimination?*

Milk: I think the main advantage of the gay rights ordinance in this city is not to force people to hire gays, but rather to protect those gays who are already employed from being fired. Probably the most sensitive area is the medical profession. There are a lot of gay doctors and psychiatrists who work for major institutions; in the past they would have been fired if it became known that they were gay. So they had to be closeted. Now, partially because of the Briggs situation, a lot of these gay professionals are coming out, because they know they are protected. If they've been working for an institution for a number of years—getting promotions and good evaluations—and now they are fired after they come out, the reason is pretty obvious. They're protected under the anti-discrimination ordinance.

Let's face it—it's not going to be perfect. There are blacks who are discriminated against. There are Latinos and women who are discriminated against, and there are laws on the books against all of that. To think that a gay rights law is going to cure everything all at once is naïve. But I think it's vital that the professional class

[307]

be protected, because when they come out, they break down the commonly held stereotypes about gay people.

Giteck: *Was it a mistake to pass gay rights ordinances around the country in the first place?*

Milk: The Constitution of the United States was not meant for the majority; it was meant to protect minorities. I'm sure if we put it to a vote, we could outlaw black teachers in some places, and Jewish teachers in others, and Holy Rollers in others. It's easy to legislate against a minority. That's what the Constitution was set up to prevent.

But even if gays lose in these initiatives, people are still being educated. Because of Dade County, the entire nation was educated about homosexuality to a greater extent than ever before. In the weeks before and after Dade County, more was written about homosexuality than during the total history of mankind. More people said "damn queers" than ever before, and for many it was the first time they'd use the word "queer." That's the beginning of a dialogue. Maybe the result was wrong, but it was the beginning of an education. The first step is always hostility, and after the hostility you can sit down and talk about it.

That's why after Dade County the campaign in Wichita was slightly different. It was different in Saint Paul and Eugene. Each time more myths were shattered, and they had to reach further and further for their arguments. Maybe we'll lose fifty races, but by the end there will be no more myths. No one will be able to claim we're child molesters.

[308]

Giteck: *In light of the political defeats gays have suffered around the country, where do you see the gay rights movement going now?*

Milk: The call for a march on Washington [D.C.] is taking place, so the next major step will be a mass meeting in Washington, we hope around the Fourth of July of the coming year. This will not only be a mass gathering, but will also include seminars, workshops and the setting up of a national political network.

On the local level, you're finding that the battle against Briggs in this city is putting a lot of gay people into the political process—people who have never been in it before. There will be a carry-over that will affect all political races in The City. Once people become

politicized many of them stay politicized. That means there will be more gay people involved—not only in running for office, but also involved in initiative campaigns, proposition campaigns and working for candidates. I guess the best way of putting it is, you're going to see the maturing of the gay political consciousness because of the Briggs initiative.

38.

A *living wage*

This letter providing the shortest interview in this book (just one question) was published in the December 21, 1978 letters column of the *Bay Area Reporter*. It gives a brief demonstration of Milk using his quick wit to shift our perception to his point of view.

A FEW DAYS before he died, I asked Harvey Milk what his reaction was to the *Chronicle* editorial against pay raises for the supervisors. His answer went something like this:

"The supervisors' salaries were set in 1964. I am going to ask the *Chronicle* how much their advertising rates have been raised since then."

We had a good laugh, and I left thinking that the chances were pretty good that the supervisors would get their raises.

The time is long past due to raise the supervisors' salaries to a reasonable level. Why doesn't the *Chronicle* lead the way with a new editorial favoring a pay raise equal to the percentage increase in their advertising rates since 1964? Fair is fair.

BILLY ALLEN
SAN FRANCISCO

39.

A last interview with our supervisor

On November 12, *San Francisco Examiner* reporter Corrie Michael Anders, moonlighting for the *Noe Valley Voice*, conducted one of the last interviews Milk ever gave. Anders' article "A last interview with our supervisor" was printed in the December 1978 issue of the *Voice* under the pseudonym Corey Michaels to hide the reporter's identity from his *Examiner* bosses.

O N ONE of those incredibly clear and crisp November Saturdays, the day before the first heavy rains came, Harvey Milk was ebullient and talkative. He sat in the blue marbled décor of the Café San Marcos on Market Street, across from his old camera store, brunching on eggs, steak and coffee light.

In one of his last interviews, Milk talked to the *Noe Valley Voice* for 90 minutes. He talked about crime, about George Moscone and Dan White, about past supervisors and those of the future, about wealthy lawmakers and those who found public service a financial drain.

Milk dwelled at length on the latter subject—one that a few days later would bring him face to face with death. He died over a relatively minor political rift.

Financially, Milk had much in common with Dan White, the former supervisor accused of killing Milk and Mayor George Moscone Nov. 27. White quite the Board because he could not support his family on the supervisor's $9,600-a-year salary, and Milk also was struggling to make ends meet.

Before he became a supervisor, Milk enjoyed the luxuries of the middle class. Though never wealthy, he went to the movies about once a week, dined frequently in restaurants, and earned $15,000 or so annually operating a camera store with a partner.

That changed after he won the right last year to represent District 5.

He went to the movies once every two months, if that often, he said. He rarely ate out, and a bowl of chowder at home proved a money-saving stomach-filler. He gave up his leased Volvo and got around town on Muni using a FastPass. He also scouted the thrift stores for bargains on clothes.

And last month, because he was devoting so much time to his official duties and not to his camera store, Milk and his partner closed the shop's doors forever, leaving the supervisor deeply in debt.

The problem was that Milk worked as a fulltime supervisor, putting in 60 or more hours a week, he said, but received a salary less than the earnings of an artichoke field hand. In fact, the $9,600 pay for the job was smaller than the salaries paid his two top aides.

The part-time pay for a fulltime job has hurt other newcomer supervisors also, like Carol Ruth Silver of District 6, Gordon Lau of District 1, and Dan White.

For their duties, Milk and other supervisors do not get to join the City's pension plan, but do participate in a health care plan and receive a "free parking space."

"I can live on $9,600 but not well," Milk had said, "but I certainly couldn't if I had a family."

The salary the supervisors receive is ridiculous when you consider the enormity of the job they must do. The eleven supervisors in effect are the board of directors for a corporation that spends one billion dollars a year. Levi Strauss, Hewlett Packard, and Polaroid would fall off their profits in hysterical convulsions at paying its directors less than the janitor.

Milk suggested that one of two standards could be used to bring a San Francisco supervisor's salary into the 1970s. It could be set at forty per cent of the mayor's $55,496 salary. Or an appropriate supervisorial salary could be based on salaries of fulltime supervisors in other comparable cities. Fulltime council members in Los Angeles, admittedly far larger than San Francisco, receive $33,000 annually.

Any salary increases would have to win voter approval to change the charter, and San Francisco voters do not seem to be in a pay boost mood.

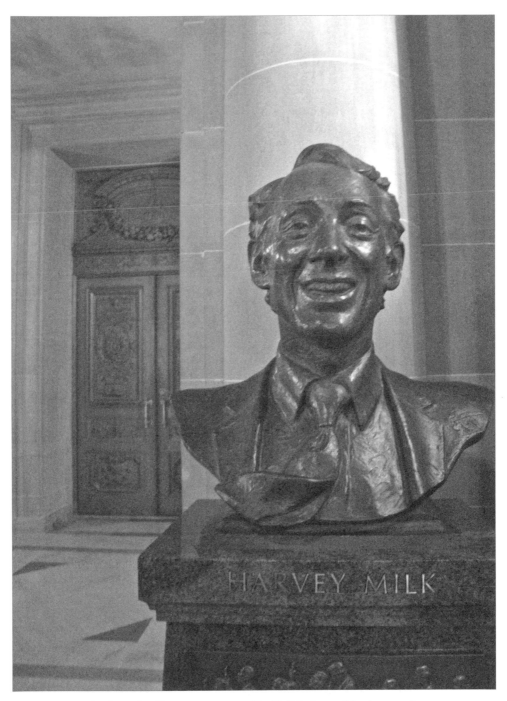

This bust of Milk greets visitors in City Hall in front of the doors to the supervisors' chambers. It was sculpted by Eugene Daub, Rob Firmin, and Jonah Hendrickson based on the iconic photo of Milk taken by Daniel Nicoletta.

That mood has been exacerbated by the tenured supervisors, downtown business interests, and the major media in this town who want to retain what's left of their power base, Milk had said.

Milk said he had to close his camera store after business became "worse and worse" because he was not devoting enough time to it. He had to hire extra personnel to manage the store, but despite the additions, the strain was too much for himself and his partner.

He said "sure" he could have cut back on his 60-hour supervisorial duties. "But I think it's important that I go to meetings and meet people."

The problems facing the City now, he said, were caused by those wealthy part-time supervisors who ran the City prior to district elections. "Maybe part-time supervisors was [a good idea] in the 40s and 50s, but it's not good in the 70s," he said. "Part-time supervisors are responsible for today's sorry state of Muni, mental health, automobile and transportation problems. They were concerned with their outside jobs."

Milk said crime had been reduced in many areas of District 5, specifically the Castro Street and Duboce Triangle areas. "That comes from being out there."

Ditto the "dogshit" law, he said. Cow Hollow and the Russian Hill neighborhoods have noted an 80 per cent improvement since his pooper-scooper ordinance went into effect, with the Haight and Castro showing a 50 per cent improvement.

[314]

"If that's what the supervisors regard as make-work, I think the people will want it," he said, referring to contentions by several old-time supervisors that they would have to make up work to do if the job were fulltime.

White said he also spent so many hours as a supervisor that he did not have enough time to run his fast-food concession at Pier 39. But when his family said they would pitch in and help at the eatery, White asked Moscone to withdraw his resignation.

Milk led the fight against White's getting his job back. In a friendly but blunt meeting, Milk told Moscone that the mayor faced the certain loss of the strong gay bloc vote if he ignored selecting someone with liberal credentials and [re]appointed the conservative White.

Unlike White, Milk never entertained any thought of quitting. In fact, he had solidified his intentions to run next year by getting the support of several of last year's rivals.

He was making do financially by cutting out fat in his own life-style, sharing expenses with a roommate, and was looking around for part-time consulting work or a job as a guest columnist for a newspaper, he said.

The shift to fulltime supervisors with fulltime pay is going "to happen sooner or later," he told the *Voice*.

If it doesn't, he predicted that the Board once again would belong to those who could afford to serve—"all white, downtown business types."

Or, he said, his face breaking into a grin, the Board would become "all gay and single."

＊ ＊ ＊

People wept over Harvey Milk's death. But people remembered his life.

The Harvey Milk they remembered was no saint. He was impatient, sarcastic, attention-seeking, short-tempered, and confrontational.

But people remembered also that Milk cared. They remembered that he was courageous. And they remembered that he stood for something.

Even though he received hundreds of death threats, even though he was sure of a violent death, Harvey Milk remained standing until his last day, until he was killed by a man with bruised pride. Decades later, he still stands for something.

He has been memorialized by countless events, places, and organizations that have adopted his name. Perhaps the tribute that would have meant the most to him was held on October 14, 1979: The National March on Washington for Lesbian and Gay Rights—an event some gay leaders feared would fail, but which Milk predicted would succeed—attracted 100,000 participants to Washington, D.C. Thousands of people marched

through our nation's capital beneath the rainbow flag designed by Gilbert Baker at Milk's request. Some carried big photos of Milk and shouted, "Harvey Milk lives! Harvey Milk lives! Harvey Milk lives!" He would have loved all the attention.

As I write these words a third of a century after Milk's death, his life and his work continue to inspire people around the world. Why is that so? Perhaps a plaque in front of Milk's Castro Street residence states it best: "His life is an inspiration to all people committed to equal opportunity and an end to bigotry." He stood for something.

Remember what he stood for. Stay inspired by his courage. Follow his challenge to "Keep involved!" and take action to make your world a better place.

As long as we take action, Harvey Milk lives.

Appendix: Milk's supervisorial activities

IN HIS 1999 *Time* magazine profile of Harvey Milk, John Cloud made the howlingly inaccurate statement that Harvey Milk as a legislator "sponsored only two laws": San Francisco's Human Rights Ordinance, which prohibits discrimination on the basis of sexual orientation, and a "pooper scooper" law. Dozens of misguided writers have picked up Cloud's whopper and spread it.

Reality was different. As Mike Weiss describes on page 192 of *Double Play*, Milk "proposed a blizzard of substantive legislation." The following pages illustrate Weiss' evaluation by chronologically cataloging some of Milk's legislative activities. This list is derived from the items listed with Milk's name in the *Journal of Proceedings, Board of Supervisors*. It also includes Dan White's items that relate to Milk.

As a record of accomplishments, the catalog here is far from complete. It does not include Milk's activities as commissioner of the Board of Permit Appeals in 1976. It omits many small items (probably more than a hundred) listed in the *Journal* with Milk's name. The *Journal* also reports hundreds of motions, resolutions, and ordinances with no supervisor's name attached, some of which undoubtedly involved Milk. Because they do not include his name, they are not included here. This catalog also does not include Milk's behind-the-scenes efforts, such as his formation of an alliance to stop a hike in Muni fares proposed by Dianne Feinstein and George Moscone, or his successful fight to keep a school in his district from being closed, or his work to amend or defeat other supervisors' proposals. It does not contain Milk's work as the chair of the Board of Supervisors' Urban and Consumer Affairs Committee, as the vice chair of its Streets and Transportation Committee, or as a member of the Board's Community Services Committee. Also omitted are Milk's activities as the Board's representative on the State of California's North Central Coast Regional Commission.

This record may be incomplete but it does highlight most of Milk's most important legislative activities. It shows Milk's brief time as a

legislator was, in fact, prolific, and that in addition to sponsoring ordinances he used other tools to nudge officials and agencies. Note how many times Milk uses a letter from the Board, a request for a report, or a specific query to let an official know that a person or a project had fallen under his (and therefore the Board's) scrutiny. Activities are listed by date, so we can see how they relate to other events in Milk's life.

Finally, this chronological catalog proves for once and for all that, yes, Milk's activities did include gay rights and dog poop, but they also affected a world that was much, much wider.

Monday January 9. At 2:00 p.m., the year's first regular session of the Board of Supervisors begins. Milk, together with either fellow Supervisor Bob Gonzales (according to the *San Francisco Chronicle*) or fellow supervisor Carol Ruth Silver (according to *Journal of Proceedings, Board of Supervisors*), introduces a bill proposing a "Human Rights Ordinance" which will prohibit discrimination based on sexual orientation in employment, housing, and public accommodations. Drafted under Milk's direction by attorney Matt Coles, and expanding Dianne Feinstein's 1972 ordinance prohibiting, in a more limited way, sexual orientation discrimination, the Human Rights Ordinance is sent by the supervisors to the city attorney's office for review, and is referred to the Board's Fire, Safety, and Police Committee for approval. Milk also speaks against an ordinance permitting more apartments to be converted into condominiums. Together with Supervisors Silver, Gonzales, and John Molinari, Milk asks Gilbert Boreman, the Board's clerk, to send a letter to the Public Utilities Commission inquiring about the actual cost of implementing a proposal to extend a cable car line to Fisherman's Wharf, the method of funding any cost overruns, and whether there is public support for the project from anyone other than the businesses that would benefit financially. No objection is raised by other supervisors, so the clerk is directed to send the letter. Supervisors Silver, Gonzales, Molinari, and Milk also present a request for a hearing on the proposed extension of the cable car line. The Board refers their request to the appropriate Board committee. Milk's first Board meeting adjourns at 5:10 p.m.

[318]

Tuesday January 10. Board of Supervisors President Dianne Feinstein names Milk a member of the Community Services Committee, the vice-chairman of the Streets and Transportation Committee, and the chairman of the Urban and Consumer Affairs Committee. Because Milk's Human Rights Ordinance will amend the Police Code, it must be reviewed by the Fire, Safety, and Police Committee. As chairman of that committee, Feinstein selects Dan White.

Monday January 16. At the Board of Supervisors meeting, Milk requests that a hearing be held to consider closing part of Haight Street on April 30 for the First Annual Haight Street Fair. Milk's request is referred to the Fire, Safety, and Police Committee. As chair of the Urban and Consumer Affairs Committee, Milk announces that his committee will meet at 6:00 p.m. on the first Thursday of every month. Milk requests that the city attorney be asked to prepare legislation imposing an income tax on businesses and persons earning income in the City and County of San Francisco. The other supervisors do not object, so the Board's clerk is directed to comply. Milk moves that the Board of Supervisors award certificates of honor to Oscar Norman, Michael Huston, Sam McDaniel, and Willie Richardson, to which the Board unanimously agrees.

Monday January 23. The Board of Supervisors appoints Milk as its representative on the North Central Coast Regional Commission, which regulates environmental issues and construction near the coastlines of Sonoma, Marin, and San Francisco counties. Milk requests that the Board ask the city attorney to draft legislation to increase penalties for dog littering and to consolidate all functions dealing with animal littering, loose, barking, or biting animals, and animal cruelty under one section of the Police Department, to be designated "Animal Cruelty." The Board directs its Clerk to comply. Milk requests that the Board ask the city attorney to prepare a charter amendment which would 1) rescind Mayor's power to appoint persons to fill vacancies on the Board of Supervisors and 2) establish a procedure to fill vacancies on the Board by election by voters in the district in a general or special election, to be held within 60 days of the creation of the vacancy. There is no objection from other Board members, so the Board's clerk is directed to ask the city attorney to draft Milk's proposed charter amendment. (If Milk's proposed amendment would have been passed before Dan White resigned from the Board, it could have prevented the assassinations that followed.) Milk requests that the city attorney prepare a charter amendment creating a Municipal Railway Commission and relinquishing to it all Muni matters now under the control of the Public Utilities Commission. There is no objection, so the Board's clerk is directed to contact the city attorney.

Monday January 30. At the Board of Supervisors' meeting, Milk requests that the Board ask the city attorney to draft legislation raising the cable car fare to fifty cents; that the Board ask the city attorney for his opinion on the suspension of a staff member of the Human Rights Commission for "unauthorized disclosures to the press;" that the Board ask the Director of the Human Rights Commission to explain the suspension of a staff member of the Human Rights Commission for "unauthorized disclosures to the press;" that the Board ask the city attorney to draft legislation exempting food vendors at street fairs and school and church events from part of the Municipal Code; that the Board ask the city

[319]

attorney to draft legislation to require that city departments notify tenants as well as property owners when public hearings will be held on matters which affect the quality of life in their neighborhoods; and that the Board ask the city attorney to prepare an opinion on the effect of State Assembly Bill 1107 on Municipal Railway fares. No supervisors object to any of Milk's six requests, so the clerk is directed to comply. Milk also proposes a resolution opposing enactment of United States Senate Bill 1437 (which will become the Federal Criminal Code Reform Act of 1978), and a resolution asking the United States State Department to close the South African consulate in San Francisco in protest of apartheid. (Milk's second resolution will become influential nationally, stimulating many local and state government agencies to take action protesting apartheid in South Africa.) The Board refers both of Milk's proposed resolutions to its State and National Affairs Committee.

Monday February 6. At the Board meeting, Milk requests the Board to ask the city attorney to provide a legal opinion on when the city's cable TV franchise with Viacom Cablevision is due for renewal and what conditions the Board can require for renewal of the TV franchise. Milk also requests the Board to ask the city attorney to draft legislation to create a 50 percent premium parking tax in commercial parking stations, to be applied to all persons entering downtown parking stations between 6 a.m. and 10 a.m. and to have funds derived from this tax provided to the Municipal Railway for the maintenance of the city's transit facilities. No Board members object to Milk's requests, so the Board directs its clerk to comply.

Tuesday February 14. Supervisors Milk, Gordon Lau, and Silver submit a resolution urging the U.S. Secretary of Transportation to designate San Francisco as the pilot city for a free public transit program. The Board passes their resolution, but the federal Department of Transportation never launches its pilot program.

Tuesday February 21. Milk asks the Board to hold a hearing to review the "costs, purposes, and effectiveness" of the Police Department's decoy program. The Board sends Milk's request to its Fire, Safety, and Police Committee for review. Milk presents the Board with a charter amendment taking public transit from the Public Utilities Commission and creating a Municipal Railway Commission. The Board refers Milk's proposed amendment to its Legislative and Personnel Committee for review.

Monday February 27. Milk requests the Board to ask the budget analyst to report on the amount of cash received to date for construction of the Performing Arts Center, and to indicate whether there are sufficient funds for completion of construction; to ask the city attorney what action the Board may take to curtail liquor licenses in a specific area of the city; and to ask the city attorney what action the Board can take to require the airport bus terminal to remain at a downtown location.

There are no objections from Board members to any of Milk's three requests, so the Board directs its clerk to comply. Milk also arranges for the Board to issue a certificate of honor to Winship Travel.

Monday March 6. In dramatic contrast to the blizzard of legislative ideas from Milk, his fellow supervisor Dan White focuses on one major issue: Stopping the Sisters of the Good Shepherd from selling their school for wayward girls to social agencies that would turn it into the San Francisco Youth Campus, a residence for disturbed youths which could house possibly violent delinquents in White's district. The Board takes up the Youth Campus issue, and in spite of White's attempt to halt progress, votes to continue consideration in its March 13 meeting. At this meeting of the Board, Milk proposes for the Board to ask the budget analyst to report on the financial arrangements between the city and parking lot operators; to ask the budget analyst to report on the city's expenses for renting space for city departments and whether it might save money for the city to build a new office building; to ask the city attorney whether it is legal for city employees to use city-owned cars for personal purposes; and to ask the city attorney to draft legislation requiring Sunset Scavenger, Viacom Cablevision, and other privately-owned utilities that contract with the city to advise customers in advance of any proposed rate changes. There are no objections to any of Milk's requests, so the Board directs its clerk to comply with them. Milk also proposes that the Board hold a hearing to consider restructuring or abolishing the Civil Service Commission, which the Board refers to its Legislative and Personnel Committee for review. Milk, Ella Hill Hutch, Feinstein, and Silver propose a resolution urging that the city withdraw investments in and disapprove of future investments in corporations and banks doing business in or with South Africa. The Board refers their proposal to its State and National Affairs Committee for review.

Thursday March 9. Milk attends a 2:00 p.m. meeting of the Police, Fire, and Safety Committee, which is scheduled to vote on his anti-discrimination bill. After the committee's Chairman Dan White makes a speech in favor of gay rights, such a large number of people crowd Room 228 of City Hall to observe and testify that Milk suggests White move the meeting to the much larger supervisors' chambers. White agrees. After hours of testimony, White and his committee vote unanimously to recommend that San Francisco enact Milk's historic bill. (This committee meeting is described in *Double Play* on pages 142–144.)

Friday March 10. Milk with his aide Dick Pabich and Dan White with his aide Ray Sloan meet in White's office. Milk encourages White to think Milk will vote against the Youth Campus on Monday, when in fact Milk plans the opposite. (This meeting is described in *Double Play* on page 144.)

Monday March 13. Expecting the Youth Campus to be voted down, Dan White packs the supervisors' chambers with supporters to witness his

triumph, but is stunned and furious when Milk instead votes to approve the Youth Campus. The bill passes, six votes to five. White is so angry with Milk that he refuses to speak to him for weeks. (This meeting is described in *Double Play* on pages 144–145.) The San Francisco Giants baseball team threatens to leave the Bay Area, so Milk moves that the Board ask the mayor to propose keeping the Giants in the area by splitting the team's home games between San Francisco and Oakland. The Board votes seven to four in favor of Milk's resolution. Milk proposes for the Board to ask the mayor for a policy statement on the city's employment practices pertaining to outside hiring; to ask the city attorney to draft legislation creating a Department of the Aging, responsible for all matters pertaining to senior citizens and expenditure of all State and Federal funds for senior services in San Francisco; and to ask the city attorney to advise the Board on restrictions on the use of city and county vehicles for personal business. The Board raises no objections to Milk's three requests, so its clerk is directed to comply. Milk and Silver introduce a resolution opposing Proposition 13, the Jarvis-Gann property tax initiative, which the Board refers to its Finance Committee for review. Milk and Molinari request a hearing to explore providing dedicated parking spaces for motorcycles throughout the city, which the Board refers to its Fire, Safety, and Police Committee. Milk requests a hearing to consider establishing curbside collection of recyclable items (an idea San Francisco will implement decades later) and recycling centers. The Board refers his request to its Governmental Services Committee for review. Milk arranges for the Board to issue certificates of honor to David Alex, William Kidd, Richard Klapp, Ray Mullane, and Frank Palma.

Monday March 20. The Board of Supervisors considers the measure (now sponsored jointly by Milk, Gonzales, and Silver) proposing a Human Rights Ordinance to prohibit discrimination based on sexual orientation in employment, housing, and public accommodations. Dan White moves to return the measure to the Fire, Safety, and Police Committee, which he chairs and where he can block it. His attempt to return the Human Rights Ordinance to his committee dies because none of the other supervisors will second his motion. Supervisors Hutch, Lau, and Milk attempt to strengthen the Human Rights Ordinance by deleting three lines, but they are voted down, eight to three. The Board moves the Human Rights Ordinance forward to the next step in the approval process by a ten-to-one vote; only White votes against it. Supervisor Quentin Kopp requests that the *Journal of Proceedings* reflect the statement by the legislation's co-authors that there is no Constitutional basis for implementation of the legislation, and that it is not the intent of the authors to require hiring of a specified number of individuals of a particular sexual orientation. Gonzales requests that the *Journal of Proceedings* reflect his view that good grooming and appearance belong with other bona fide requirements for employment. Kopp requests that

the Board send a letter to the Human Rights Commission, asking if Milk's Human Rights Ordinance is finally passed that the Commission is to report on its effectiveness six months later, any related complaints, and any actions taken. No Board members object to the requests by Kopp and Gonzales, so the Board's clerk is directed to comply with them. Milk requests the Board to ask the Mayor to declare the week of April 30–May 7, 1978 San Francisco Energy Week, and the day of May 3, 1978 San Francisco Sun Day; to ask the director of public works to ask the Division of Street Repair to assist in the planting of street trees by cutting and removing concrete in sidewalks; and to ask the director of public health to survey hospitals in clinics in San Francisco about their use of electroshock therapy. There are no objections to Milk's three requests, so the Board's clerk is directed to comply with them. Milk proposes two ordinances, one exempting food vendors at authorized street fairs and school and religious group events from license fees, and one providing that any vacant supervisor's position will be filled by a special election. The Board sends both proposed ordinances to the proper committees.

Monday March 27. Milk's proposed Human Rights Ordinance "prohibiting discrimination based on sexual orientation in employment, housing, and public accommodations" is considered for second reading by the Board. Supervisor Kopp proposes twelve different amendments to the text of the ordinance. The Board accepts all but one. Then the Board moves the Human Rights Ordinance forward to the next and final step in its approval process by a ten-to-one vote; only Dan White votes against it. Milk proposes a resolution endorsing the enactment of a bill pending in the state legislature to fund the Small Utility Consumer Action Group. The Board sends Milk's resolution to its State and National Affairs Committee for review. Milk requests the Board to ask the city attorney to draft legislation banning the use of electroshock therapy in San Francisco; to ask the city attorney to draft legislation to simplify the permit process for solar water heating systems; to ask the mayor to apply for federal funds under President Carter's new national urban policy; to ask the Social Services Commission if it can assign a general assistance worker to the county jail; and to write to the presiding judges of the municipal and superior courts expressing concern that proposed increases in bails would unfairly affect poorer people. There are no objections to Milk's requests, so the Board directs its clerk to comply with them. Milk obtains the Board's approval to award certificates of honor to Matthew Coles (the attorney who drafted the anti-discrimination Human Rights Ordinance), Don Knutson, Donald Solomon, Jerel McCrary, the *Bay Area Reporter* newspaper, Professor Billy C. Henderson, and the Haight Ashbury Arts Workshop.

Thursday March 30. At the Board meeting, Milk requests that the *Journal of Proceedings, Board of Supervisors* express his concern that some craft workers are making less than they earned four years ago. He also

[323]

requests the Board to ask the controller how much actual cash is on hand for construction of the Performing Arts Center; to ask the city attorney whether construction on Performing Arts Center can legally begin before all cash revenues have been received for it; to ask the mayor why construction has been started on the Performing Arts Center's site when it has not been determined that all funds for construction have been collected; to ask the Parking Authority to estimate lost revenues if the Performing Arts Center garage is not constructed and the revenue loss for each day that the garage is in use before the center is constructed; to ask the city attorney if a conflict of interest has occurred because Tudor Engineering Company was responsible for a feasibility study of the project and now has a contract for its creation; and to ask the mayor to apply for federal funds for an emergency operations center. There are no objections to Milk's requests, so the Board directs its clerk to take care of them.

Monday April 3. The anti-discrimination Human Rights Ordinance from supervisors Milk, Gonzales, and Silver "prohibiting discrimination based on sexual orientation in employment, housing and public accommodations; and providing remedies therefor" is taken up by the Board for final passage. It passes ten to one; the only vote against it comes from Dan White. It will become law if signed by the mayor within ten days.

At the same Board meeting, Milk's proposed ordinance changing the composition of citizens advisory committees in rehabilitation assistance program (RAP) areas (such as the Haight Ashbury RAP in Milk's district) is sent back to the Board's Planning, Housing and Development Committee for further review. Milk requests that a letter be sent to the chief of police asking for copies of police department reports on animal control; that a letter be sent to the city attorney asking to draft legislation to abolish the Animal Control and Welfare Commission; that a letter be sent to the city attorney asking to prepare legislation prohibiting the deposit of dog excrement; that letters be sent from the Board to all supermarket chains in San Francisco "urging their cooperation in the effort to reduce dog litter by selling and promoting containers available for disposal of dog litter;" that letters be sent from the Board "to major dog food manufacturers, urging their cooperation by promoting and selling disposable containers for dog excrement with their products;" that the Board send a letter to the "Alcoholic Beverage Commission, asking that it give consideration to suspending issuance of on-sale and off-sale licenses" in the Haight Ashbury neighborhood and in the Noe Valley neighborhood "for a period of one year, in view of widespread community opposition to such issuance;" that a letter be sent to the chief of police "asking for [a] report on unsolved cases of gay-related murders;" that a letter be sent to the mayor asking him to declare the week of April 17–23, 1978 National Rail Passenger Week; and that a letter be sent to the

general director of the San Francisco Opera "suggesting that the opera and other theatrical companies set aside a certain percentage of their tickets in every price category for non-subscriber sales." There are no objections to any of Milk's nine requests, so the clerk of the Board is directed to comply with them. Milk also presents a proposed ordinance revising the rate of real estate transfer tax, which the Board refers to its Finance Committee for review.

Monday April 10. At the Board meeting, Milk presents a resolution "disapproving flat fares on Bay Area Rapid Transit (BART) District," which the Board refers to its Streets and Transportation Committee for review. Milk proposes an ordinance to raise revenue by charging a license fee to people "who engage in the City and County in any trade, occupation or profession," which the Board refers to its Finance Committee for review. Milk asks the Board to hold a hearing to consider appointing an Energy Advisory Committee to study the city's energy problems. The Board refers Milk's idea to its Urban and Consumer Affairs Committee (which Milk chairs) for review. Milk asks the Board to ask the Municipal Railway to consider charging less for a Muni Fast Pass after the first week of each month; to ask the assessor for information about the amount of lost tax revenues caused by the condemnation of housing units to make way for the Performing Arts Center; and to ask the mayor to declare "one day in April a free parking day, with all parking meters being free." There are no objections to any of Milk's three requests, so the Board's clerk is directed to comply.

Tuesday April 11. At a ceremony in the mayor's office, Mayor George Moscone signs Milk's anti-discrimination Human Rights Ordinance into law.

Monday April 17. As its first order of business, the Board unanimously adopts a resolution in memoriam of the death of Bertram Feinstein, M.D., the late husband of Dianne Feinstein. Milk requests the Board to ask the city attorney "to draft legislation to make permanent the provisions of Ordinance 320–75, prohibiting discrimination in housing against families with children, which ordinance will expire in July of this year;" to ask the Recreation and Park Department about the controls over the collection of fees at city golf courses; to ask the Bureau of Building Inspection "how it determines which homes will be inspected, and whether this determination is public knowledge, in light of many instances in which property owners who receive inspection citations are contacted soon thereafter by real estate agents;" and to ask the city attorney for an opinion how charter commissioners would be elected to revise the city charter if Proposition L is approved by voters in June. There are no objections to Milk's requests, so the Board's clerk is directed to comply. Milk presents a resolution supporting California State Senate Bill 2053, which would ban discrimination in employment based on sexual orientation; his proposal is referred to the Board's State and National Affairs Committee. Milk requests that the Board

[325]

hold a hearing to consider a pedestrian walkway from City Hall to the opera house across Van Ness Avenue, one of San Francisco's busiest streets. The Board referred Milk's idea to its Fire, Safety, and Police Committee; a walkway bridge was never built and is still needed today.

Monday April 24. Milk re-introduces his resolution asking the U.S. Department of State to close South Africa's consulate in San Francisco. Supervisor Kopp introduces a motion to postpone consideration of it to May 1, which passes. Supervisors Hutch, Feinstein, Milk, and Silver re-introduce their resolution "urging immediate withdrawal of all City funds invested in corporations and banks doing business in or with South Africa;" their resolution is sent back to its committee. The Board's State and National Affairs Committee presents Milk's proposed resolution opposing the federal government's Criminal Code Reform Act of 1977. Dan White introduces a motion to delay consideration to May 8, which passes. Milk presents a resolution supporting the United Nations special session on disarmament, which the Board refers to its State and National Affairs Committee. Milk requests the Board to ask the chief of police to establish a procedure for reviewing permits for amplified music; to ask the general manager of the Civil Service Commission whether transit planning engineers without a professional background in planning can fill the needs for a director of planning for the Municipal Railway; and to ask the assessor whether the assessment on the Uptown Theatre at Sutter and Steiner Streets "has the effect of contributing to the blight of the neighborhood." There are no objections to Milk's three requests, so the Board's clerk is directed to comply.

Monday May 1. Milk's resolution requesting the U.S. Department of State to close the Republic of South Africa's consulate in San Francisco is adopted by a six-to-three vote. Milk proposes a resolution opposing the state ballot initiative entitled "School Employees Homosexuality" (which later becomes known as "Proposition 6" and the "Briggs Initiative"); the Board refers Milk's proposal to its State and National Affairs Committee. Milk requests that the Board send a letter to the mayor "inquiring as to the views of Mr. Alan E. Rothenberg, the mayor's appointee-designate to the Port Authority, with respect to responsibility for operation of the fireboat." There are no objections, so the Board's clerk is directed to comply. Milk moves that the Board should award certificates of honor to the Hunger Project and to the San Francisco Municipal Railway Planning Division, which the Board unanimously approves.

Monday May 8. On the resolution proposed by supervisors Hutch, Feinstein, Milk, and Silver "urging immediate withdrawal of all City funds invested in corporations and banks doing business in or with South Africa," the Board postpones consideration to May 15. On Milk's resolution opposing the enactment of United States Senate Bill 1437 (the Criminal Code Reform Act of 1977), the Board postpones consideration to May 22. Milk requests a hearing to consider temporarily

closing certain streets for the Gay Freedom Day parade and celebration on Sunday, June 25. The Board refers Milk's request to its Fire, Safety, and Police Committee, which is chaired by Dan White. Milk requests the Board to ask the city's purchaser how much money city departments spend with printers outside San Francisco; to ask the city attorney for an opinion as to the "legality of establishing [a] requirement that all printing by city departments be done by San Francisco firms;" and to send a letter on former Navy Lieutenant Milk's behalf to the Secretary of the Navy "similar to the one directed by acting clerk of the Board to the then Secretary of the Navy on June 18, 1974, with respect to visit of the Chilean ship *Esmeralda* to San Francisco." There are no objections to Milk's requests, so the Board's clerk is directed to comply.

Monday May 15. The Board postpones consideration of the resolution by supervisors Hutch, Feinstein, Milk, and Silver "urging immediate withdrawal of all city funds invested in corporations and banks doing business in or with South Africa" to May 22. Consideration of Milk's proposed ordinance imposing "a transfer tax on short-term speculative profits from the sale of residential real estate" is postponed until May 22. Consideration of Milk's resolution supporting California State Senate bill 2053, which bans discrimination in employment based on sexual orientation, is postponed until May 22. In budget hearings, Milk attempts to delete funding for some positions, especially public relations officers from the Municipal Railway and the Public Utilities Commission, and to add funding for additional automotive mechanics to the Municipal Railway budget. All of Milk's proposals are defeated. Milk's resolution supporting State Assembly Bill 1289 "which provides funding for the Small Utility Consumer Action Group" is adopted unanimously. Milk's resolution supporting the United Nations special session on disarmament is adopted unanimously. Supervisors Silver and Milk propose an ordinance "providing for revision of budget data format to permit review of proposals for increase and decrease in budget allocations" and an another ordinance "providing for economy in government and limitations on spending," both of which the Board refers to its Finance Committee. Milk requests a hearing to consider closing Market Street between The Embarcadero and Sixth Street to all but Muni, police, and fire vehicles and ambulances during rush hours "to encourage use of Muni and provide for faster Muni service downtown." The Board refers Milk's request to its Fire, Safety, and Police Committee. Milk requests that the Board send a letter to the chief administrative officer "requesting information as to the necessity for security gates in City Hall." There is no objection, so the clerk is directed to comply. Ironically, when security gates are installed in City Hall, they will fail to protect Milk from Dan White, who will evade them by sneaking through a window with his gun. This lengthy Board meeting adjourns at 1:20 a.m.

[327]

Monday May 22. The Board meets on Milk's 48th birthday. Consideration of Milk's proposed ordinance imposing "a transfer tax on short-term speculative profits from the sale of residential real estate" and establishing a Property Transfer Tax Appeals Board is postponed until May 30. Milk's resolution supporting California State Senate Bill 2053, which bans discrimination in employment based on sexual orientation, is adopted by a ten-to-one vote, the only "no" vote coming from Dan White. The Board discusses Milk's proposed resolution opposing the enactment of the federal government's Criminal Code Reform Act of 1977. Board President Feinstein states "the Board should not get involved in a bill as complicated as this; that the provisions are directed at a wide variety of crimes, both violent and nonviolent," and Milk's resolution is voted down, six to four. Milk's resolution urging a trial closure of the Great Highway extension between Sloat and Skyline Boulevards is voted down, nine to two. Milk requests that a letter to be sent from the controller giving the accuracy of the funds for contractual services for the Commission on the Aging; that letters be sent to the mayor and the chief administrative officer "asking them to consider studying the simplification of the permit and inspection process and encouraging new housing starts;" and that a letter be sent to the mayor asking him to declare June 16th Operation Concern Day. There are no objections to Milk's three requests, so the clerk is directed to comply. The Board meeting adjourns twenty minutes before one o'clock in the morning.

Tuesday May 30. After a great deal of debate and several amendments to Milk's proposed ordinance imposing "a transfer tax on short-term speculative profits from the sale of residential real estate" and establishing a Property Transfer Tax Appeals Board, the Board votes Milk's proposal down, eight to two. Milk requests that the Board ask the city attorney to draft legislation to change the cutoff times for periods protected by noise control regulation from 7:00 a.m. to 8:00 a.m. Milk requests that a letter be sent to the director of planning asking how many loans have been granted in the Upper Ashbury rehabilitation assistance program (RAP) area, and a report on the progress and effectiveness of the program in that area. There are no objections to Milk's two requests, so the clerk is directed to comply.

[328]

Monday June 5. After discussion and amendments, the proposed resolution by supervisors Hutch, Feinstein, Milk, and Silver establishing a policy of the City and County of San Francisco not to invest City funds "in corporations and banks doing business in or with South Africa" is adopted nine votes to two. Milk proposes an ordinance increasing taxes on parking stations during specified hours, and providing that certain parking tax revenue shall be transferred to the Municipal Railway; the Board refers Milk's proposal to its Legislative and Personnel Committee for review. Milk proposes an ordinance abolishing the Animal Control and Welfare Commission, which is referred to the Board's Health and Environment Committee. Milk presents an ordinance "amending

Section 40 of Health Code to provide penalties for owner or custodian of any dog who permits said dog to defecate on public or private property, or who walks a dog without carrying a container suitable for removal and disposal of dog excrement," which the Board refers to its Health and Environment Committee. Milk requests the Board to send a letter to the city attorney asking what steps the Board can take "to alter or terminate the rehabilitation assistance program in designated areas." There is no objection, so the Board's clerk is directed to comply.

Tuesday June 6. As part of the primary election, California state voters pass Proposition 13, the Jarvis-Gann Tax Initiative, reducing property tax revenues and restricting state and local governments' ability to increase property tax rates.

Wednesday June 7. The Board's Fire, Safety and Police Committee, chaired by Dan White, votes to refuse Milk's request for temporary street closures for the Gay Freedom Day Parade and Fair on June 25.

Friday June 9. The Board of Supervisors holds an emergency meeting so Mayor George Moscone can address the Board concerning the financial emergency resulting from voter approval of Proposition 13, the Jarvis-Gann Initiative. The Board passes several tax increases quickly to avoid Jarvis-Gann restrictions. Milk pulls his request for temporary street closures for the Gay Freedom Day Parade and Fair out of Dan White's Fire, Safety and Police Committee and schedules it to be considered by the entire Board on June 19. Milk requests for a letter to be sent to the district attorney asking for an investigation of alleged kickbacks by vans taking passengers to the San Francisco International Airport; for a letter to be sent to the State Public Utilities Commission, "citing the allegation that vans have violated their own permits and that the State PUC refuses to enforce its own rules despite appeals over a three-year period;" for a letter to be sent to the State Supreme Court, urging it to make a decision on lawsuits about the Jarvis-Gann initiative; to the city attorney, asking "for an opinion as to whether the city may enact legislation to require landlords to pass on to their tenants the property tax savings received as a consequence of passage of Proposition 13." There are no objections to Milk's requests, so the clerk is directed to comply.

[329]

Monday June 12. Supervisor Dan White does not attend this Board of Supervisors meeting due to the birth of his first child, Charles Edward White. A proposed resolution by supervisors Milk, Lau, and Silver opposing Proposition 6, the Briggs Initiative, is postponed until June 19. Supervisors Lau and Milk move to send a letter to the registrar of voters "inquiring as to steps taken to comply with 1975 Federal Voting Rights Act and requesting response to allegations of non-compliance with the Act during the June 6, 1978 election." There is no objection, so their motion is carried. Milk requests that a letter be sent to the chief of police "inquiring whether it is departmental policy to have police lieutenants serve as chauffeurs for captains, and, if so, asking

whether regular officers could not be used for this purpose, thus freeing lieutenants for other duties." Milk also requests that a letter be sent to the general manager of the Hetch Hetchy water system "inquiring as to the amount of money spent and projected to be spent for studies of proposed dams on the Tuolumne River, as well as [a] status report on the project." There are no objections to Milk's requests, so the clerk is directed to comply. Supervisor Lee Dolson motions on behalf of all supervisors that the Board award a certificate of honor to Master Charles Edward White. All supervisors present vote to award the certificate to Dan White's new baby son.

Wednesday June 14. The Board's Special Committee to Implement State Proposition 13 submits Milk's proposed ordinance to increase taxes on parking stations and transfer revenue from the Parking Tax Fund to the Municipal Railway. The Board sends Milk's ordinance back to committee for further review. Milk requests that letters be sent to Governor Jerry Brown, to the speaker of the state senate, and to the speaker of the state assembly "urging enactment of legislation to legalize gambling in the State of California" to make up for tax revenue lost due to Proposition 13. Milk also requests that the Board's clerk obtain the city attorney's opinion "as to the legality of poker parlors in San Francisco, and if appropriate, ask that he draft legislation authorizing their operation." There are no objections, so the clerk is directed to comply.

Monday June 19. The resolution by supervisors Milk, Lau, and Silver stating that the Board opposes Proposition 6, the Briggs Initiative, passes unanimously. Supervisor Dan White states that he was a dissident vote on Milk's "Gay Rights" ordinance when it was before the Board, but that he is voting for this resolution opposing the initiative pertaining to school employees because he feels that the Briggs amendment carries the matter too far, and asks that his statement be incorporated in the *Journal of Proceedings.* Milk's resolution granting permission for temporary street closings for the Gay Freedom Day parade and celebration on June 25 (which Milk had called out of the Fire, Safety, and Police Committee, where Dan White had blocked it), is adopted by a ten-to-one vote. Only White votes against it. Milk's proposed ordinance to raise taxes on parking stations and transfer revenue from the Parking Tax Fund to the Municipal Railway is tabled by a unanimous vote of all eleven supervisors. Milk requests that a budget analyst conduct a management audit of the Police Department. The Board refers Milk's request to its Rules Committee. Milk requests that the Board send a letter to the city's chief administrative officer, asking about the feasibility of leasing emergency health centers to private contractors. There are no objections, so the Board's clerk is directed to comply. Milk requests that a letter be sent to the city attorney, asking if San Francisco could legally establish a city lottery, and if the answer is affirmative, to ask the city attorney to draft appropriate legislation for Milk to introduce. There are no objections, so the clerk is directed to comply.

Monday June 26. Attempting to find a way to make up for lost tax revenue due to Proposition 13, Milk proposes an ordinance establishing and regulating card rooms in San Francisco. The Board refers his proposal to its Fire, Safety, and Police Committee. Milk presents a resolution opposing State Senate Bill 1757 relating to cable television, which is referred to the Board's State and National Affairs Committee. Milk requests temporarily closing Castro Street on Sunday, August 20, for the Fifth Annual Castro Street Fair. His request is referred to the Fire, Safety, and Police Committee. Milk requests that a letter be sent to the Public Utilities Commission to find what steps are being taken to refund excess fees charged for Muni Fast Passes; that a letter be sent to the chief administrative officer asking what is being done to recycle paper at City Hall; that a letter be sent to the chief of police "concerning lack of response to calls about cars being parked in driveways and on sidewalks illegally and asking what overall policies the department has to enforce, such as parking laws, in light of the fact the Department will be funded next year at [only] 99% of its current budget'; and that another letter be sent to the chief of police "concerning the recent flurry of arrests for prostitution and/or loitering in the Geary-O'Farrell Street area, requesting number of arrests, charges, how many incidents, and whether a considerable amount of personnel, time and money are spent and to point out it has had the effect of harassment of persons and businesses in the area." There are no objections to Milk's requests, so the clerk is directed to comply.

Monday July 3. Supervisors Milk and Molinari request that the Board ask the city attorney to prepare the legislation needed to call for the election of charter commissioners for the November 1978 election. There is no objection, so the clerk is directed to comply. Milk requests that the mayor and the chief administrative officer be asked to "establish suggestion boxes for suggestions by city employees on ways to improve efficiency and that financial rewards be established for those suggestions acted upon;" that the city attorney be asked to draft legislation to submit to voters in the November 1978 election "to place responsibility for the setting of refuse collection rates with the Board of Supervisors rather than the current rate board;" and that the Department of City Planning be asked to produce "a study of the desirability of revising height limits, bulk limits, floor area ratios, and bonus systems for high-rise construction in the central business district." There are no objections to Milk's three requests, so the clerk is directed to comply. Milk, as chair of the Urban and Consumer Affairs Committee, announces that to reduce overtime costs, future meetings of his committee will begin at 2:00 p.m. instead of 6:00 p.m.

Monday July 10. Discussion on a proposed ordinance by Milk regulating street artists and craftspersons is postponed until July 24. Discussion of a proposed charter amendment by Milk to repeal certain restrictions on cable car fares is postponed to July 17. Milk presents an ordinance

regulating and licensing card rooms for playing draw poker, which the Board sends to its Fire, Safety, and Police Committee. Milk requests that the city attorney be asked to "prepare legislation which would establish a moratorium on the establishment of bars, restaurants and liquor stores for one year on 24th Street between Church and Diamond Streets" in Noe Valley, a neighborhood in Milk's district. Milk also requests that a letter be sent to the director of city planning asking for a report on the delay in processing the environmental review for Dr. Rider's Parnassus Heights project. There are no objections to either of Milk's requests, so the clerk is directed to comply. Supervisors Milk and Silver present three proposed ordinances providing tax credits, which are referred to the Board's Finance Committee.

Monday July 17. Milk's resolution opposing State Senate Bill 1757 relating to cable television is adopted by a unanimous vote of all supervisors present. Milk requests that the Board ask the director of public works and the general manager of the Recreation and Park Department to review a proposal for bike racks to be installed by a private firm at no expense to the city in exchange for selling advertising space on the racks. Milk also requests that the city attorney be asked whether legislation would be required for the bike racks project and if there are restrictions on the installation of bike racks on private property and sidewalks. Milk requests that a letter be sent to the director of the DeYoung Museum asking whether recent layoffs of staff were made because the employees laid off were close to retirement age. Milk requested that the city attorney be asked to prepare legislation which would impose a citywide rollback of residential rents, and also establish a procedure for landlords to impose rent increases to compensate for increased taxes or property improvement expenses. There are no objections to Milk's requests, so the clerk is directed to comply. Supervisor Dan White requests that the Board ask the city attorney for "an opinion as to whether members of the Board may personally support a convicted drug dealer," referring to Milk and Silver's support of marijuana supplier Dennis Peron. No objections are raised, so the clerk is directed to comply.

Monday July 24. A proposed resolution by supervisors Gonzales, Molinari, and Milk establishing a renters' hotline, and urging the emergency services office of the mayor to log renter complaints is adopted by a unanimous vote of all supervisors present. A proposed ordinance by Milk covering "fixed source noise level" is referred to the Fire, Safety, and Police Committee. Discussion on a proposed ordinance by Milk regulating street artists and craftspersons is postponed until July 31. Milk requests that the city attorney be asked to draft legislation for him to introduce "to make it illegal for hotel doormen to require kickbacks from taxicab drivers before placing passengers for airport rides." Milk also requests that a letter be sent to Governor Jerry Brown and to San Francisco's delegation in the state legislature expressing concern over

the disparity "between the salaries of city-employed nurses and those in the private sector, and requesting support for legislation which would exempt San Francisco nurses from the wage freeze established as a result of Proposition 13." There are no objections to Milk's requests, so the Board's clerk is directed to comply.

Monday July 31. After debate and amendments, Milk's proposed charter amendment repealing certain restrictions on cable car fares is voted down. After debate and amendments, Milk's proposed ordinance "regulating street artists and craftspersons; establishing an advisory committee of street artists and craftspersons examiners; prescribing certification procedures, including renewal and revocation, and procedure for designation of sales areas; establishing a revenue fund for street artists program; and repealing initiative approved as Proposition L at the election held on November 4, 1975" is passed by a six-to-four vote. Supervisors Silver and Milk present a resolution opposing the advertisement and sale of South Africa's kruggerand gold coin in San Francisco. Their proposed resolution is referred to the Board's State and National Affairs Committee. Milk and Silver request that the city attorney prepare a resolution stating that the Board intends to make a feasibility study for the City and County of San Francisco to take over the electricity generation facilities of Pacific Gas & Electric Co. at Hetch Hetchy. No objection is made, so the clerk is directed to comply. Milk requests the city attorney be asked to give an opinion as to whether salary standardization is legally defined as a cost-of-living increase, and whether the State of California's guidelines for allocation of state surplus funds allow internal adjustments. Milk also requests that the city attorney be asked to draft legislation to require code inspections prior to the sale of any residential property, which would make the buyer aware of all code violations before the sale. He also requests that letters be sent to Pacific Gas and Electric Co. and to Pacific Telephone asking whether they will ask to reduce their rates as a result of the savings they receive from Proposition 13. There are no objections to Milk's requests, so the clerk is directed to comply.

[333]

Monday August 7. A charter amendment proposed by supervisors Kopp, Ron Pelosi, and Milk to create a transit commission is tabled. A resolution by supervisors Milk and Molinari to urge the Bay Area Rapid Transit (BART) District not to approve a proposed common fare of fifty cents or a flat fare is discussed, amended, and then adopted by a unanimous vote of all eight supervisors present. Milk presents a proposed ordinance "temporarily prohibiting approval of permits for establishment and operation of amusements, places of entertainment, dance halls, cabarets and restaurants on 24th Street, between Church and Diamond Streets for six months" in the Noe Valley neighborhood in Milk's district. Milk's proposal is referred to the Fire, Safety, and Police Committee. Supervisors Gonzales, Hutch, and Milk present a proposed ordinance rolling back rents for a six-month period.

Their proposal is referred to the Board's Planning, Housing, and Development Committee. Supervisors Silver and Milk ask for a letter to be sent to the San Francisco Unified School District, suggesting that the district alleviate its financial crisis by selling its office space at 135 Van Ness Avenue to the city. There is no objection, so the clerk is directed to comply. Supervisors White and Milk ask that a letter be sent to the Federal Aviation Administration asking for an investigation of allegations that aircraft routes specifically designed to reduce noise for the west end of San Francisco are not being followed. There is no objection, so the clerk is directed to comply. (This request is unusual for two reasons; first, it is very unusual for White and Milk to jointly make a request; second, the west end of San Francisco is in neither of their districts.) Milk asks that a letter be sent to the Public Utilities Commission about street cars on order from Boeing; and that a letter be directed to the city's chief administrative officer asking why the Yerba Buena Center (after Moscone's assassination, renamed the Moscone Center) groundbreaking has been scheduled for August 10, "four days before [the] expiration date for filing [a] response to legal action taken by [the] Redevelopment Agency." There are no objections to Milk's two requests, so the clerk is directed to comply. This Board of Supervisors meeting adjourns at 1:50 a.m.

Monday August 14. Supervisors Molinari and Milk propose a resolution calling a special election to choose charter commissioners to revise the notoriously complicated City and County Charter, to be held with the general election on November 7. After some amendments, their resolution is adopted on a seven-to-four vote. Supervisors Molinari, Milk, and Silver present a resolution to send a letter to the state legislature and to Governor Jerry Brown urging them to approve and sign an assembly bill that would require a charter commission to complete its work within two years. The measure is referred to the Board's State and National Affairs Committee. Supervisors Silver, Feinstein, Gonzales, and Milk jointly request that a letter be sent to the city Housing Authority, asking that the Authority reconsider any travel at this time due to allegations of misappropriation of funds, reminding them that the City and County has withdrawn from all organizations to which the Authority might be traveling. There is no objection, so the clerk is directed to comply. Milk requests that a letter be sent to the Municipal Railway asking to "study the feasibility of selling special short-term Fast Passes for tourists for cable cars only;" that letters be sent to the director of public works and the general manager of the Recreation and Park Department asking them "to repair the city's fountains and restore them to use;" that the city attorney be asked to draft a charter amendment for Milk to introduce to exempt from the jurisdiction of the City and County purchaser "all purchases by the Municipal Railway, and to establish a separate purchasing office in the Municipal Railway;" and that a letter be sent to the mayor asking for a citizens' committee

"to look into alternate uses of closed school buildings." There are no objections to Milk's requests, so the clerk is directed to comply.

Monday August 21. After discussion and amendments, further discussion of a proposed ordinance from supervisors Gonzales, Hutch, and Milk providing a six-month moratorium on rent increases and a six-month rollback of rental rates is postponed until September 5. Milk moves to delete the Upper Ashbury district from the RAP program. Board President Feinstein rules Milk's motion out of order. Milk presents eight proposed arguments to appear on the November ballot: an argument supporting an initiative to create a street artist ordinance; one supporting a charter amendment "pertaining to removal of boards and commissions appointed by the mayor to serve at his pleasure;" one supporting a charter amendment reorganizing the Public Utilities Commission and creating a Transportation Commission; one supporting a ballot measure creating a Charter Commission and electing charter commissioners to revise the City and County charter; one supporting a "charter amendment pertaining to absence of officers from the state;" one supporting a marijuana initiative; a "skeleton ballot argument supporting renters' initiative;" and a "skeleton ballot argument supporting mayor's 'Home Rule Preservation Ordinance'." All eight proposed arguments are referred to the Board's Legislative and Personnel Committee for review. Milk requests a hearing to consider giving free Muni Fast Passes to all city employees. The Board refers Milk's request to its Streets and Transportation Committee. Milk requests a hearing to consider whether a budget analyst should conduct a management audit of the rehabilitation assistance program (RAP). The Board refers Milk's request to its Rules Committee. Supervisors Silver, Feinstein, and Milk request that letters be sent to the Board of Education and to the superintendent of schools asking for the Board of Supervisors' budget analyst's staff to given access to its records to conduct a management audit of its child care program. There is no objection, so the clerk is directed to comply. Supervisors Silver and Milk request that the Board ask the city attorney to prepare a charter amendment to have San Francisco Airport pay all revenues realized from the airport into the general fund. There is no objection, so the clerk is directed to comply. Milk requests that a letter be sent to the chief administrative officer suggesting that the former Park Emergency Hospital be turned into a senior center; and that letters be sent to the Department of Public Works, to the Recreation and Park Department, and to Wastewater Management soliciting their comments on findings issued by the Ocean Beach Erosion Control Conference. There are no objections to Milk's two requests, so the clerk is directed to comply.

Monday August 28. Milk's proposed ordinance changing the health code "to provide penalties for owner or custodian of any dog who permits said dog to defecate on public or private property or who walks a dog without carrying a container suitable for the removal and disposal of dog

[335]

excrement" is unanimously passed for its first reading by all supervisors present. Milk requests that a letter be sent to the general manager of the Recreation and Park Department asking why hours at city pools have been cut back and for a schedule of when the pools are open. There is no objection to Milk's request, so the clerk is directed to comply. The meeting adjourns at 6:55 p.m.

Tuesday September 5. Milk's proposed ordinance requiring dog owners to clean up after their dogs is brought back for two amendments and the amended version is passed for a second reading by an eight-to-one vote, with only supervisor Gonzales voting against it. The proposed ordinance from supervisors Gonzales, Hutch, and Milk providing a six-month moratorium on rent increases and a six-month rollback of rental rates is postponed until September 11. Milk presents a proposed substitute ballot argument favoring the street artist ordinance. The motion authorizing the submission of Milk's ballot argument is approved unanimously by all supervisors present. Milk presents a proposed substitute ballot argument favoring the measure creating a Charter Commission and electing charter commissioners to revise the City and County charter. Milk's ballot argument is approved unanimously by all supervisors present. Milk requests that a letter be sent to the chief of police asking to explain an incident reported in the September 1 *San Francisco Progress* about the detention of suspects in the Candlestick Park area, and expressing Milk's concern about the difficulty the public encounters trying to get information from the Police Department about such incidents. There is no objection, so the clerk is directed to comply. Milk makes a motion that the Board adjourn its meeting in respect to the memory of John Lira, Jr. Milk's motion is unanimously adopted by a rising vote as the Board adjourns at 11:50 p.m.

[336] **Monday September 11.** Milk's ordinance establishing "penalties for owner or custodian of any dog who permits said dog to defecate on public or private property or who walks a dog without carrying a container suitable for the removal and disposal of dog excrement" is given final passage by an eleven-to-one vote. After a great deal of discussion and several amendments, the proposed ordinance from supervisors Gonzales, Hutch, and Milk providing a six-month moratorium on rent increases and a six-month rollback of rental rates is refused passage for a second reading. Supervisors Silver, Hutch, and Milk present a resolution asking the Chilean government to cooperate in the investigation of the Letelier-Moffitt assassinations, which the Board refers to its State and National Affairs Committee. Milk requests that letters be sent to the general manager of the Recreation and Park Department and to the director of museums asking them to institute free admission for senior citizens one day each week at the zoo and museums. There is no objection, so the clerk is directed to comply.

Monday September 18. Authorization of temporary closing of streets in North Beach for three hours on September 24 for the Third Annual Columbus Day Cycling Races is, in spite of fevered opposition from Dan White, passed by a seven-to-three vote. (See pages 202–204 of *Double Play* for details.) Milk asks for letters to be sent to the Department of Public Works, to the Public Health Department, and to the Fire Department asking for their policies "regarding investigation of anonymous complaints and seeking their response to the suggestion that all complainants be required to file their names and addresses before any investigation begins." There is no objection to Milk's request, so the clerk is directed to comply. The Board meeting adjourns at 2:05 a.m.

Monday September 25. With two minor amendments, Milk's proposed ordinance "temporarily prohibiting the approval of permits for establishment and operation of amusements, places of entertainment, dance halls, cabarets, bars and restaurants on that portion of 24th Street between Church Street and Diamond Street for six months" is passed for its second reading unanimously by all supervisors present. Milk requests that a letter be sent to the chief of police asking for his department's policies on street musicians. There is no objection, so the clerk is directed to comply.

Tuesday October 10. Milk's ordinance temporarily prohibiting the approval of permits in Noe Valley is approved by a unanimous vote of all supervisors present. Milk presents a resolution closing Castro Street for Halloween, which is immediately adopted by a unanimous vote of all supervisors present.

Monday October 16. Supervisors Silver and Milk present a proposed resolution asking the United States Congress to desist from providing "further aid to Nicaragua as long as the Somoza government is in power." The Board refers the proposal to its State and National Affairs Committee. Milk requests that the Board ask the city attorney to draft legislation to establish a program of deposits on beverage bottles similar to one recently enacted in Marin County; that a letter be sent to the general manager of the Recreation and Park Department asking about plans for the future use of long-abandoned Kezar Stadium, the former home of the San Francisco 49ers football team; and that the city attorney be asked to prepare legislation for Milk to introduce creating a Commission on Youth, "to be composed totally of youth members." There are no objections to Milk's requests, so the clerk is directed to comply.

Monday October 30. Supervisors Pelosi, Molinari, and Milk request that the Board send a letter to the mayor "proposing that he ask the Public Library Commission to appropriate funds to purchase a book over one hundred years old, which records the first meeting of the Board of Supervisors, which book is currently in the John Howell Book Store on Post Street, and will shortly be auctioned off to the highest bidder;

or alternatively, that the mayor appoint a citizens' committee to raise money to purchase said book." There is no objection, so the clerk is directed to comply. Milk requests that the city attorney be asked for an opinion as to steps to be taken by the Board to "limit and/or stop construction of new high-rise buildings in the downtown area, north of Market Street." There is no objection to Milk's request, so the clerk is directed to comply.

Friday November 10. Dan White hands Mayor Moscone a letter resigning White's seat on the Board of Supervisors. (For the most thorough explanation of why and how White resigned, see *Double Play*, pages 206–216.) Late Friday afternoon, Gilbert Boreman, the clerk of the Board of Supervisors, hears about White's resignation, obtains a copy of his letter, timestamps the copy as received at 4:57 p.m., and files it as the first action item for the Board to take up on its Monday meeting. Because the Board normally meets once a week, Boreman's fast action prevents White's resignation from a one-week delay in being processed by the Board.

Monday November 13. The Board meeting begins with Boreman reading a copy of White's resignation letter. Supervisor Kopp, seconded by Supervisor Hutch, moves to accept and file White's resignation. There is no objection, so Kopp's motion is carried.

Supervisors Milk and Silver present a resolution urging the chief of police and the district attorney to assign low priority to enforcement of laws against marijuana, and calling on the state legislature to decriminalize the use, possession and cultivation of marijuana. Their proposed resolution is referred to the Fire, Safety, and Police Committee. Milk and Molinari present a resolution honoring Fred Methner, which is adopted by a unanimous vote of all supervisors present. Milk calls his proposed ordinance for the "regulation and licensing of card rooms for the playing of draw poker" out of the Fire, Safety, and Police Committee and asks to add it to the agenda for the Board meeting on November 20. There is no objection, so the clerk is directed to comply. Milk requests that the city attorney be asked to draft legislation for him to introduce to "to require that city departments act within ten days on matters pertaining to granting of police permits;" that a letter be sent to the director of airports asking what plans have been made about "recent increases in routes and flights approved for San Francisco International Airport;" and that a letter be sent to the mayor, with copies to the controller and the director of the Commission on Aging, asking about "contracts for use of $650,000 in parking tax funds for [an] escort program; and an additional $400,000 in parking tax funds to be allocated for a nutrition program; urging that open public meetings be held to insure adequate public participation in determination as to use of such funds." There are no objections to any of Milk's requests, so the clerk is directed to comply.

Tuesday, November 14. Dan White decides he wants to remain a supervisor, and retrieves his resignation letter from Mayor Moscone. Because the Board has already accepted White's resignation, it cannot be withdrawn.

Monday November 20. Gilbert Boreman, the clerk of the Board, presents a letter from former Supervisor Dan White, outlining his desire to be reappointed to the Board of Supervisors. In response to an inquiry from supervisor Kopp, Deputy City Attorney Jim Lazarus advises the Board that the city attorney is preparing a legal opinion on the Dan White situation, and that the opinion will find that action reappointing White would have to be taken by the mayor. Milk's proposed ordinance about "card rooms for the playing of draw poker" is refused passage by a five-to-three vote. Milk requests that the city attorney be asked to "research the legality, and if legally feasible, draft legislation" for Milk to introduce "which would permit the city to declare a building which has been vacant five years or more a public nuisance and to sell the same;" that the Board ask the city attorney to draft legislation for Milk to introduce "to establish a two-year moratorium on the granting of licenses or permits to operate for bars and restaurants which serve wine, beer and/or liquor in the 18th and Castro Streets area;" that the Board ask the chief administrative officer "to reconvene the Citizens' Task Force to update the Solid Waste Management Plan;" and that the city attorney be asked to draft legislation amending San Francisco's cable television franchise to provide:
 A. An annual review;
 B. A regulatory commission of three members;
 C. A continuance of the five percent franchise fee, with the regulatory commission and the Board to determine how an extra two percent will be allocated;
 D. The cable company (Viacom) to agree to wire the entire city and to submit its wiring plans annually for public comment.

[339]

There are no objections, so the clerk is directed to comply with Milk's final requests.

Further reading and viewing

Aretha, David. *No Compromise: The Story of Harvey Milk.* Greensboro, North Carolina: Morgan Reynolds, 2010. This earnest biography of Milk is written for young adults. Includes 48 photos, 7 of which have nothing to do with Milk's story. The ugliest cover photo of Milk ever.

Bellefountaine, Michael with Bellefountaine, Dora. *A Lavender Look at the Temple: A Gay Perspective of the Peoples Temple.* Bloomington: iUniverse, 2011. An eight-page chapter "Harvey Milk and Peoples Temple" discusses Milk's relationship with the Temple and its leader Jim Jones. This is the only book with a detailed discussion of this topic. Although it presents unique information, specific sources are often not cited, making verification of its claims almost impossible.

City and County of San Francisco. *Journal of Proceedings, Board of Supervisors,* volumes 72 and 73, January-December 1978. The official record of all Board meetings during Milk's supervisorship.

Epstein, Rob and Schmiechen, Richard. *The Times of Harvey Milk.* New York: Criterion, 2011. This deeply moving documentary is the second most-important resource on Milk's life. The two-DVD Criterion edition restores the Academy Award-winning 1984 film and adds audio commentary by Rob Epstein, Deborah Hoffman, and Dan Nicoletta; Milk interview excerpts not used in the film; items about *The Times of Harvey Milk* and Gus Van Sant's *Milk*; audio and video recordings of Milk (including short interview videos, an audio recording of Milk's speech before the Texas Gay Conference in Dallas, and Milk's tape-recorded political will); video interviews with six people not featured in the film (Scott Smith, Rob Ross, Amber Hollibaugh, Cleve Jones, Lillian Sing, and Hank Wilson); news clips about Dan White; excerpts from a 2003 panel discussion about White's trial; and more. It also includes a 32-page color booklet with 40 photos and articles by B. Ruby Rich, Stuart Milk, and Ross Lipman. Highly recommended.

Jones, Cleve, with Dawson, Jeff. *Stitching a Revolution: The Making of An Activist.* New York: HarperSanFrancisco, 2000. Cleve Jones, the founder of the NAMES Project Foundation, was pulled into political activism by Milk. He became a key member of Milk's inner circle. He worked closely with Milk and Sally Miller Gearhart to fight against Proposition 6, assisted Milk in City Hall, led the candlelight march after Milk's murder, and was present for the White Night Riots. Though the bulk of his autobiography deals with the AIDS crisis and the AIDS memorial quilt, the 28 pages Jones devotes to his time with

Milk give a close, heartfelt look at the man. Jones is particularly good in describing Milk battling Proposition 6, why people were attracted to Milk, and the aftermath of his assassination.

Meason, Christopher, editor. *Milk: A Pictorial History of Harvey Milk.* New York: NewMarket, 2009. This informative and good-looking book collects diverse parts. It features an introduction by Dustin Lance Black, a foreword by Armistead Maupin, the making of Gus Van Sant's movie *Milk* by Jason Simos and James Ferrera, and a brief biography of Milk bolstered by an oral history compiled by Black of quotations from Milk (including his complete "Hope" speech), from 12 people who knew him, and from news media. The book is a visual feast, thanks to 108 photos showing Milk's life and times, and another 32 photos from the movie *Milk* and its production. Useful for research and enjoyable.

Rathbun, Mary, and Peron, Dennis. *Brownie Mary's Marijuana Cookbook and Dennis Peron's Recipe for Social Change.* San Francisco: Trail of Smoke, 1996. Pages 30–36 contain three photos of Milk and information on Milk and marijuana decriminalization not provided elsewhere.

Shilts, Randy. *The Mayor of Castro Street: The Life and Times of Harvey Milk.* New York: St. Martin's, 1982. Shilts' stirring biography is the first book anyone should read about Milk. Shilts was a participant in several of the events he describes, knew Milk, and conducted groundbreaking research. Unfortunately, he makes many minor factual errors. (The most notorious is his implication that John "Jack" Galen McKinley was sixteen years old when he moved in with Milk. McKinley was born October 18, 1946, so he was 17 or 18 when he first met Milk in late 1964. 17 is the age of consent in New York, so Milk's relationship was not with someone underage.) Shilts includes a remarkably small number of specific dates (I highlighted all dates in my copy and was surprised by how few I could find), so he sometimes scrambles sequences of events. However, *The Mayor of Castro Street* remains the essential work on Milk. Includes five of Milk's speeches and 19 photos.

Weiss, Mike. *Double Play: The Hidden Passions Behind the Double Assassination of George Moscone and Harvey Milk.* San Francisco: Vince Emery Productions, 2010. This new edition of Weiss' 1984 book is revised, updated, and expanded. It provides much information available nowhere else. Weiss gives the first mention anywhere of Milk's earliest time in San Francisco in the 1950s, the fullest account of Milk and Scott Smith's first year in San Francisco, the most complete coverage of Milk's activities as a supervisor, the best explanation of the complex, shifting relationship between Milk and Dan White, and the only detailed account of White's trial, life after prison, and suicide. Includes 90 photos and illustrations, and a 2-hour DVD with interviews of White and Moscone, recorded phone calls from City Hall just after the killings, police dispatch recordings of police responding to the murders and hunting for the killer, Dianne Feinstein on discovering Milk's body, and White's confession to shooting Moscone and Milk.

Acknowledgements

I OWE incalulable gratitude to Susan Goldstein and Tim Wilson of the San Francisco History Center/James C. Hormel Gay & Lesbian Center and to Rebekah Kim of the Gay, Lesbian, Bisexual, Transgender Historical Society. Without their kindness and assistance *The Harvey Milk Interviews: In His Own Words* would not exist.

Many thanks to Marc Cohen, David Fechheimer, Richard Layman, Daniel Nicoletta, Craig Sinclair, and Mike Weiss; without their thoughtful help this book would be thinner and less accurate.

Thanks to Peter Fagerdal of Torpedo Design (torpedodesign.dk) for designing the book logo and the dust jacket's front cover. The book's interior design and composition are by Desktop Miracles.

My gratitude and love for Rita Sinclair cannot be captured between two covers.

Grateful acknowledgment is made to the following parties for interviews and photographs:

The Associated Press for permission to reprint the 1977 article "S.F.'s first gay supervisor sees self as symbol" by Robert McEwen (Used with permission of The Associated Press. © 2012. All rights reserved.)

Atlantic/Teldec for the photograph on page 205. Photo by Ron Scherl.

Bold Type, Inc. for permission to reprint two articles from the *Berkeley Barb*: October 24, 1975 "Harvey Milk: One gay candidate runs to win" by David Johnston; and January 27, 1978 "S.F. Supervisor Harvey Milk: You can throw bricks at City Hall or you can take it over" by John Bryan (© 1975, 1978 Berkeley Barb, © 2010 Bold Type, Inc.; used by permission).

Michael W. E. Edwards and Regent Media for permission to reprint two articles from *The Advocate*: October 10, 1973 "S.F. gay campaigning for the straight vote, too" by an anonymous author (© 1973 The Advocate, a division of Regent Media); and April 7, 1976 "In San Francisco, Milk gets canned but keeps on running" by Sasha Gregory-Lewis (© 1976 The Advocate, a division of Regent Media).

Vince Emery for *The Harvey Milk Interviews: In His Own Words* logo (trademark of Vince Emery, © 2012 Vince Emery); photos on pages 24, 48,

139, and 150 (© 2010 Vince Emery); and photos on pages 27, 62, 94, 160, 298, and 313 (© 2012 Vince Emery).

Janet Fries for permission to print her photos of Milk and friends with signs on Market Street, October 1975; Milk in front of Castro Camera, December 19, 1975; and Milk from September 1977 (© 1975, 1977 Janet Fries).

Herbert Gold for permission to excerpt the Milk interview from his article "A walk on San Francisco's gay side," which appeared in the November 6, 1977 *New York Times Magazine* (© 1977 Herbert Gold).

Greg Gordon for permission to make a transcript from his February 1978 interview with Milk for *This Way Out* (recording © 1978 Greg Gordon; transcript © 2012 Vince Emery).

Tom Hayden for permission to reprint his interview with Milk from the April/May 1978 *CED News* (© 1978 Tom Hayden).

Rebekah Kim and the GLBT Historical Society for permission to make a transcript from the 1977 Paul Avery interview of Milk from the Randy Alfred Collection, 1991-24, The Gay, Lesbian, Bisexual, Transgender Historical Society (recording © 2012 The Gay, Lesbian, Bisexual, Transgender Historical Society; transcript © 2012 Vince Emery), for permission to print the text of Geoff Mains' February or March 1978 interview with Milk from the Oral History Project of the Gay, Lesbian, Bisexual, Transgender Historical Society (© 2012 The Gay, Lesbian, Bisexual, Transgender Historical Society), for permission to photograph Milk's belt buckle, and for providing a copy of the video of the November 1, 1978 Milk-Briggs debate in Garden Grove.

Tim Lewis for permission to make a transcript from his recording of the September 15, 1978 Milk-Briggs debate in Walnut Creek (recording © 1978 Tim Lewis; transcript © 2012 Vince Emery).

The Harvey Milk Archives–Scott Smith Collection, James C. Hormel Gay & Lesbian Center, San Francisco Public Library for permission to print Milk's response to the August 7, 1973 questionnaire for candidates for the San Francisco Board of Supervisors; Milk's responses to four questions from the October 21, 1974 Tunbridge in San Francisco questionnaire; and Milk's March 17, 1978 letter to Kenneth Cravey. The photo of Milk by an unknown photographer used on pages 3 and 22; the three photos of Milk by Henry Marx on pages 96, 99, and 101; and the 1978 photo of Milk's supervisor's office by Janet Kagan on page 200 appear courtesy of the Harvey Milk Archives–Scott Smith Collection, James C. Hormel Gay & Lesbian Center, San Francisco Public Library. The San Francisco Public Library owns the copyright to the Harvey Milk Archives–Scott Smith Collection.

Ed Miskevich and KOCE-TV for permission to make a transcript and reproduce screen shots from the November 1, 1978 videotape of the Milk-Briggs debate in Garden Grove (videotape © 1978, 2012 KOCE-TV, Orange County PBS; transcript © 2012 Vince Emery).

[344]

Daniel Nicoletta for permission to print his photos on pages 143 and 144 of Milk on election night 1977 (© 1977, 2012 Daniel Nicoletta).

Northeastern University Libraries, Archives and Special Collections Department for permission to reprint the February 25, 1978 *Gay Community News* article "Harvey Milk talks about politicians and lying" by Joe Martin (© 1978 Bromfield Street Educational Foundation).

Jim Pimentel and the *San Francisco Examiner* for permission to reprint the July 27, 1973 article "Shopowner runs for supervisor" by an anonymous author and the photo on page 34 by an anonymous photographer (© 1973 San Francisco Examiner); the November 30, 1977 article "An 'unofficial supervisor' gets a shot at real power" by W.E. Barnes and two accompanying photos by Judith Calson (© 1977 San Francisco Examiner); and the November 29, 1978 article "An interview with Harvey Milk" by Lenny Giteck, introduction by Pamela Brunger, and photo on page 300 by Gary Cameron (© 1978 San Francisco Examiner).

Ron Ress, Jeff Giles, and Comcast for permission to make a transcript and reproduce screen shots from the March 30, 1978 *Newsdesk* television program (program © 1978 Viacom, © 2012 Comcast; transcript © 2012 Vince Emery).

Juana Samayoa for permission to make a transcript of and reproduce a screenshot from her 1978 *News Talk* interview with Milk (video recording © 1978, 2009 Juana Samayoa; transcript © 2012 Vince Emery).

The San Francisco Bay Area Television Archive for providing a copy of the surviving videotaped excerpts from the September 6, 1978 New San Remo Milk-Briggs debate.

The *San Francisco Chronicle* for permission to reprint the October 23, 1975 article "The second time around for Milk" by Julie Smith and the June 10, 1976 article "The summing up: Harvey Milk blames 2 factors in defeat" by Ron Moskowitz (© 1975, 1976 Chronicle Publishing Co.).

Bill Sievert for permission to include his article "Divided they stand: the Milk-Stokes split," which appeared in the July 12, 1977 *The Advocate* (© 1977 Bill Sievert).

Sally Smith and the *Noe Valley Voice* for permission to reprint Milk's September 1977 survey answers (© 1977 Noe Valley Voice), his November 1978 "Election Poll" answers (© 1978 Noe Valley Voice), and "A last interview with our supervisor" by Corrie Michael Anders (© 1978 Noe Valley Voice).

Tom R. Spitz and KPIX/CBS 5 San Francisco for permission to make a transcript from the surviving videotaped excerpts from the September 6, 1978 New San Remo Milk-Briggs debate (video recording © 1978 KPIX/CBS 5 San Francisco; transcript © 2012 Vince Emery).

Jack Veasey, Mark Segal, and the *Philadelphia Gay News* for permission to reprint the March 15, 1978 article "*Body Politic* raid triggers tourism boycott" by Veasey (© 1978 PGN–The Philadelphia Gay News).

Mike Weiss for permission to make a transcript of Aaron Berg's 1978 interview with Milk (recording © 2012 Mike Weiss; recording of the interview provided courtesy of the San Francisco History Center, San Francisco Public Library, Mike Weiss *Double Play* Collection; transcript © 2012 Vince Emery).

Calvin Welch for permission to reprint the March 1978 interview with Milk from the *Haight Ashbury Newspaper* (© 1978 Calvin Welch).

Michael Yamashita and the *Bay Area Reporter* for permission to reprint the February 19, 1976 article "Harvey Milk vs. The Machine" by George Mendenhall (© 1976 The Bay Area Reporter, a division of Benro Enterprises, Inc.); the April 1, 1976 article "What makes Harvey run . . ." by Wayne Friday (© 1976 The Bay Area Reporter, a division of Benro Enterprises, Inc.); and the December 21, 1978 letter "A living wage" by Billy Allen (© 1978 The Bay Area Reporter, a division of Benro Enterprises, Inc.).

Endnotes and Errata

ENDNOTES for *The Harvey Milk Interviews: In His Own Words* will be available online at:

www.emerybooks.com

Just go to this book's main page and look near the bottom of the page for a link called **Endnotes**.

An errata document will also be published online. In addition, if you find errors in this book you can tell us. Just go to the main web page for *The Harvey Milk Interviews: In His Own Words* and look near the bottom of the page for a link called **View or submit errata**.

Index

[351]

[354]

About the Authors

HARVEY MILK (1930 – 1978) was named "one of the 100 most important people of the twentieth century" by *Time Magazine*. His life and work have inspired millions of people around the world.

When Milk was elected a supervisor of the City and County of San Francisco, he became the first openly gay person elected to office in California. In spite of death threats, he supported a wide range of human rights, environmental, labor, and free speech issues across North America. Milk and San Francisco Mayor George Moscone were assassinated in 1978.

Since his death, Milk has been portrayed in films by Sean Penn in an Academy Award-winning performance in *Milk*, and by Peter Coyote in *Execution of Justice*. Milk's life has also been the subject of books, plays, a grand opera, and the Academy Award-winning documentary *The Times of Harvey Milk*. In 2009, President Barack Obama posthumously awarded Milk the Presidential Medal of Freedom, America's highest civilian honor.

A plaque before Milk's San Francisco residence states: "His life is an inspiration to all people committed to equal opportunity and an end to bigotry."

VINCE EMERY, the editor of *The Harvey Milk Interviews: In His Own Words,* also wrote the bestseller *How to Grow Your Business on the Internet* and edited *Lost Stories* by Dashiell Hammett. He has contributed research and articles to several books about San Francisco history and authors. Emery lives near San Francisco.

THE HAIGHT NEWS

MONTHLY BY AND FOR RESIDENTS OF THE HAIGHT

NAME THE NEWSPAPER CONTEST
$50 Prize SEE BELOW

"A LOT OF PEOPLE DON'T REALIZE THE IMPORTANCE OF OPENING DIALOGUES. IT'S THE ONLY WAY YOU CHANGE PEOPLES VIEWS"